People to People

PEOPLE TO PEOPLE

Essentials of Personal
and Public
Communication

Jack G. McAuley
Grossmont College

Wadsworth Publishing Company, Inc.
Belmont, California

Communications Editor: Rebecca Hayden

Production Editor: Connie Martin

Designer: Joe di Chiarro

Illustrator: Timothy Michael Keenan

Cartoonist: Sidney Harris

© 1979 by Wadsworth Publishing Company, Inc., Belmont, California 94002. All rights reserved. No part of this book may be reproduced, stored in a retrieval system, or transcribed, in any form or by any means, electronic, mechanical, photocopying, recording, or otherwise, without the prior written permission of the publisher.

Photo Credits (Page numbers are given in parentheses.)

Jean-Claude Lejeune / © 1977 Stock, Boston, Inc. (2); © David Powers, 1978 / Jeroboam, Inc. (5); Ellis Herwig / © 1977 Stock, Boston, Inc. (12); Ellis Herwig / © 1977 Stock, Boston, Inc. (20); © Arthur Tress / Woodfin Camp, Inc. (24); Jeff Albertson / © 1977 Stock, Boston, Inc. (34); Owen Franken / © 1977 Stock, Boston, Inc. (46); © Arthur Tress / Woodfin Camp, Inc. (50); © Marc and Evelyn Bernheim / Woodfin Camp, Inc. (61); Cary S. Wolinsky / © 1977 Stock, Boston, Inc. (68); Peter Menzel / © 1977 Stock, Boston, Inc. (73); Nicholas Sapieha / © 1977 Stock, Boston, Inc. (82); Cary S. Wolinsky / © 1977 Stock, Boston, Inc. (92); Owen Franken / © 1977 Stock, Boston, Inc. (99); Jeff Albertson / © 1977 Stock, Boston, Inc. (104); Elizabeth Hamlin / © 1977 Stock, Boston, Inc. (126); Tim Carlson / © 1977 Stock, Boston, Inc. (135); Peter Southwick / © 1977 Stock, Boston, Inc. (139); © Emilio Mercado, 1978 / Jeroboam, Inc. (148); Gabor Demjen / © 1977 Stock, Boston, Inc. (151); © Karen R. Preuss, 1976 / Jeroboam, Inc. (167); W. B. Finch / © 1977, Stock, Boston, Inc. (174); Michael Dobo / © 1977 Stock, Boston, Inc. (181); Jean-Claude Lejeune / © 1977 Stock, Boston, Inc. (189); © Arthur Tress / Woodfin Camp, Inc. (200); Ellis Herwig / © 1977 Stock, Boston, Inc. (207); Frank Siteman / © 1977 Stock, Boston, Inc. (217); Donald Patterson / © 1977 Stock, Boston, Inc. (232); Owen Franken / © 1977 Stock, Boston, Inc. (239); Julie O'Neil / © 1977 Stock, Boston, Inc. (251).

Printed in the United States of America
2 3 4 5 6 7 8 9 10—83 82 81 80

Library of Congress Cataloging in Publication Data

McAuley, Jack G
  People to people.

  Includes index.
  1. Communication. I. Title.
P90.M17   001.5   78-14842
ISBN 0-534-00619-1

P90
M17

To Millie and Michael

Contents

Chapter Four

The Subject   69

Section A
Interpersonal Focus

We choose to talk about something: a discussion of subjects for interpersonal communication with emphasis upon self-disclosure.

■ What we talk about ■ the rewards and risks of self-disclosure ■ guidelines for self-disclosure

Section B
Person-to-Group Focus

The speechmaker chooses a subject: a discussion of purpose and subject in person-to-group communication.

■ The subject ■ the topic ■ the purpose statements ■ places to look for speech subjects

Suggested Assignments

Chapter Five

Perception and Structure   93

Section A
Interpersonal Focus

Our perception structures our reality: a discussion of human perception and how it influences interpersonal communication.

■ Human perception is personal and in-complete ■ controlling factors ■ perception affects communication

Section B
Person-to-Group Focus

The speaker guides audience perception with speech structure: a discussion of organization and its effects on person-to-group communication.

■ Organizational patterns guide audience perception ■ organizational patterns are based on knowledge of perception ■ the four-part deductive pattern ■ variations of the basic pattern ■ outlining

Suggested Assignments

Chapter Six

Listening   127

Section A
Interpersonal Focus

Listening encourages communication: a discussion of listening and its effects on interpersonal communication.

■ Active listening described ■ the benefits of active listening ■ negative listening games

Section B
Person-to-Group Focus

When we listen, we learn: a discussion of factors that influence how people listen to speeches.

■ The importance of data-listening ■ positive data-listening practices ■ negative data-listening practices

Suggested Assignments

Chapter Seven

Abstraction and Support   149

Section A
Interpersonal Focus

Awareness of abstraction affects interpersonal communication: a discussion of the abstraction concept and its implications for interpersonal communication.

■ The abstraction process ■ the abstraction ladder ■ interpersonal uses for the concept

Section B
Person-to-Group Focus

The speechmaker utilizes the abstraction ladder: a discussion of how the speaker uses the abstraction concept by employing supporting materials.

■ Moving up and down the ladder ■ types of supporting materials ■ sources of supporting materials

Suggested Assignments

Preface

The dual focus design of this book is based on the belief that the differences between interpersonal communication and public speaking are primarily differences of degree rather than of kind and that improvement in one area often facilitates improvement in the other area. It provides for the concurrent study of interpersonal and public communication, and it makes possible a variety of additional choices concerning course emphasis.

With the exception of the Introduction, each chapter is divided into an A and B section. In every case the A section contains the interpersonal focus and the B section contains the public speaking focus. In some chapters the A and B sections treat separate but similar communication elements; in other chapters they present different applications for the same element. In every chapter the A and B sections compliment one another—they are mutually enhancing. Students and teachers who wish to place equal emphasis upon interpersonal communication and public speaking may do so by considering each chapter in its entirety. Those who wish to emphasize interpersonal communication can do so by eliminating consideration of selected B sections. Those who wish to place more emphasis on public speaking than on interpersonal communication can do so by eliminating consideration of appropriate A sections.

Suggested assignments are presented at the end of each chapter. They are designed to help students think about communication concepts in connection with their own lives while they are practicing communication skills. These assignments allow students to practice public speaking skills while thinking and talking about interpersonal communication. They promote personal involvement with interpersonal concepts while providing speech topics that are exceptionally meaningful to most people.

Chapters are arranged so that speaking assignments progress from the simple to the more complex. For the most part, however, the chapters are independent; they can be pursued in any order the reader deems appropriate.

Throughout the book the term *person-to-group communication* has been substituted for the words *public speaking*. For many people the words public speaking have limited meaning. They suggest formal occasions almost exclusively. Of course, the skills traditionally presented in connection with public speaking are often utilized in formal speaking situations. It is my belief, however, that person-to-group or public speaking skills are important whenever one person presents material in a relatively uninterrupted fashion to a group of people. The situation needn't be formally defined as a public speaking situation.

I have been particularly careful to avoid technical language and to present the material in an informal, conversational manner, so that readers who are unfamiliar with the field will be comfortable with the book. I have also tried to make the material as clear as possible.

Perhaps no other study is as important

to as many people as is the study of human communication. Communication pervades every area of human activity. Our patterns of communication are directly related to the quality of life we each experience. Communication is a force in our vocational, social, and civic lives. It is also an important factor in the process of self-realization. Our ability to communicate with, and to relate to, others is a vital element in how we see ourselves and how we grow as persons.

In recent years technological developments have created a communication explosion. The laser, communication satellites, television, and other devices have made it possible for people around the world to exchange messages almost instantaneously. Unfortunately, these advances haven't done much to solve our most fundamental communication problems. They have helped us to send and receive messages; they haven't helped us to understand those messages.

We still have wars, we still hurt those we love, we still frequently feel isolated, alone and misunderstood. The most crucial communication problems, then, are not mechanical problems; they are human problems. They grow from our need to create shared messages—to know and to understand one another. Technology alone cannot meet this need. Human communication will improve only to the extent that we learn to abandon negative, self-defeating patterns of communication and replace them with productive, supportive patterns.

Happily, experience shows that such learning *is* possible. Communication behavior is learned behavior. We communicate the way we do because we have learned to communicate that way. We have learned from our culture—from families,

friends, schools, and the media. Our culture has, however, provided negative as well as positive models, and consequently many of us have developed both productive and nonproductive communication habits and patterns. The college speech course is important because it offers an opportunity to examine alternatives and to begin the task of eliminating negative patterns and replacing them with more satisfying communication behaviors.

At many institutions the basic speech course has undergone considerable change in the past few years. Only a decade ago most beginning college speech courses were devoted almost exclusively to instruction in public address. Today many basic courses emphasize what has come to be known as interpersonal communication. Advocates for both of these approaches are easily found. Some are convinced that the basic course should be an interpersonal course; others are sure it should be a public speaking course.

Over the years I have modified my own position concerning the basic course. After teaching both courses separately for several years, I have come to believe that it is unrealistic and counterproductive to talk and to think about communication in interpersonal and public settings as two separate and unrelated processes. They are, after all, simply different points on the same continuum. Furthermore, I have found that improved communication in one setting often results in improved communication in other settings. The concepts traditionally offered in connection with interpersonal communication are often helpful to the student whose primary concern is public speaking. The reverse is also true. The principles and methods of public speaking are often of great value to the student whose primary interest is communication in interpersonal settings. Finally, because college students are whole people who function in both personal and public settings, I believe they are best served by the course that offers some insight and training in both areas. I have written this book to accommodate these beliefs. To my knowledge at this writing no other book is organized as this book is organized. I sincerely hope that it will prove to be of value to those who wish to secure the advantages of combining, in various degrees, a consideration of communication in both personal and public settings.

I would like to thank my colleagues from throughout the country, most of whom I have not met, for reading the manuscript and offering suggestions. These are: Smith Brand, Thornton Community College; Ralph Hillman, Middle Tennessee State University; David Mrizek, San Antonio College; Warren Smith, Chemeketa Community College; Roy K. Stave, Portland Community College; and Anthony Tripolone, Onondaga Community College.

I owe a special debt of gratitude to Lawrence Payne of West Hills College. During the Fall Semester of 1977 Mr. Payne used the manuscript in his classes on a trial basis. His suggestions and the suggestions from his students were encouraging and helpful. I would also like to thank Jean Britt for her diligent and careful work as researcher and Carolyn Villa Lobos for her invaluable help. Extraordinary thanks go to Cecily Hadley, who somehow managed to type the manuscript from my garbled dictation. Without her help I would still be working on Chapter 1. Finally, I want to offer profound thanks to Rebecca Hayden and Connie Martin of Wadsworth Publishing Company for their cheerful and expert guidance.

People to People

Chapter One

Introduction

In each of the following chapters we are going to discuss suggestions for improving communication in both interpersonal and public settings. In this chapter we will prepare for that study by considering an overview of the dynamic process that is human communication.

■ The importance of communication ■ some communication models ■ characteristics of the general process ■ some definitions ■ the format of the book

Suggested Assignments

An
Overview

Language, as well as the faculty of speech, was the immediate gift of God.

Noah Webster

This book is about the most awesome force the world has known: human communication. Communication can be used to liberate or to enslave, to create or to destroy, to improve the quality of life on earth or to diminish it. Communication is not only the process by which we define ourselves, it is the means by which we become ourselves. It enables us to know others and to be known by them. It makes possible group living, and it is the universal instrument of social cooperation and coordination. Communication is a vital factor in economic and vocational success. It enables us to govern ourselves and to discharge our civic responsibilities. With it we are able to pass information from person to person and from generation to generation. It is the characteristic that most significantly distinguishes us from the other creatures of the earth.

Communication is everywhere; it is unavoidable. No one can afford to relinquish concern for communication to the specialist or expert. To lack communication skill is to be handicapped. Our communication behavior is directly related to the quality of life we experience. Fortunately, more effective communication behavior is well within the reach of most

people. In each of the chapters that follow we will discuss suggestions for improving communication in both interpersonal and public settings. In this chapter we will consider an overview of the communication process.

It would seem logical to begin with a definition. Communication, however, is so omnipresent, so dynamic, so pervasive in our lives that it is difficult to capture it in a single definition. Furthermore, definitions are usually most meaningful to those who already somewhat understand what is being defined. Consequently, we are going to postpone a definition of communication until later in the chapter. Specifically, in this chapter we will (1) look at some communication models, (2) discuss some characteristics of the general process, (3) consider some definitions, and (4) consider the format of the book.

Communication Models

Communication models represent an attempt to freeze the dynamic process that is communication. In a sense, models are like still photographs of an ever-moving, ongoing event. As such, they are oversimplifications. They are often useful, however, in enabling us to see some of the components involved and some of the relationships that exist between those components. Before looking at some models, let's consider some terms that are often used in connection with them. (We will consider all of these terms at greater length later in the book.)

Some Useful Terms

Message The message is the *stimulus* being transmitted. It is the feeling or idea or desire or impression that is communicated. The message cannot be given meaning apart from the situation and the people involved.

Source The source is the *originator* of the message. It is usually a person or a group of persons, but sometimes it is a lower animal or a thing or an event. The source is sometimes called the *sender*.

Channel The channel is the *means* used to convey the stimuli. It is the pathway along which the message travels. Spoken words, for example, travel on air waves; gestures and facial expressions travel on light waves. Although the most common channels are visual and auditory, other channels utilize tactile, gustatory, and olfactory senses. For example, in an embrace, a message is con-

Messages are often carried on more than one channel.

veyed by touch. The important thing to remember is that human communication is multichanneled. If the same message is carried simultaneously on more than one channel, the chances for successful communication are increased. To illustrate: when you supplement a verbal description of your brothers and sisters with a photograph of them, communication is enhanced. On the other hand, when channels simultaneously carry conflicting messages, communication is diminished. For example, when the verbal message is "What's the hurry, stick around for awhile," but the visual message presented by the speaker's body and face is "Boy am I tired, I wish these people would go home," the result is decreased message clarity.

Symbol A symbol is something that represents something else. It can be verbal or nonverbal. Words are symbols; the flag is a symbol; certain uniforms, gestures, and objects are symbols. Symbols have communication value to the extent that communicators agree upon what they represent. Often, however, the same symbols represent different things to different people.

Encoding Encoding is the *process* of selecting symbols to express the idea or feeling the source wishes to communicate. It is the process of putting what the source wishes to communicate into symbols. Sometimes this process is almost automatic and at other times it is deliberate. When you are answering an essay question on a test, you are apt to take some time in fitting words to your thoughts. On the other hand, when

"Dictionary."

you see a friend, you say, "Hi," without giving the symbol much thought. As we will note many times in this book, there is always the chance that the symbols you select to express your meanings will be given different meanings by those who receive your symbols.

Receiver   The receiver is the person who *receives* and *interprets* the stimuli sent by the source. As we have just noted, the receiver may or may not interpret the symbols provided by the source in the way the source intended. There are many reasons for differences in interpretation, some of which we will discuss in the chapters that follow. For now let's note that one of the primary reasons is that we give meaning to symbols in accordance with our life experiences— and, of course, no two of us have had exactly the same experiences. At this point we should also note that the receiver is usu-

ally also a sender and the sender is also a receiver. This is to say that in most situations we both send and receive messages.

Decoding   Decoding is the process by which the receiver *translates* the symbols provided by the source. It is the process by which the receiver attaches her or his own meaning to the sender's symbols. In other words, the source encodes and the receiver decodes. If the meanings produced by the receiver in the decoding process are the same as the meanings intended by the source in the encoding process, communication has been successful.

Feedback   Feedback is the *response* the source receives as a result of the original message. Feedback itself is a message. When receiving feedback, the original source becomes the receiver, and when producing feedback, the original receiver becomes the source. Feedback is important to communication because it provides both sender and receiver with important information about the progress of the communication. For example, when you don't understand what your friend is saying, your puzzled look may provide appropriate feedback. Your friend can then rephrase and try to make the point clearer, and you will both benefit. Feedback also provides information about how people perceive themselves and how they are perceived by others.

Noise   Noise is anything that *interferes* with the communication process. It can be either external or internal. External noise is anything in the external environment that interferes with initiating, transmitting, or receiving the message. It can be an un-pleasant sound, a distracting mannerism displayed by either the sender or the receiver, or uncomfortable seating. Internal noise is any barrier that exists within the source or the receiver, such as a headache, fatigue, unpleasant past experiences with the subject, or a strong dislike for someone involved in the communication process.

Now that we understand some of the terms that are usually used in connection with communication models, let's turn our attention to some representative models.

The Shannon and Weaver Model

One of the earliest communication models was developed by Claude E. Shannon and Warren Weaver as a means of describing electronic communication.[1] It is frequently referred to as the telephone model because it explains telephone communication so well. In Figure 1.1 you can see that this model utilizes six components: (1) source, (2) transmitter, (3) signal, (4) receiver, (5) destination, and (6) noise.

The Shannon and Weaver model can easily be adjusted to represent nonelectronic human communication. We can think of the human nervous system as the source, the vocal apparatus as the transmitter, the sound waves as the signal, the hearing apparatus of the listener as the receiver, and the entire nervous system of the receiver as the destination. Although this model was originally developed for use with engineering problems, it stimulated much thought concerning the nature of human communication and is a forerunner of many modern models.

The Lasswell Model

The Lasswell model is a verbal model.[2] It is frequently presented in the form of a question: "Who says what to whom through

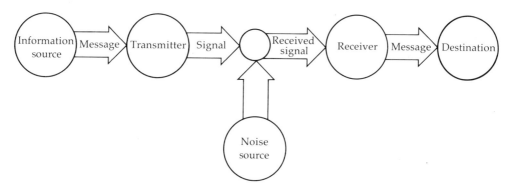

Figure 1.1

Source: Claude E. Shannon and Warren Weaver, *The Mathematical Theory of Communication*, p. 5. Copyright 1949 by the Board of Trustees of The University of Illinois. Reprinted by permission of the University of Illinois Press.

Figure 1.2

Source: Harold D. Lasswell, "The Structure and Function of Communication in Society," in *The Communication of Ideas*, ed. Lyman Bryson, p. 37. Reprinted by permission of Harper & Row Publishers, Inc.

what channels with what effect?" This model (see Figure 1.2) introduces some elements that are not represented in the Shannon and Weaver model. It introduces the idea that "who" and "whom" are important. The person who sends the message and the person who receives it are often as important as the message itself. For example, we sometimes receive instructions differently from people we respect than from people we don't respect. Many studies in public speaking indicate that the credibility of the source is very influential. The receiver, of course, is also important. You can send the same message to five different people, and they all will interpret it differently simply because they are different people. The Lasswell model indicates that source and receiver are significant variables. Lasswell also calls attention to the element of effect. It is not enough to deliver a message in an attractive fashion; what counts is the effect the message has. To be

realistic we must evaluate communication by results or effects.

The SMCR Model

The SMCR model was developed by David Berlo.[3] The letters of the label represent the major elements in the model: the source, the message, the channel, and the receiver. This model indicates that several factors affect the source and the receiver: communication skills, attitudes, knowledge, the social system in which they live, and the cultural environment (see Figure 1.3). Berlo's model does not take note of noise or feedback.

The McCroskey Model

The McCroskey model, first presented in 1968, details some of the steps involved in encoding and decoding.[4] It also shows some of the things that occur in the source prior to communication and in the receiver after communication. The most important feature of this model is that it illustrates feedback. Feedback is usually described as the response the receiver gives to the message. Since feedback itself is a message, it stimulates more feedback or more messages, which in turn stimulate more feedback or messages; the process can go on and on. You say something to a friend and your friend responds. Your friend's response is feedback stimulated by your message, and at the same time it constitutes a new message from your friend to you. Your response to your friend's message is also at once

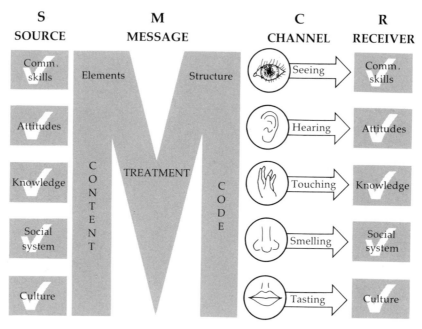

S SOURCE	**M** MESSAGE	**C** CHANNEL	**R** RECEIVER

Figure 1.3

Source: *The Process of Communication: An Introduction to Theory and Practice* by David K. Berlo. Copyright © 1960 by Holt, Rinehart and Winston, Inc. Reprinted by permission of Holt, Rinehart and Winston, CBS, Inc.

feedback and a message. The process is circular. The McCroskey model also includes noise. It indicates that noise can be present in the source and the receiver as well as in the channel (see Figure 1.4).

The Reciprocal Model

The last model we will consider is a simple one (see Figure 1.5). I devised it to illustrate the cyclical nature of communication, which we discussed in connection with the McCroskey model. The models we have considered thus far tend to be linear. Communication is not, however, linear; it is circular. In most situations we are simultaneously source and receiver. We send messages in response to other messages, and our messages stimulate responsive messages, which in turn stimulate additional messages from us—on and on. Trying to separate stimulus from response is like trying to separate the chicken and the egg. This is as true for public speaking situations as it is for intimate interpersonal situations: the speaker affects the audience, but the audience also affects the speaker.

In review, we have considered some communication models and some of the terminology that is usually associated with them. Scores of additional models are avail-

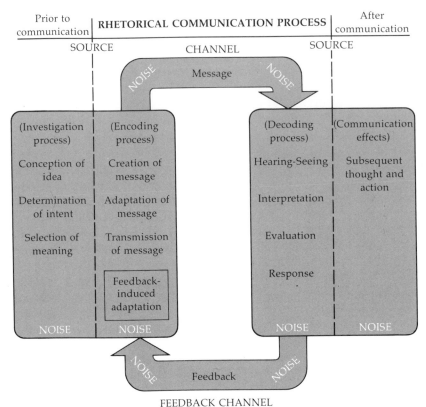

Figure 1.4

Source: James C. McCroskey, *An Introduction to Rhetorical Communication*, 2nd ed., p. 25. © 1972. Reprinted by permission of Prentice-Hall, Inc., Englewood Cliffs, New Jersey.

able, some incredibly complex. As we noted earlier, all communication models, even the most complex, have inherent limitations because they are static representations of a dynamic process. Nevertheless, it is hoped that our brief look at these models has given you a clearer picture of the process that is human communication. To understand this vital process further, let's discuss some of its general characteristics.

Some General Characteristics of Human Communication

Communication Is Multileveled

Communication occurs on more than one level. Three such levels are the intrapersonal level, the interpersonal level, and the person-to-group level.

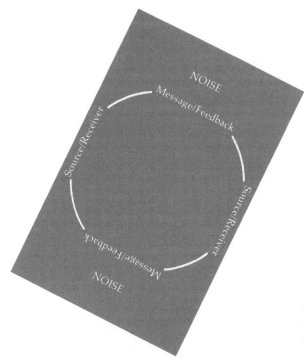

Figure 1.5

one another. Interpersonal communication is usually dyadic; that is, it usually involves just two people. It can, however, occur in a small group when the participants respond directly to one another as individuals. Interpersonal communication, then, usually takes place between two people or in very small groups. It assumes the form of a dialogue. Most importantly, it occurs when people communicate personally and directly as individual persons. When you discuss a matter of mutual interest with two of your best friends, when you talk over your term project on an individual basis with your instructor, when you talk on the telephone with a dear friend, when you discuss vacation plans with a spouse, you are engaged in interpersonal communication.

The Intrapersonal Level Intrapersonal communication occurs when we communicate with ourselves. It is communication that takes place within the individual. At the intrapersonal level, we process and interpret raw data and make decisions. It is the level at which encoding and decoding take place. Intrapersonal communication is the basis for the communication that takes place on all the other levels.

The Interpersonal Level Interpersonal communication is the communication that occurs in situations that allow people to respond directly to one another as individuals. It usually takes the form of a dialogue, and it is characterized by verbal give and take—people often interrupt

The Person-to-Group Level Communication on this level is frequently referred to as *public speaking*. We are going to call it *person-to-group communication* instead because the terms *public communication* or *public speaking* often denote a speaker's platform, an audience of hundreds, and all the trimmings. While person-to-group communication may include all of this, more often it does not. Person-to-group communication occurs when one person presents ideas, feelings, and information in a relatively uninterrupted fashion to a group of people. This can occur in a classroom, at a union meeting, in a business conference, in a family counsel, at a pep rally, or in many similar situations. The term *person-to-group* as opposed to the term *public* includes the total range of formal and informal situations.

Most of what can be said about interpersonal communication can in some degree be said about person-to-group communication. Most of what can be said about person-to-group communication can be said in some degree about interpersonal communication. The differences are of degree rather than of kind. In person-to-group communication situations, individuals usually cannot communicate directly and personally with one another as successfully as they can in interpersonal settings. Usually in person-to-group settings, speakers present longer units of communication than they do in interpersonal settings. In person-to-group settings listeners usually do not interrupt speakers.

Usually person-to-group settings involve more people than do interpersonal situations. This is not always the case, however. Sometimes interpersonal communication can become person-to-group communication in the twinkling of an eye. To illustrate: A committee of four meets to discuss an item of importance. At first the communication is individually focused; it assumes the form of a dialogue. This is interpersonal communication. At one point, however, one of the committee members says, "Hey, wait a minute, I have been thinking about this and I want to explain something to you," and proceeds to present material without interruption for several minutes. The member speaks to the others as a group. They in turn listen without interrupting. Interpersonal communication has become person-to-group communication.

Since people usually have more time to prepare for person-to-group communica-

Person-to-group communication situations are often informal.

tion, it is usually more organized than interpersonal communication. For this same reason style is sometimes more formal in person-to-group situations than it is in interpersonal situations.

In summary, person-to-group communication occurs when one person presents material to a group of people with relatively little interruption. Person-to-group situations can be formal or informal and usually involve more people than interpersonal situations do. Person-to-group communication is generally better organized than interpersonal communication. When you speak at a rally on behalf of a political candidate, when you call the office staff together to explain new procedures and guidelines, when you make an announcement in class, when you talk to your Little League team as a group, when you speak on behalf of a motion in a club meeting, you are engaged in person-to-group communication.

Communication Is Cyclical

Communication is not something one person does to someone else; it is something people do together. The speaker affects the listeners, but the listeners also affect the speaker. Each of us is simultaneously source and receiver. It is impossible to fail to respond to a message. Silence or failure to respond overtly is in itself a response, and any response is at the same time a message, which in turn engenders a response that is a message, which in turn engenders a response that is a message—and on and on. Communication is not a straight line; it is a circle.

Communication Is Unavoidable

You cannot not communicate. Even your silences say something. So do your facial expressions, your clothes, your posture, and the many other nonverbal attributes you inevitably present. Were you to decide to get away from it all and live by yourself on a deserted island, your withdrawal and absence would say something. When you sit alone in your room and think, you are communicating with yourself on the intrapersonal level. Communication is inescapable.

Communication Is Indirect

As we observed in connection with some of the models, communication does not transfer meaning directly from one mind to another. The process of translation is always involved. It works like this: (1) Susan has some meaning she wishes to express to David. (2) She selects some words to express that meaning. (3) She sends the words to David. (4) David receives her words and puts his own meaning on them. If David's meanings for Susan's words are the same as Susan's meanings for those same words, communication has been successful. But, for reasons we will discuss later in the book, Susan and David often have different meanings for the same words.

Communication Is Integrated

Communication does not exist in isolation. It is interrelated with every other aspect of life. For example, the way we respond to others affects the way they respond to us; the way they respond to us affects the way we respond to them. The way we see ourselves affects the way we respond to others, and the way others respond to us affects the way we see ourselves. Our communication affects our jobs, and our jobs affect our communication. Our ability to communicate affects our education, and education affects our ability to communicate. Our health affects our communication, and our ability to communicate affects our health. Our ability to communicate with ourselves affects our ability to communicate with others, and our ability to communicate with others affects our ability to communicate with ourselves. Our capacity for communication affects government, and government affects our capacity for communication. In short, communication affects and is affected by every aspect of life.

We have been discussing some general characteristics of the communication process. We noted that communication is multileveled, reciprocal, and unavoidable. It does not transfer meaning directly, and it is an integrated process. Let's turn our attention next to some definitions of the process.

Definitions

Definitions must be treated with caution. We sometimes assume that, because something has been defined in one way, it cannot be defined in another way. This, of course, is not true. Most things can be correctly defined in many ways. Additionally, we sometimes assume that, because we have the definition, we have the thing defined. This is also untrue. The definition is not the thing defined. The definition of a banana is not a banana. Finally, because they are invariably incomplete, definitions may be misleading. This is particularly true of definitions concerning communication. Communication occurs in so many ways and places, it is so dynamic and complex that to contain it in a single definition is difficult. Nevertheless, several excellent definitions have been proposed, most of them having both strengths and weaknesses. Consider the following representative examples:

> Human communication is a subtle set of processes through which people interact, control one another, and gain understanding.[5]
> Communication occurs whenever persons attribute significance to message related behavior.[6]

> The word communication will be used here in a very broad sense to include all of the procedures by which one mind may affect another.[7]
> Communication is the process of sharing meaning through the intentional and unintentional sending and receiving of messages.[8]

Each of these definitions has something to recommend it, and many other splendid definitions are available. Our own definition is as follows: *Successful human communication is a transaction in which shared meanings are created in response to the stimulation of verbal and/or nonverbal interaction.* Like most other definitions, this one leaves much to be desired. It is included here because it implies many of the factors we will be emphasizing throughout the book. When you have finished this chapter, perhaps you will want to develop your own definition. Formulating definitions can be fun, and it usually stimulates thought concerning the phenomena being defined.

Notes on the Book

A few words concerning the format of this book may be useful.

The Focus

The book utilizes a dual or twin focus. Each chapter presents concepts and ideas relevant to both interpersonal and person-to-group communication. Each of the remaining chapters is divided into A and B sections. In every case, the A section contains the interpersonal focus, and the B section contains the person-to-group focus. In some chapters the A and B sections represent different sides of the same coin. In other instances, they treat different but related factors. In every case the A and B sections complement each other. In each chapter an understanding of one section will help the reader understand the other section. The A and B sections are interrelated and mutually enhancing.

Language

Most technical jargon has been eliminated from this book. However, as you have already observed, we frequently use the words *interpersonal communication* and *person-to-group communication*. As we noted earlier, the term *person-to-group communication* is more inclusive than *public communication* or *public speech*. Person-to-group communication can occur in very formal situations complete with speaker's platforms and large audiences, or it can occur at a sales meeting or a church supper. Person-to-group communication occurs when one person talks to several other people at one time. The occasion can be formal or informal.

As we observed earlier, interpersonal communication is less monologic than person-to-group communication; there is more verbal give and take. Interpersonal communication usually takes place between two people or within very small groups. Its most distinguishing characteristic is that people communicate directly and individually with one another; they react to one another as individuals. Interpersonal communication is usually less organized than person-to-group communication. The differences between interpersonal and person-to-group communication are primarily differences of degree rather than differences of kind. For a more thorough discussion of these differences, review pages 10–13.

Throughout the book when we use the words *interpersonal partners,* we are referring to any persons who are mutually engaged in interpersonal communication. The partners can be well known to each other or only casual acquaintances. For our purposes, if they are communicating interpersonally, they are interpersonal partners for the time they are communicating.

Chapter Arrangement

The chapters are arranged so that speaking assignments progress from the simple to the more complex. However, for the most part the chapters are independent. They can be pursued in any order that seems appropriate.

Assignments

In the chapters that follow, suggested assignments appear at the end of each B section. Three kinds of assignments are included: integrated assignments, interpersonal assignments, and person-to-group assignments. The integrated assignments are designed to help you explore the ideas presented in both the A and B sections. They call upon you to think and talk about the ideas presented in the A section, while you are at the same time utilizing the suggestions for improved person-to-group communication that were presented in the B section. The interpersonal assignments deal primarily with interpersonal communication, and the person-to-group assignments deal primarily with person-to-group considerations.

In this chapter we looked at communication models, we discussed some general characteristics of the communication process, we examined some definitions of communication, and we talked about the format of the book.

Key Ideas in Review

☐ **The ability to communicate is the characteristic that most significantly distinguishes us from the other creatures of the earth.**

☐ **The quality of life we enjoy is directly related to our ability to communicate.**

☐ **Communication models are unrealistic in that they are static representations of a dynamic, complex, ongoing process; nevertheless, they are sometimes useful because they enable us to see some of the components involved and to note relationships that exist between those components.**

☐ **Human communication is multileveled.**

☐ **Human communication is cyclical.**

☐ **Human communication is unavoidable.**

☐ **Human communication does not transfer meaning directly.**

☐ **Communication is an integrated process.**

☐ **We have defined successful human communication as "a transaction in which shared meanings are created in response to the stimulation of verbal and/or nonverbal interaction."**

☐ **Each of the remaining chapters will focus on both interpersonal and person-to-group communication.**

Suggested Assignments

The suggested assignments that accompany the remaining chapters are designed to help you think about the material presented in the chapters while you are practicing appropriate communication skills. The assignments accompanying this chapter are designed to help you become better acquainted with your classmates and the general process of communication while you become accustomed to communicating with members of the class.

1. The class is divided into pairs, and partners talk with each other for ten minutes. Partners then introduce each other to the class. Information about hobbies, interests, place of birth, academic major, and so forth should be shared.

2. The class is divided into five groups. Group members introduce themselves and chat for five minutes. At a signal from the teacher two members from each group join a different group and introduce themselves. This process of discussion and regrouping is repeated several times.

3. The class is divided into small groups. Each group will develop and present to the class an original definition of communication.

4. The class is divided into small groups. Each group will develop and present to the class a model of human communication.

5. Select a short paragraph that interests you from a newspaper or magazine. Read the paragraph to the class and spend a few moments discussing it. This exercise is designed to help you become accustomed to communicating with the class.

6. This exercise will also help you become accustomed to speaking with the class. Select one of the following topics and chat informally about it to the class:

   a. For you, what would be the ideal meal?
   b. If money were no object and next weekend were a three-day weekend, what would you do with the time?
   c. What are your occupational goals?
   d. If you could relive one day of your life, what day would you relive, and why?
   e. What do you most like and dislike about your college?

7. Give a short, informal talk on a topic related to the general subject of communication. Sample topics are (1) the best or the poorest communicator you have encountered, (2) the relationship between communication and democracy, (3) personal benefits to be gained from improved communication, (4) what you would most like to gain from your college communication course.

Suggested Readings

Berlo, David K. *The Process of Communication: An Introduction to Theory and Practice*. New York: Holt, Rinehart & Winston, 1960. One of the best introductions to the study of the communication process. The author integrates material from the behavioral sciences, linguistics, and the philosophy of language. Highly recommended for the beginning student.

Budd, Richard W., and Ruben, Brent D., eds. *Approaches to Human Communication*. New York: Spartan Books, 1972. A fine collection of 24 essays by scholars from several disciplines. Each author provides a view of communication from her or his own field.

Reid, Ronald F., ed. *An Introduction to the Field of Speech*. Glenview, Ill.: Scott, Foresman, 1965. A collection of essays that demonstrates the breadth of the field of communication and tends to show how various areas in the field are related to common concepts.

Note Directory

1. Claude E. Shannon and Warren Weaver, *The Mathematical Theory of Communication* (Urbana: University of Illinois Press, 1949), p. 5.

2. Harold D. Lasswell, "The Structure and Function of Communication in Society" in *The Communication of Ideas,* ed. Lyman Bryson (New York: Harper & Row Publishers, 1948), p. 37.

3. David K. Berlo, *The Process of Communication: An Introduction to Theory and Practice* (New York: Holt, Rinehart & Winston, 1960), p. 72.

4. James C. McCroskey, *An Introduction to Rhetorical Communication: The Theory and Practice of Public Speaking* (Englewood Cliffs, N.J.: Prentice-Hall, 1968), p. 25.

5. Alfred G. Smith, ed., *Communication and Culture: Readings in the Codes of Human Interaction* (New York: Holt, Rinehart & Winston, 1966), p. v.

6. C. David Mortensen, *Communication: The Study of Human Interaction* (New York: McGraw-Hill Book Co., 1972), p. 14.

7. Shannon and Weaver, *Mathematical Theory,* p. 95.

8. Kathleen S. Verderber and Rudolph F. Verderber, *Inter-Act: Using Interpersonal Communication Skills* (Belmont, Calif.: Wadsworth Publishing Co., 1977), p. 4.

Chapter Two

**Concept
of
Self
and
Speaker**

How we perceive ourselves and others affects our ability to communicate by influencing how we both send and receive messages. In Section A of this chapter we will consider how our self-concept affects communication in interpersonal settings, and in Section B we will consider how our concept of the speaker's self affects communication in person-to-group settings.

Section A: Interpersonal Focus

We perceive ourselves: a discussion of the self-concept and how it affects interpersonal communication.

■ The nature of the self-concept ■ the self-concept evolves ■ the self-concept affects communication ■ the self-concept can be improved

Section B: Person-to-Group Focus

The audience perceives the speaker: a discussion of how audience perception of the speaker's self affects person-to-group communication.

■ Audience perception of the speaker's self makes a difference ■ image factors to be encouraged

Suggested Assignments

Section A

Interpersonal Focus

What a man thinks of himself, that it is which determines, or rather indicates, his fate.

Thoreau

Of the many elements that influence human communication, the self-concept is one of the most significant. In Section A of this chapter let us consider what the self-concept is, how it develops, how it affects communication, and how it might be improved.

The Self-Concept Defined

Your self-concept is the picture you have of yourself. Viewed from a distance this portrait may appear to be a single image. A closer look, however, reveals that it is an exceedingly complex dynamic. It is the rich, ever-shifting, ever-changing collage of images, ideas, and feelings you have about yourself. This mosaic includes impressions of your worth, your talents, your shortcomings, your relationships with others, your body, your sexuality, and all the countless other components of your self. Some of these impressions are willingly shared with others, some are privately held, and still others exist below the level of consciousness.

Sometimes a distinction is made between ideas about the self and feelings about the self. For most uses this distinction is unnecessary and even unrealistic. In actual practice it is impossible to separate ideas about self from feelings about self. Consequently, the term *self-concept* usually refers to the entire mixed bag of ideas and feelings we all have about ourselves.

Sometimes our self-concept contains elements that are less than realistic. Consider the example of Rachael, whom most people consider to be a very pretty young woman. During her childhood, however, she was thought to be less attractive than her two sisters. Unfortunate comparisons over the years led Rachael to accept the idea that she was unattractive. Today, although others admire her beauty, she still thinks of herself as an "ugly duckling." Frequently, formerly obese persons report that years after achieving and stabilizing a desirable weight level, they retain the negative feelings that went with being overweight.

These two examples show us that the photo album we call the self-concept sometimes includes pictures that are distorted, outdated, or unrealistic. Fortunately for Rachael and the rest of us, the self-concept is not static. The picture can be changed. Later in this chapter we will consider techniques for seeing ourselves more positively. The self-concept, then, is the total conglomerate of perceptions one has about oneself; it may contain incorrect pictures, and its development is continual.

The Development of the Self-Concept

To repeat, the self-concept is not static. It is constantly evolving. You are not born with a self-concept in the same way that you are born with blue eyes or brown eyes. Your self-concept must be developed. Several forces shape the development of the self-concept, and in this section we will consider some of the most important ones. An understanding of these factors will help us understand how others have influenced us and, perhaps more importantly, illuminate the responsibility we each have for those whose lives we influence.

People

People have the most significant influence on our sense of self. As we interact with others, we learn (correctly or incorrectly) what we are. This process starts at birth. Our parents, or the other "big people" who care for us through infancy, communicate to us with a number of nonverbal clues. The way the infant is held, the tone of a parent's voice, the state of comfort that is maintained—all communicate a degree of acceptance. Dr. Thomas Harris, in his popular book *I'm OK—You're OK*, explains the phenomenon in this fashion:

> During the first two years of life he does not have conceptual "thinking" tools—words —to construct an explanation of his uncertain status in his world. He is, however, continually recording the feelings which grow from the relationship between himself and others, primarily mother, and these feelings are directly related to stroking and nonstroking.[1]

In short, the way a child is treated in infancy becomes translated into positive or negative feelings of worth.

As we pass from infancy into childhood, the big people in our lives continue to communicate to us about who we are. Sometimes this communication is intentional and sometimes it is unintentional. Sometimes it is verbal and sometimes it is nonverbal. Sometimes it is realistic and sometimes it is not realistic.

For example, most adults remember chance remarks about themselves overheard in childhood. Curtis provides an example. Although he can't remember the specific details, he vividly remembers some words his parents spoke when he was a child. Apparently the words were given in response to a question about whether the boys (Curtis and his brother) would be going to college. The answer was "We are going to try to help James. We'll be lucky if Curtis makes it through grade one." Curtis is over sixty now and he still remembers that statement. The statement in itself may not be important, but the attitude that prompted it is. Parents' perceptions of children are often "picked up" by the children and believed. These parental perceptions are frequently accepted by the child without question and incorporated into his or her own self-concept. In this way, parental perceptions sometimes become boundaries for the child. They limit and define for the child what she or he is, or can become. Curtis knew even before he was enrolled in elementary school that success in school was outside his own reality. Today, over fifty years later, he is finally learning how unrealistic and unnecessary that limitation was and is.

Another example involves Don. At one time Don was almost convinced that he was a manual moron. His father, a skilled craftsman, was anxious that Don become skilled also. He was impatient with Don's early, clumsy attempts at toy repair, birdhouse construction, and similar projects. Don soon learned that he could not please his father, and by the time he enrolled in junior high he was convinced of his manual inadequacy. This example illustrates the gap that sometimes occurs between what parents expect and what children can deliver. Because small children are inexperienced, it seldom occurs to them that something is wrong with the expectation; they invariably assume the blame themselves. Gerald S. Blum states the matter as follows:

We learn cultural roles.

> The child lacks the equipment and experience necessary to form an accurate picture of himself, so his only guide is the reactions of others to him. There is very little cause for him to question these appraisals, and in any case he is far too helpless to challenge them or to rebel against them. He passively accepts the judgments, which are communicated empathetically at first, and by words, gestures, and deeds in this period.[2]

From parents and family, children also begin to learn about their cultural roles. These roles help us decide what we are and what we can become. Theresa learns that little girls do not climb trees and that women become nurses instead of doctors. Michael learns that little boys do not cry and that men must be aggressive and dominant. A sort of "catch-22" or irony is sometimes connected with these early role lessons.

At the very time Michael is learning that he is not supposed to feel pain, he does feel pain from time to time—and he knows

it. He also knows that on these occasions it feels good to cry. Caught between what he believes he ought to be and what he knows he is, Michael is apt to feel that something is wrong with him—that he is somehow inadequate. It takes some of us much of a lifetime to realize that we are all right, even though we do not perfectly fit the prevailing cultural stereotypes.

A vivid illustration of how powerfully parents can affect a child's sense of worth is provided by the sensitive and moving book *Dibs: In Search of Self* by Virginia Axline. Axline is a noted play therapist. Her book is not fiction; it is a case history. It is the story of a boy whose parents had inadvertently denied him any significant sense of self-worth. When the history begins, counselors, teachers, and psychologists are convinced that Dibs is mentally retarded. When it ends, Dibs is in a school for the gifted. This informative book validates the idea that the most significant gift children can receive from their parents is a sense of their own worth.

Parents and family, of course, are not the only adults in a child's life. Teachers, for example, have enormous impact on the developing self-images of their students. For most of our childhood, teachers are significant dispensers of praise and blame, of love and rejection. Talented indeed is the teacher who can let us know that we are important and still all right even though we are having problems with arithmetic or history. As stated by George A. Borden and John D. Stone, "In essence, the teacher becomes a significant other to the student and has a great deal to do with the student's picture of him or her self."[3] We will further consider the influence of teachers and schools when we look at cultural institutions in connection with the self-concept.

Although they have a tremendous influence, adults are not the only people in our childhood. We have siblings and playmates. These "little people" seldom hesitate to tell us about ourselves. Merna, a girl with a slight speech defect, responded positively to speech therapy, but it took considerable time for the negative feelings that accompanied the speech defect to disappear. These negative feelings had been induced in part by the taunts of other children. "Funny Merna—Merna talks funny."

When for better or for worse we leave childhood and become adults, other people continue to contribute to our self-perceptions. Our friends and acquaintances, our employers and fellow workers, and most of all our significant interpersonal partners help us define who we are and how we feel

"Sticks and Stones may break my bones, but names can give me an inferiority complex."

about ourselves. The kinds of messages we are able to send and receive in our interpersonal relationships provide for most adults a significant source of ideas and feelings about the self. In this sense interpersonal relationships can be growth-promoting—or just the opposite. For example, if in our interpersonal relationships we find acceptance, if the messages we receive affirm our importance and worth, then those relationships are sources of strength and positive feelings about the self. Conversely, if our relationships fail to provide acceptance, if we must wear disguises to gain approval, if the messages we receive are depreciating and negative, those relationships if not altered or terminated will be destructive. Perhaps this is what the psychologist Bonaro Overstreet means when he says, "We are not only our brother's keeper; in countless small and large ways, we are our brother's maker."[4] More of this later when we consider ways to improve the self-concept. Let us turn now to those social institutions that impinge upon our sense of self.

Social Institutions

Direct contact with people provides the most significant source of perceptions about who we are. Many other factors, however, are relevant. The many institutions in our society that tend to perpetuate cultural norms influence our self-concepts. Examples are the church, the school, and the media.

Many churches appear to have assumed responsibility for telling us who we are and what we ought to become. Some church doctrines apparently describe humankind as being evil or constantly on the verge thereof. Other doctrines are more hopeful and define us as being essentially good, or at least capable of becoming so. For many, the church is a definite source of positive or negative feelings about self.

Our schools constitute yet another source. For many, our schools provide success and acceptance. For far more, however, school provides alienation, failure, and debasement. Jonathan Kozol discusses this thesis in *Death at an Early Age*.[5] Many schools operate with the presumption that it is more edifying to emphasize a student's failures than to emphasize her or his strengths. These schools tend to limit rather than expand the student's sense of possibility. This is tragic not only for the students involved but for the rest of us as well.

Consider the following quotation:

People will behave only in ways that are appropriate to their own picture of themselves. People who have learned to think of themselves as competent, successful, and acceptable will undertake more tasks and persist longer against difficulties than those who have learned that they are incompetent and unsuccessful. It is a profligate waste of our national resources to teach millions of people to think of themselves as mediocre, incompetent, or failures at activities which are socially desirable and even essential. Every person who accepts such a concept of himself cuts down the standard of living, the safety, and security of his fellow citizens. He becomes less of an asset and more of a liability. Yet this is precisely what many of our schools are now doing by requiring all children to compete in a narrow range of verbal activities and giving recognition only to the winners.[6]

Another societal institution that affects most of us is the media. From the media we get, among other things, messages that tell us what we ought to be, what we should value, and of course what we should buy.

The organs of mass communication—printing, television and radio—provide the means of selecting, recording, viewing, and sharing man's notions of what is, what is important, what is right and what is related to what else.[7]

Our Selves

Thus far we have focused on forces outside the individual that help to form the self-concept. This is not to imply that we are helpless pawns swimming against a current over which we have no control. On the contrary, it should be emphasized that we ourselves must accept considerable responsibility for our feelings of self-worth.

We all choose to act in ways that either enhance or diminish our feelings of worth. For example, if I promise myself that I will quit smoking and I fail to do so, I disappoint not only my doctor and my family but also myself, and I lose a little respect for myself. On the other hand, when I succeed in doing something I consider worthwhile, I gain a little respect for myself. To illustrate further: From time to time most of us undertake self-improvement programs. We go on diets or start exercise regimes. The feelings of well-being that often accompany these programs frequently go beyond the immediate physiological benefits involved. We feel better about ourselves because we have chosen to act responsibly. As William Glasser states:

> A responsible person also does that which gives him a feeling of self-worth and a feeling that he is worthwhile to others. He is motivated to strive and perhaps endure privation to attain self-worth. When a responsible man says that he will perform a job for us, he will try to accomplish what was asked, both for us and so that he may gain a measure of self-worth for himself. An irresponsible person may or may not do what he says depending upon how he feels, the effort he has to make, and what is in it for him. He gains neither our respect nor his own, and in time he will suffer or cause others to suffer.[8]

We will return to this topic later in the chapter when we discuss ways of altering the self-concept. In review, the evolution of the self-concept begins at birth and continues throughout life. It is the product of social interaction. The major imprints result from interaction with others, from exposure to social institutions, and from the quality of our own behavior.

The Self-Concept and Communication

Thus far we have considered a definition of the self-concept and some of the forces that shape its evolution. The next question is, So what? Does it really matter? The answer is emphatically, yes. The self-concept does make a difference. Evidence from a variety of sources indicates that the self-concept is an important determinant of human behavior. We seem to be strongly motivated to act in ways that are consistent with our concept of self. When we feel good about ourselves, we reach higher, persist longer, and accomplish more than when we feel dissatisfied with ourselves. Support for this conclusion is found in an early study conducted by William W. Wattenberg and Clare Clifford, which concludes that measurements of the self-concept predict success in school more accurately than measurements of intelligence do.[9]

The importance of the self-image is further emphasized by Bernard Borislow.

> Using seventh-grade students in an urban school system, it was found that . . . there is a significant and positive correlation be-

tween self-concept and performance in the academic role; this relationship is substantial even when measured I.Q. is controlled.[10]

Research has also been done in areas other than academic achievement. J. Sterling Livingston,[11] Douglas McGregor,[12] and R. K. Merton[13] among others have studied the effect of the self-concept on performance in business and in other areas. The fact is that self-concept affects human behavior in any arena. As E. C. Kelly states:

> An inadequate concept of self, so common in our culture, is crippling to the individual. Our psychological selves may become crippled in much the same way as our physical selves may be crippled by disease or by an accident. They are the same, in effect, because each limits what we can do.[14]

In this section we are going to consider three means by which the self-concept affects human communication.

**The Self-Concept as
a Self-Fulfilling Prophecy**

Sometimes the self-concept acts as a self-fulfilling prophecy—a prophecy that comes true simply because the prophet believes it will come true. R. K. Merton, a sociologist at Columbia University, put the matter clearly, "The self-fulfilling prophecy is, in the beginning, a false definition of the situation evoking a new behavior which makes the originally false conception come true."[15]

For example, if Ann expects to do poorly in her history class, her expectation may cause her to behave so that she will do poorly. She may skip history assignments in favor of assignments for other classes. She may be reluctant to volunteer in class or to discuss the subject outside of class. In short, Ann may not approach her history class in the positive, constructive way she would approach a class about which she felt better. Thus, her prophecy concerning the class is self-fulfilling.

It is easy to see how this phenomenon could affect communication. If my self-concept is such that I feel others won't want to relate to me, I may act toward them in such a way that they won't want to relate to me. The opposite, of course, is also true. A salesperson who feels good about himself or herself approaches work with the persistent, confident enthusiasm that results in sales. This phenomenon is self-perpetuating. The better I feel about myself as a salesperson the more sales I make, and the more sales I make the better I feel about myself as a salesperson. If my self-concept is such that I feel people won't want to talk with me, I tend to behave in ways that discourage people from talking to me. Their behavior toward me in turn reinforces my original belief about myself.

Message Filter

In addition to sometimes functioning as a self-fulfilling prophecy, the self-concept affects communication by acting as a message filter. Each of us is motivated to maintain and protect the picture we have of ourselves. One of the ways we do this is by rejecting or distorting messages that jeopardize our picture of self while welcoming messages that reinforce our concept of self.

A man had been trim and athletic most of his life. When his doctor told him he had grown 28 pounds overweight, he refused to believe it. He rejected the message because it violated his self-concept. It took a considerable amount of nagging from his family for him to accept the fact that he was overweight. As S. I. Hayakawa states, "No man or woman can easily be persuaded to do something, to accept something, which violates or threatens his self-concept."[16]

A Factor in Defensiveness

The effect of the self-concept on communication can also be seen in the relationship between the self-concept and human defensiveness. Human response to threat is an important area for communication study. Perceived threat and the defensive reactions it invokes comprise one of the most fundamental barriers to successful communication. When people are threatened psychologically, they react with any number of defensive responses. Usually these defensive reactions are damaging to communication. We will pursue this subject in the next chapter.

Although no human being can be entirely free from defensive responses, some people become more easily threatened, and consequently more defensive, than others. Furthermore, most of us are more easily threatened in some situations than in others. When we feel positive about ourselves, we are less apt to be threatened than when we are unsure of ourselves. Generally speaking, therefore, people who possess positive self-concepts tend to be less defensive than people who have negative feelings about self. This idea is substantiated by Carl Rogers, Maslow, Rollo May, Sidney Jourard, and others who, when writing about the "psychologically mature person," have observed that self-acceptance and high self-esteem are often accompanied by acceptance of and tolerance for others with divergent viewpoints.

In summary, the self-concept affects communication by acting as a self-fulfilling prophecy, by serving as a message filter, and by affecting our responses in threatening situations.

Enhancing the Self-Concept

Thus far we have discussed what the self-concept is, how it develops, and how it affects communication. In this section we shall consider some suggestions for building positive feelings of self-worth. Sometimes talk about the self-concept gets pretty gloomy. If we don't emphasize that the self-concept can be changed, we may conclude that we are hopeless prisoners of the past. Nothing could be further from the truth.

Each of us can do something about the way we see ourselves. Consider two case histories. A man had spent a great deal of his life in assorted jails and prisons. One day, with the help of a counselor, he decided that he could change the way he saw himself. Today, in middle age, he has a college degree and is in charge of a program that helps other released prisoners. A woman spent most of her life serving her family. She thought she wasn't good for anything but waiting on others. With her family's support, she joined a self-improvement group and concentrated on changing her self-perception. She was so successful that last year she received her law degree. Both she and her family are pleased with her new self-image.

Changing the self-concept isn't always easy. It frequently requires considerable time and effort. People with stubborn, deep-seated feelings of self-doubt are advised to seek professional help. People without unusual problems, however, can usually learn to think more positively about themselves simply by making a conscious effort. For example, studies utilizing the Tennessee Self-Concept Scale conducted in my own department indicate that significant changes in the self-concept can occur in a one-semester college speech course.

The following suggestions have proven helpful for many. There is something self-fulfilling about them. When you have a little success, you feel better about yourself, and the better you feel about yourself the more you feel like trying. The more you try the better you feel—it is like yeast. The only trick is getting started. You probably won't want to try all the suggestions at once. Pick one or more that seem appropriate to begin with and get going!

The first suggestion is simply to decide to *take charge of and be responsible for your own life.* We can do something about most of the things that get us down—that is, we can do something once we break the spell that has some of us believing that what we become is up to someone else. Glasser and others who practice reality therapy believe that most people are happier when they take charge of themselves and accept responsibility for their own lives. That very stance is an act of self-affirmation. Once you realize that what you become is up to

you, you are on your way.

A second suggestion is to *develop self-acceptance.* This means accepting yourself as you are—crooked teeth and all. It doesn't mean that you must be wild about all aspects of yourself; it does mean that you accept that human beings have successes and failures, strengths and weaknesses, and that you are a human being. It helps to realize that you do not need to be like anyone else. You are important because you are unique. To forgive the past also helps. Some people cannot enjoy themselves today because they are stuck on something in the past. The general semanticists' concept of a process view of the world is useful here. This means that nothing stays the same, that everything is change. You are not the same person today that you were yesterday, or five years ago. Why waste time worrying about a you that no longer exists? Why not begin to accept the you that exists today? Self-acceptance is a comfortable thing and an important step. As Everett Shostrom says, "We must accept ourselves as we are, not regret that we are not gods. The paradox is that when we do accept ourselves we find ourselves growing and changing."[17]

A third suggestion, closely allied with the first, is to *work on one thing at a time.* Once we decide to take charge of our lives, we can start making whatever changes we choose. If, for example, you are discouraged about yourself because you are overweight, you can lose weight. If you think that people do not like you, you can find out why and act differently. One trick in making changes is to work on one thing at a time. Often we fail because we attempt a complete transformation all at once. A man decided to go on a diet, to stop smoking, and to start an exercise program all at once. He failed and continued to fail until he decided to work on those behaviors one at a time. After that it was easier. Once a desired behavior pattern has become habitual, go after another one. It also helps to be *specific* about what needs to be changed. Goals stated vaguely often seem unattainable. The statement "I want to become a better husband to my wife" is so broad it doesn't give much direction. On the other hand, if we say, "I am going to stop criticizing my wife in front of her friends," we have something specific enough to work with.

A fourth way we can alter our self-concept is to *assume control of the messages we send to ourselves.* There is little doubt that the language we use influences our thinking in many ways. The messages we send not only report our perceptions; they also influence them. This is partly explained by the theory of conditioning. If you receive an electric shock every time you smoke a cigarette, before long you will develop negative feelings about smoking. Negative messages, just like the electric shock, condition your perceptions to be negative. We are constantly transmitting messages about ourselves. When we transmit to others, the process is called communication; when we transmit to ourselves, it is called *thinking* or intrapersonal communication. The messages we send by either process influence self-perception. One way to build positive feelings about yourself is consistently to send positive *self-messages.* Self-messages are positive if they imply that what you think, feel, or want is important; they are negative if they imply that what you think, feel, or want is not important. Examples are given in the table.

Negative Self-Messages	Positive Self-Messages
Thoughts	
"You know more about that stuff than I do, Alice. If you think that sofa will work, O.K."	"Alice, I know you have had a lot of experience with this stuff, but I honestly think that it is too big for our room. Let's talk some more about it."
Feelings	
You decide that what you feel is not important enough to chance rocking the boat. You say nothing to your partner, and this, of course, says a lot to you.	"Vince, I want to talk to you. I feel awfully embarrassed when you act the way you did last night."
Desires	
"Gosh, it is up to you. I will eat whenever you want to."	"I am really hungry this afternoon. I would like to eat by five. O.K. with you?"

Upon first examination, some of the examples that are identified in the table as positive may appear to be negative. This is because, for reasons that are not entirely logical, many of us have been taught that denying our own importance is somehow virtuous. This comment is not meant as encouragement for conceit or self-indulgence. The point is that many of us have learned to act in ways that devalue our own worth. The messages inherent in these acts have been identified as self-messages—messages that either affirm or deny self-worth. They can emerge as thoughts we send to ourselves or as verbal and nonverbal cues we send to others.

Learning to send positive messages about the self is important in developing more positive self-perceptions. If you decide to make changes in this area, remember the advice given in the third suggestion: be specific and work on one area at a time. If, for example, you normally send negative self-messages when deciding with your partner how to spend leisure time, work on this area until you see improvement and then begin work on another. Success in one area, of course, tends to carry over into other areas. A word of caution is in order here: sending messages that affirm the importance of the self is important in building positive self-awareness, but care must be taken that in the process we do not deny the importance of others. Ideally our messages should say, "I am worthwhile, and so are you."

The fifth and last suggestion is to *utilize interpersonal relationships* to build self-esteem. Blessed indeed are those who find acceptance and affirmation within their interpersonal relationships. When within a relationship you are appreciated for what you are, when the communication you receive affirms your value, then the overriding message from that relationship is that you are worthwhile. Sometimes this kind of a relationship seems just to happen, but people can waste time merely waiting for it to happen. More often it must be developed. Partners can agree to work at building a relationship that will affirm the worth of each of them. Partners who are truly committed to working at it can develop just about any kind of relationship they desire. Simply acknowledging that relationships require some attention and tending is often a positive step toward growth. Partners should begin by agreeing on specific, realistic, attainable goals. Remembering that success grows on previous success, begin modestly and build.

Sometimes one partner can initiate change almost unilaterally. This happens because behavior within relationships tends to be reciprocal. If, for example, one partner is particularly punishing, other partners to the relationship can be expected to react defensively by finding their own ways to punish. In reaction, the original partner often becomes even more punishing, and thus the ugly cycle begins. A more positive communication climate can develop in the same manner. This was demonstrated by a woman who was enrolled in one of my classes. We had talked in class about the difficulty many of us have in expressing and receiving positive feelings. For her term project she decided to keep a diary of her efforts to express more freely her positive feelings toward members of her family. Her record shows that almost single-handedly she changed the communication climate within her family. As she more freely expressed positive feelings when she honestly felt them, others in the family felt free to do the same. Before long, the entire message structure within the family had improved.

Unfortunately, not all relationships are amenable to growth. Sometimes one or more of the partners are reluctant to work for change. In these cases professional counselors can often help the partners discover alternatives.

Once again, you are not stuck with a self-image over which you have no control. In this section we have considered five ways to develop more positive feelings about self. These suggestions have been: accept responsibility for your own life, develop self-acceptance, attempt specific changes one at a time, assume control over self-messages, and utilize interpersonal relationships for building self-esteem.

Key Ideas in Review

☐ **The self-concept is the complex collage of ideas and feelings one has about oneself.**

☐ **The self-concept sometimes includes unrealistic elements.**

☐ **The development of the self-concept begins at birth and continues throughout life.**

☐ **Major factors in the development of the self-concept are interaction with others, exposure to social institutions, and the quality of one's behavior.**

☐ **The self-concept influences communication because it is a factor in human defensiveness, because it acts as a self-fulfilling prophecy, and because it serves as a message filter.**

☐ **One can consciously alter one's self-concept.**

☐ **Five suggestions for developing a more positive self-concept are: accept responsibility for your own life, develop self-acceptance, attempt specific changes one at a time, assume control over self-messages, and utilize interpersonal relationships for building self-esteem.**

Section B

Person-to-Group Focus

What you are stands over you—and thunders so I cannot hear what you say to the contrary.

Emerson

The speaker's image exists in the minds of the listeners.

In Section A of this chapter we considered the fact that what we think about ourselves influences how we communicate with others. In this section we will explore the idea that what we think of others influences how they communicate with us. Our focus here will be on person-to-group communication, or public speaking. Specifically, we will note the importance of the listener's perception of the speaker's self and we will consider image factors to be encouraged.

The Importance of the Listener's Perception of the Speaker's Self

The listener's perception of the speaker's self is an important element in communication. Over the years it has been referred to variously as the *ethos* of the speaker, the speaker's *character*, the *personality* of the speaker, and the speaker's *attitude*. Regardless of how it's labeled, it is an important factor in communication. In addition to hearing speech, listeners hear a person speaking; and they react not only to what they hear but also to the way they feel about the person who is speaking.

This element of person-to-group communication has long been appreciated. The early Greek and Roman orators and teachers were aware of its importance. Over 2,000 years ago Aristotle said, "Character is the most potent of all means to persuasion."[18] Modern research has validated what speech scholars have known intuitively for centuries: that the listener's perception of the speaker's self makes a difference. Experimental studies have shown repeatedly that audience reaction to identical speeches varies widely when speaker credibility is manipulated by the experimenter.

Both experience and research illuminate numerous image factors. The matter is further complicated by the fact that these image factors interact with other variables in the speech situation. For example, the expertise and expectations of the audience, the occasion, and the speech subject and purpose intersect with such image factors as the speaker's perceived knowledge, honesty, friendliness, and motives to produce the audience-perceived speaker's image. To illustrate: a college football player speaking about football is perceived differently when talking to a Pop Warner team than when talking to a group of coaches or an audience of housewives. His image is further altered when he switches from the subject of football to politics or to an insurance policy he is trying to sell. In other words, your image as a speaker is not constant; you do not possess a good or a bad image as you possess blue or brown eyes. The speaker's image exists in the minds of the listeners and is affected by innumerable variables. The important thing to note is that the speaker can anticipate and partially control most of these variables. For example, if out of enthusiasm for a particular viewpoint the speaker overreaches the evidence or becomes too emphatic or too intolerant of opposition, the audience may react negatively. The image factors in this circumstance are well within the control of the speaker.

In the remainder of this chapter we will discuss some significant image factors that most speakers can usually control.

Perceived Image Factors to Be Encouraged

A review of pertinent literature suggests that perceived speaker confidence, authority, trustworthiness, tolerance, friendliness, and interest are significant image factors that the speaker can control to some degree.[19]

Perceived Confidence

In most circumstances a reasonable amount of confidence and composure will win for the speaker a measure of audience acceptance. On the other hand, audiences frequently react to speakers who are unsure and unusually nervous by becoming uncomfortable and disinterested. These facts are usually not seriously questioned. The question that does arise is "How can I reflect confidence when my stomach is full of butterflies?" Because most of us face this dilemma from time to time, let's briefly consider that old bugaboo—communication apprehension. What is it and what can we do about it?

Communication Apprehension Much of the excitement we feel as speakers is simply that—excitement. It is the normal exhilaration we experience in important situations that require us to produce specific results. Actors and athletes experience the same feelings before the curtain goes up or the game begins. These feelings are not altogether undesirable. They often stimulate us to do a better job. They help us become more animated and alert. The process works something like this:

1. We feel threatened. We learned in the first section of this chapter that we need the support and approval of others. As we will learn in the next chapter, we consequently consider evaluative situations to be threatening. When we experience situations in which we are going to be evaluated, we feel threatened because there is always the possibility that we will be evaluated negatively, that others might find us unworthy and withhold their approval. In practically every person-to-group situation, the speaker

exposes himself or herself to the possibility of rejection and disapproval. Consequently, for most of us, person-to-group communication situations contain an element of threat.

2. Our bodies react to the threat. Frequently in speaking situations our bodies respond as though the threat were real and as though it were physical. Often then, we experience the age-old "fight or flight" reaction we learned about in biology class. When we are endangered, our bodies become energized so that we can take action. Various organs of the body release stimulants into the bloodstream and the metabolism accelerates. If the situation were physical, we would utilize this extra energy by engaging in physical activity, such as running or fighting. The speaking situation, however, is usually not physical enough to utilize all the extra energy. In short, we are "stuck" with extra energy. This supercharged condition accounts for most of our discomfort—the pounding heart, the extra perspiration, the high-pitched voice, and the trembling arms and legs. As the body attempts to utilize the extra energy, opposing sets of muscles strain against each other and produce tension. In summary, most of the uncomfortable feelings associated with person-to-group speaking result from the body's having been tricked into the flight or fight reaction.

3. Special circumstances frequently intensify feelings of anxiety. These special circumstances are sometimes called *precipitating causes* or *immediate causes*. They include such things as lack of preparation, lack of knowledge about the subject, an unusual concern with self, an unrealistic achievement expectation, or a hostile audience.

Reducing Communication Apprehension As we have observed, some anxious feelings associated with person-to-group communication are normal and desirable. However, undue anxiety is debilitating because it can cause people to avoid communication. Fortunately, practically everyone can learn to control communication apprehension. If you are particularly apprehensive about communicating in person-to-group situations, carefully consider the following suggestions:

1. One of the most significant things you can do is to develop a positive attitude toward yourself as a speaker. One way to contribute to such an attitude is to realize that you don't need to be anything but yourself. Sometimes people suffer undue anxiety because they falsely believe that the speaking situation requires them to play the "role" of speaker. Role playing of this kind is unnecessary and harmful. You don't need to be anything but yourself. When you are yourself, you ring true; you are, of course, better at being yourself than anybody else. Instead of putting on an act, simply concentrate on your listeners and on accomplishing the purpose of your speech. Remember, a speech is simply a

convenient means for sharing your thoughts and feelings with others.

Another way to acquire a positive mental attitude is to realize that your listeners seldom perceive you to be as nervous as you think you appear. Numerous studies show that people rate their nervousness much higher than their audiences do.

Finally, you can sometimes achieve a favorable mental attitude with purposeful fantasizing. Sit quietly and entertain a daydream or fantasy in which you give a very satisfying, successful speech. See yourself being comfortable and happy in front of the class. Note the pleased reactions from your listeners as well as your feelings of satisfaction with the speech when it is finished. Fantasy rehearsals of this kind have proven to be remarkably effective for many people. They help replace unpleasant associations with pleasant ones.

2. Another way you can develop feelings of confidence is to gain experience. We are usually anxious in unfamiliar situations. Take full advantage of your speech class and get as much speaking experience in it as you can.

3. Still another way you can experience feelings of confidence is to be prepared. If you are thoroughly prepared you have little to fear.

4. An additional way to reduce tension is to select subjects you are really qualified to talk about. When you know your subject thoroughly, you can usually face your listeners with increased confidence.

In review, if you will establish a positive mental attitude, if you will gain all the experience you can this term, if you are prepared, and if you talk about subjects that you are qualified to talk about, the chances are high that you will develop confidence during the course of your speech class.

Perceived Speaker Authority

Audiences respond to speakers partly on the basis of how authoritative they perceive the speaker to be. I once demonstrated this tendency by playing a short, taped lecture on first aid in 30 undergraduate classes. In each case students were asked to rate the value of the lecture on a standard rating form. The only variable in the presentation was the reputation I provided for the speaker. One-half of the classes were told that the speaker was a medical doctor. The other half were told that the speaker was a junior high physical education teacher. The students who thought they were listening to a medical doctor rated the value of the speech significantly higher than did the other students. Sometimes audiences will overlook factors that otherwise would be negative if they perceive the speaker to be authoritative.

A man who was paroled after spending several years in prison for committing a number of robberies is presently in great demand as a speaker on "How to Prevent Robberies in Commercial Establishments." His audiences respond favorably because they believe he thoroughly knows whereof he speaks.

A valuable review of many interesting studies in this area is provided by Bert Bradley in his excellent text on the credibility of ideas.[20] Speakers can control this factor of the speaker's image simply by speaking only on topics they are thoroughly qualified to discuss.

Perceived Speaker Trustworthiness

The perceived trustworthiness of the speaker is another important factor of speaker credibility. Recent research confirms what common sense tells us: that we are more apt to be influenced by someone we trust than someone we do not trust. Once again, circumstances are important. One who is perceived as trustworthy in one situation may be seen as less trustworthy in a different situation.

The perceived motive of the speaker seems to be important in the perception of trustworthiness. The more self-serving we perceive the speaker to be, the less apt we are to bestow trust. A number of studies confirm this point. In one, subjects were presented messages from a convicted criminal. When the messages appeared to be self-serving, they evoked little opinion change within the subjects. When the messages implied that the sender was speaking against his own interest, significant opinion change occurred.

Speakers can promote audience trust by being objective and problem-oriented, by being honest with evidence and claims, by speaking for the common good, and by openly admitting personal interests when they exist.

Perceived Speaker Tolerance

Another image factor is perceived tolerance. Intolerance often leads to audience resistance. We want our leaders to stand for something, but we don't want them to have "tunnel vision." Speakers usually get the best results when they deal as tolerantly as possible with opposing ideas and viewpoints. They are also most apt to be perceived as being realistic, honest, and objective when they give credit where credit is due to opposing arguments, products, and ideas.

When speakers twist evidence to support a viewpoint or treat opposing viewpoints unfairly, they run the risk of being perceived as less than reliable. Research indicates that this is particularly true when audience members are well educated. In one study, groups of college students heard the summary for the prosecution and for the defense in a fictitious trial. Some groups heard one-sided arguments and other groups heard arguments on both sides. Students who heard the arguments for both sides changed their opinions more than did students who heard the one-sided arguments.

Perceived Speaker Friendliness

As we will observe many times in this book, human behavior tends to be reciprocal. Behavior begets like behavior. When we are supportive of people, they are more apt to be supportive of us. When we growl at people, they usually growl back. When the speaker approaches the audience with genuine goodwill, he or she does much to dissipate hostility and resistance. If nothing more, perceived friendliness usually wins for the speaker initial interest and attention.

The contagious nature of genuine friendliness and goodwill was often demonstrated by James O'Hara, who as a congressman from Michigan served as chairman of the House Subcommittee on Post-Secondary Education during the early 1970s. No stranger to controversy, O'Hara frequently took strong stands. Nevertheless, he was widely respected and in great demand as a speaker. As one observer pointed out, "He has the uncanny ability to communicate to each audience a genuine sense of respect and goodwill." Although he and his listeners sometimes disagreed about substantive matters, he usually received a courteous and thoughtful hearing. It was difficult for people to feel hostility toward one so cheerful and charming.

The person-to-group speaking situation need not be a contest. It is a time for sharing ideas and feelings, and the sharing usually goes better when the speaker approaches the occasion in a spirit of friendship and goodwill.

Perceived Speaker Interest

Interest is catching. Listeners can catch it from the speaker. When the speaker is genuinely interested in the subject and in discussing it with the audience, listeners are likely to become interested also.

In the next chapter we shall discuss the kinds of behaviors that people often find threatening. You will learn, for example, that we are often threatened by indifference. We like to feel that we count for something, that others care about us. When speakers simply "go through the motions," when verbally and nonverbally they signal that they don't care about talking to us, we are likely to respond defensively. Both you and your listeners are more likely to enjoy the communication when you talk about something that really interests you and when you allow your listeners to sense your interest.

In this section of the chapter, we have examined perceived speaker confidence, authority, trustworthiness, tolerance, friendliness, and interest as significant image factors. Each of these factors can be controlled to some degree by the speaker.

Key Ideas in Review

□ Audience perception of the speaker's self is an important element in the communication process.

□ The speaker's image exists within the minds of the listeners.

□ The speaker's image isn't constant but varies from situation to situation.

□ Research has isolated many interacting factors that contribute to audience perception of the speaker's self.

□ Many important image factors can be controlled in part by the speaker.

□ Six significant image factors are perceived speaker confidence, authority, trustworthiness, tolerance, friendliness, and interest.

Suggested Assignments

Integrated Assignments

The following assignments are designed to help you further understand and explore the concepts presented in both sections A and B of this chapter. These assignments call upon you to think and to talk about Section A while you are utilizing the suggestions for improved person-to-group communication from Section B. Please note that the speaking assignments in this book reflect a progressive, "building block" approach. They progress from the very simple to the more demanding. Don't think of the first few assignments as speeches; think of them as conversations before the class. They are designed to help you learn to speak naturally, conversationally, and comfortably before the audience, while at the same time exploring principles of interpersonal communication. The speaking assignments will become progressively more complex. Soon you will be giving well-organized, fully developed speeches while at the same time learning about interpersonal communication.

Present a short, informal talk to the class. Do your best to reflect positively those elements of the speaker's image that were presented in the chapter. This should not be difficult because all the subjects listed below call for you to speak from your own experience. Speaking from your own experience is one of the quickest ways to learn to reflect positive image factors. Additionally, each of the topics listed below calls upon you to explore some aspect of the self-concept, which was the subject of Section A of this chapter.

As you begin working on this assignment, please remember that a speech is not a performance. It is simply a means by which you share with other people something that is important to you.

Speech Topics

1. Using any materials available, build a collage that represents you. Your speech will consist of explaining how the various parts of the collage represent different aspects of you.

2. Give an object speech. Bring an object to class that you feel symbolizes you. Talk about the object and explain in what ways it symbolizes you.

3. Discuss a specific part or aspect of your own self-concept. Consider such points as what forces may have shaped its development, how it affects your communication, whether you want to retain this particular element. Be specific. Whenever possible illustrate with examples.

4. In Section A of this chapter we considered some factors that normally influence the development of the self-concept. With examples from your own life, illustrate a number of those factors and explain the influence of such elements as parents, siblings, teachers, books, and TV. The important thing is to provide examples from your own life.

5. Explain how you may have influenced the self-concept of someone else. Illustrate your speech with specific examples.

6. Explain the specific measures you would take as a parent or a teacher to encourage your children or students to experience more positive feelings of self-worth. Illustrate your ideas with examples.

7. With examples from your own life or the life of someone you know well, illustrate how the self-concept influences behavior. Fill your speech with specific examples.

8. Explain how advertisers and salespersons utilize the self-concept of potential buyers to promote sales. Fill your speech with specific examples.

9. With several specific examples, illustrate the phenomenon of the self-fulfilling prophecy.

10. Demonstrate with examples how the self-concept sometimes acts as a message filter.

11. Explain how your self-concept might affect you as a public speaker. Illustrate your speech with examples.

12. Explain at least three worthwhile things you did last week. The events need not be momentous. You can describe such things as passing up an extra dessert, helping a friend with homework, or resisting an urge to skip class.

13. Discuss some things you like about yourself. Illustrate your speech with specific examples.

14. Describe some changes that could be made in a current relationship that would encourage the partners to experience more positive feelings of self-worth.

15. Explain some changes you could make in your life that would promote a more positive self-image.

Auxiliary Assignments

Interpersonal Focus

1. This exercise is divided into two parts. First, on a piece of notebook paper answer the following questions in as much detail as you can manage. No one will grade your paper; be as candid as possible. If it is easier, use shorthand or simply jot down brief notes. Try to recall as much detail as possible, however.

   a. Did people or events ever help you feel proud of yourself as you were growing up? Describe the people and the events.

    b. Did people or events ever cause you to feel ashamed? Describe and explain.

    c. Did you feel positive or negative about your body as you were growing up? Explain.

    d. Did you feel essentially smart or stupid as a youngster? Who and what helped you feel this way?

    e. As a child did you feel secure or insecure? What events and what people helped you feel this way?

    f. If you were answering these questions about your life today, would you answer in the same way?

After everyone has had a chance to answer these questions either at home or in class, the class is divided into small groups. Group members discuss their answers to the questions.

2. Following are six ideas taken from the chapter:

    a. Our parents contribute to the development of our self-concepts.

    b. Schools contribute to the development of our self-concepts.

    c. As adults our sense of self can be positively or negatively affected by our interpersonal relationships.

    d. The self-concept sometimes affects communication by acting as a self-fulfilling prophecy.

    e. The self-concept sometimes affects communication by serving as a message filter.

    f. People transmit either positive or negative self-messages.

The class is divided into six groups. Each group prepares and presents a role-playing scene designed to illustrate one of the aforementioned ideas.

3. The class is divided into groups of five or six. Each group will devise a list of suggestions for home and school that might help family members and students feel more positive about themselves. When the groups are finished, each list is read and then discussed by the entire class.

4. With a horizontal line, divide a piece of notebook paper in half. On the top half list six words that you feel represent how others see you. Also on the top half of the paper draw a picture or a design that you feel illustrates how others see you. Repeat this process on the bottom half of the paper, but use words and a design that represent how you feel you really are. Papers should be submitted anonymously. If possible, they should be displayed temporarily for the entire class to view.

5. This short exercise can be repeated throughout the course. The class is divided into groups of five or six. Group members take turns telling something about themselves or something they have done of which they are proud. The exercise continues until each person has made at least three positive statements about herself or himself.

Person-to-Group Focus

1. Give a short speech in which you discuss personality traits or image factors you have observed that have influenced the speaking of others. Your materials can come from your observations of such speakers as teachers, ministers, and television personalities. Discuss traits that have been helpful as well as detrimental to communication.

2. People frequently feel better in front of an audience when they have something to do with their hands or body. Give an object speech. Select an object that lends itself to demonstration and explain what it does, how it works, or how to use it. Tools, toys, instruments, sporting goods, kitchen gadgets are samples of objects that lend themselves to this assignment.

3. One of the quickest ways to develop poise and confidence in front of an audience is to speak from your own experience. Give a short

speech to the class that you can prepare entirely from your own experience. Tell about the funniest thing that ever happened to you, or the most embarrassing, or the most exciting, or the most frightening. Tell about your pet peeve or your plans for the future, or your greatest regret. Be sure the topic is one you can develop completely from your own experience.

4. For this exercise the class should be divided into groups of four or five. Group members discuss their own experiences with stage fright.

5. Before coming to class question five people about what they consider to be desirable and undesirable speaker personality traits. The results of these interviews will be shared in a general class discussion.

Suggested Readings

Interpersonal Focus

Bird, Caroline. *Born Female: The High Cost of Keeping Women Down*. Rev. ed. New York: David McKay Co., 1971. At one time a best seller, this book describes the restrictions our culture places upon women and the restrictions it teaches women to place upon themselves.

Farrell, Warren. *The Liberated Man: Beyond Masculinity: Freeing Men and Their Relationships with Women*. New York: Random House, 1975. A highly recommended book about how our culture defines men and teaches them to define themselves. It is readable and well documented.

Laing, Ronald D. *The Politics of Experience*. New York: Random House, 1967. The author, an English psychoanalyst, tells about some of the things that happen to people when they engage in behaviors that are damaging to their self-concepts. A fine book for serious students.

Rogers, Carl R. *On Becoming a Person: A Therapist's View of Psychotherapy*. Boston: Houghton Mifflin, 1961. A collection of essays. The classic text on what it means to be an authentic person.

Stevens, John O. *Awareness: Exploring, Experimenting, Experiencing*. Lafayette, Calif.: Real People Press, 1971. One of the most comprehensive books on self-awareness. It presents a collection of exercises you can do by yourself, with a partner, or in a group.

Person-to-Group Focus

Andersen, Kenneth E. *Persuasion: Theory and Practice.* Boston: Allyn & Bacon, 1971, pp. 217–63. A comprehensive development of many factors relating to ethos.

Brooks, Robert D., and Scheidel, Thomas M. "Speech as Process: A Case Study." *Speech Monographs* 35, no. 1 (March 1968): 1–7. An easy-to-read study that shows some of the ways an image can change during communication.

McCroskey, James C. *An Introduction to Rhetorical Communication: The Theory and Practice of Public Speaking.* 2d ed. Englewood Cliffs, N. J.: Prentice-Hall, 1972, pp. 63–81. A good discussion of ethos and source credibility and their effects on communication.

Note Directory

1. Thomas A. Harris, *I'm OK—You're OK: A Practical Guide to Transactional Analysis* (New York: Harper & Row Publishers, 1967), p. 41.

2. Gerald S. Blum, *Psychoanalytic Theories of Personality* (New York: McGraw-Hill Book Co., 1953), pp. 73–74.

3. George A. Borden and John D. Stone, *Human Communication: The Process of Relating* (Menlo Park, Calif.: Cummings Publishing Co., 1976), p. 162.

4. Bonaro Overstreet, quoted in Ardis Whitman, "The Courage to Trust," *Reader's Digest,* (December 1968), pp. 140–42.

5. Jonathan Kozol, *Death at an Early Age* (Boston: Houghton Mifflin, 1967).

6. Arthur W. Combs and Donald Snygg, *Individual Behavior: A Perceptual Approach to Behavior* (New York: Harper & Row Publishers, 1949), p. 223.

7. George Gerbner, "Communication and Social Environment," in *Communication: A Scientific American Book* (San Francisco: W. H. Freeman, 1972), p. 113.

8. William Glasser, *Reality Therapy: A New Approach to Psychiatry* (New York: Harper & Row Publishers, 1965), p. xv.

9. William W. Wattenberg and Clare Clifford, "Relation of Self-Concepts to Beginning Achievement in Reading," *Child Development* 35, no. 2 (June 1964): 467.

10. Bernard Borislow, "Self-Evaluation and Academic Achievement," *Journal of Counseling Psychology* 9 (1962): 246–54.

11. J. Sterling Livingston, "Pygmalion in Management," *Harvard Business Review* 47, no. 4 (July–August 1969): 81–89.

12. Douglas McGregor, *The Human Side of Enterprise* (New York: McGraw-Hill Book Co., 1960), pp. 139–41.

13. Robert K. Merton, *Social Theory and Social Structure* (Glencoe, Ill.: Free Press, 1957), pp. 421–36.

14. Earl C. Kelly, "The Fully Functioning Self," in *Perceiving, Behaving, Becoming: A New Focus for Education,* ed. Arthur W. Combs (Washington: Association for Supervision and Curriculum Development, 1962), p. 10.

15. Merton, *Social Theory,* p. 423.

16. Samuel I. Hayakawa. *Symbol, Status, and Personality* (New York: Harcourt Brace Jovanovich, 1963). p. 46.

17. Everett L. Shostrom, *Man, the Manipulator: The Inner Journey from Manipulation to Actualization* (New York: Bantam Books, 1968), p. 177.

18. Aristotle, *The Rhetoric of Aristotle,* trans. Lane Cooper (New York: Appleton-Century-Crofts, 1932), p. 9.

19. For a review of research on speaker-image, see Kenneth Andersen and Theodore Clevenger, Jr., "A Summary of Experimental Research in Ethos," *Speech Monographs* 30 (June 1963): 59–98.

20. Bert E. Bradley, *Fundamentals of Speech Communication: The Credibility of Ideas* (Dubuque, Iowa: William C. Brown Co., 1974), pp. 272–73.

Chapter Three

**Threat
and
Defensiveness**

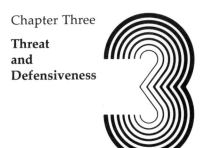

An important area for communication study is human response to threat and the effect of threat on communication. In Section A of this chapter we will consider threatening and supportive behaviors and defensive reactions in interpersonal communication. In Section B we will consider the same factors as they apply in person-to-group communication.

Section A: Interpersonal Focus

We support or threaten those around us: a discussion of threat and defensiveness in interpersonal communication.

■ The reciprocal nature of defensiveness ■ threatening and supportive behaviors ■ defensive responses

Section B: Person-to-Group Focus

The speaker threatens or supports the audience: a discussion of threat and defensiveness in person-to-group communication.

■ The Gibb study revisited ■ the conversational mode as supportive behavior ■ developing the conversational mode ■ speech preparation and the conversational mode

Suggested Assignments

Section A

Interpersonal Focus

Act so as to elicit the best in others and thereby in thyself.

Felix Adler

One of the surest ways to encourage communication is to provide a climate in which all the partners feel it is safe to communicate. Conversely, one of the surest ways to discourage communication is to fill the environment with threat and the defensive responses that are the inevitable result of threat. When we are threatened physically, we try to protect ourselves. We run or fight or cry, or do any number of other things that we have learned might work for us. When we are threatened psychologically, we react similarly. We respond with complex defense mechanisms; unfortunately, however, these reactions are usually harmful to communication. If in our relationships with others we wish to establish conditions favorable to mutually satisfying communication, we must reduce threat and replace it with support. Instead of attacking we must reinforce the security of others.

It is sometimes difficult to remove threat because we frequently threaten others without meaning to or without knowing we have done so. The difficulty is compounded by the fact that we tend to behave in fairly regular patterns. Some people are consistently easy to talk with because they have learned to behave in patterns that

are nourishing and supportive. Others have learned, (usually inadvertently) to behave in ways that are toxic and threatening. In Section A of this chapter we shall discuss the reciprocal nature of defensiveness, some threatening and supportive behaviors, and some common defensive reactions.

The Reciprocal Nature of Defensiveness

One of the reasons that defensive reactions are so destructive to communication is that they are reciprocal, or cyclical. For example, when one partner in a relationship becomes defensive, his or her behavior threatens other partners to the relationship, and they in turn become defensive. Their defensiveness is perceived by the original partner, who reacts with increased defensiveness, which in turn creates increased defensiveness in the other partners. The ugly cycle often continues until constructive communication is impossible. To put it in other words: when A is threatened, her or his consequent defensive behavior tends to threaten B, whose defensive reactions to A tend to intensify A's defensiveness. This in turn intensifies B's reactions, which in turn intensifies A's reactions, and so on. For the symbols A and B, you may substitute any number of words, such as parent and child, husband and wife, teacher and student, employer and employee, or policeman and demonstrator.

The reverse of this process is, of course, also true. We can start the cycle of reduced defensiveness simply by becoming less defensive ourselves. When we reach an impasse with another person, we often tend to increase our attack and, consequently, to intensify the defensiveness of the person we are trying to reach. By replacing the attack with an effort to understand and support, we can often reduce the other's defensiveness (and, consequently, our own) and improve the chances for meaningful communication. Most of us have observed this phenomenon in momentary arguments.

This same reciprocal phenomenon can be observed in relatively long-term situations. If over a period of time we want our partners to be nondefensive with us, we must be nonthreatening with them. In turn, if over a period of time we are going to be encouraged to behave in ways that are nonthreatening to our partners, they must be supportive of us. With our support or lack of it, we help to shape our partners and they in turn help to shape us.

Threatening and Supportive Behaviors

Many researchers have helped us identify both threatening and supportive behavior patterns. One of the most famous studies was conducted by Jack Gibb, a noted psychologist. After analyzing tape recordings of discussions that took place in a variety of settings, Gibb articulated six paired categories of threatening and supportive behaviors.[1] The categories are given in the table.

Before considering each category, we should emphasize that a variety of elements operate to diminish or intensify reactions to these behaviors. For instance, in this context when we talk about threat we are talking about perceived threat. The so-called threatening behaviors are threatening only if they are perceived as threatening. Of course, some people are more easily threatened than others, and each of us is less secure in some situations than in other situations. Also, the communication atmosphere changes continuously. Furthermore, we should note that one behavior often alters the effect of another behavior. For example, a high degree of honesty and openness in a situation could mitigate what otherwise would be threatening behavior. This interaction occurs among all the categories. We are going to discuss them separately here for convenience of study; more realistically, they intermix with a variety of effects.

Threatening Behaviors	Supportive Behaviors
1. Evaluation	1. Description
2. Control	2. Problem orientation
3. Strategy	3. Spontaneity
4. Neutrality	4. Empathy
5. Superiority	5. Equality
6. Certainty	6. Provisionalism

We are less secure in some situations than in others.

Evaluation and Description

Behavior perceived as evaluative is frequently threatening and, consequently results in defensiveness. A synonym for the term *evaluation,* as it is used here, is judgment. To be judged or evaluated is threatening for most of us. There is always the possibility that the evaluation will be unfavorable or that it will make us feel somehow inferior to the evaluator. The experience can leave us feeling diminished. From his vast background of experience in counseling and psychotherapy, Carl Rogers presents the significance of evaluation this way: "I would like to propose, as an hypothesis for consideration, that the major barrier to mutual interpersonal communication is our very natural tendency to judge, to evaluate, to approve or disapprove, the

statement of the other person, or the other group."[2]

We can convey an impression of being judgmental by what we say, by our tone of voice, by our posture, by the way we listen, by being late for an appointment, or by myriad other verbal and nonverbal means. Sometimes evaluation is perceived where none has been intended. Generally, the more insecure we are in a situation the more conscious we are of evaluation. A simple pleasantry, such as "Where have you been?" can be perceived as evaluative if the person being questioned is feeling guilty about where he or she has been. A comment, such as "George certainly takes good care of his place," can be interpreted as evaluative by me if I am feeling ashamed of my own unkept lawn.

A student once provided this example: Her father reacted sharply when she suggested that he try a particular kind of aftershave lotion. A later discussion revealed that the father, a man who was displeased to be approaching middle age, interpreted his daughter's suggestion as a criticism of his ability to remain in tune with the times.

Unlike evaluative behavior, *descriptive communication* tends to provoke minimal resistance. It carries with it no implication of judgment. Speech that is descriptive solicits information without suggesting that an evaluation of the information source is being made. It also gives no indication that the source should make a change in attitude or behavior. Counselors and therapists learn that, to encourage clients to discuss significant problems, they must listen descriptively. They must listen with interest and care, without passing judgment.

The difference between descriptive behavior and evaluation can be illustrated in this way: When my wife asks, "What are you doing in the refrigerator?" the question is evaluative. I am trying to lose weight and she is my self-appointed conscience. She wants to know what I am doing because she is going to judge me—which, of course, is what any steadfast conscience ought to do. When my son asks the same question, it is strictly descriptive. He is not interested in my diet and is not going to judge my sins in the kitchen. He merely wants information because he too is hungry.

We can't eliminate evaluative behavior entirely. On some occasions it is perfectly appropriate. It is when we become overly and unnecessarily evaluative that we pollute the communication environment.

Control and Problem Orientation

Just as too much evaluation can be detrimental to communication, so can too much control. A certain amount of control is often necessary and desirable. However, in interpersonal situations, excessive and unnecessary control can stimulate defensive reactions. Our interpersonal communication is controlling when it denies others the possibility of being persons separate from us—when it insists they think and feel as we think and feel. Specifically, we are controlling when our purpose is to have others act in ways that we have pre-chosen. We are controlling when we limit and structure the participation of others by interrupting, changing the subject, or insisting that they speak only in response to our ques-

tions. We are controlling when we dismiss or postpone consideration of issues that are of concern to our partners. The list is endless.

Unlike control, *problem orientation* is marked by respect for the sovereignty of each individual. When our behavior is problem oriented, our objective is to discover mutually satisfying solutions and positions. When control is our aim, we often lose sight of the common good and our objective becomes the personal gratification that comes from "winning" or imposing our will upon others. These two tendencies are infectious. When partners are problem oriented, the atmosphere is usually cooperative and supportive. When they try to control one another, the atmosphere is frequently competitive and threatening, and the chances for communication are reduced.

The following hypothetical examples may illustrate the difference between control and problem orientation: When group A comes together to solve a problem, its members have not only considered the problem but have arrived at individual solutions. At their meeting, they spend little time in mutually examining the problem and much time in attempting to persuade others to preconceived solutions. Little listening, little compromise, but much defending is accomplished in group A's meeting. The members of group B also think about the problem before the meeting, but they stop short of "marrying" a particular solution. They come to the meeting with knowledge of the subject but also with openness and a willingness to search for, and accept, the best solution. Group B's meeting is imbued with a spirit of cooperation. Group B spends most of its time on the problem and little time with personal defenses. The best results usually come from Group B. The same principle applies to individual encounters. When we become involved in the control game, we often damage the climate for communication.

Strategy and Spontaneity

In interpersonal encounters *strategy* is used when a person attempts to manipulate others by means of disguised techniques. These maneuvers are often carefully planned in advance. Most of us resent being treated dishonestly, and the strategist usually tries to keep real motives and feelings hidden. You are a strategist when you flatter partners simply to achieve a personal favor, you are a strategist when you pretend friendship for an acquaintance because you want to meet his sister, you are a strategist when you invite someone on an outing in the hope that he or she will volunteer the use of a car. You are also being strategic when you disguise a self-serving action with the statement, "I am doing this for your own good." Everett Shostrom chronicles a vast number of common strategies in his interesting book, *Man, the Manipulator.*[3]

Unfortunately for the strategist, we usually are quick to detect dishonest behavior. Gibb observed this point in his study: "Monitoring the tapes of feedback and evaluation sessions in training groups indicates the surprising extent to which members perceive the strategies of their colleagues. This perceptual clarity may be quite shocking to the strategist, who usually feels that he has cleverly hidden the motivational aura around the 'gimmick.'"[4]

The opposite of strategy is *spontaneity*. When communication is spontaneous, genuine, and real, when it comes from our depths without the complications of deceit, it tends to reduce defensiveness. Rogers says, "In place of the term realness I have sometimes used the word congruence. By this I mean that when my experiencing at the moment is present in my awareness, and when what is present in my awareness is present in my communication, then each of these three levels matches or is congruent. At such moments I am integrated or whole, I am completely in one piece. Most of the time of course I, like everyone else, exhibit some degree of incongruence. I have learned, however, that realness, or genuineness, or congruence—whatever term you wish to give to it—is a fundamental basis for the best of communication."[5]

Neutrality and Empathy

Perhaps a better word for what Gibb calls *neutrality* is *indifference*. The perception that others are indifferent to us can be very painful. Indeed, it has been hypothesized that the cruelest of all punishments would be a long lifetime of being completely ignored by other people. For psychological health, each of us needs the warmth of human caring, consequently, we often react defensively when we sense indifference from our partners.

Unfortunately, in this mechanized world it is not difficult to feel that nobody cares. As the humorist Sam Levinson once observed, "You can go into a modern supermarket and find 35 kinds of cottage cheese—but no one to say, hi Sam, how are the kids?" I know of elderly people in large cities who shop for clothes they will never buy simply to secure a few moments of human contact with a salesperson. I have talked to small children who have deliberately misbehaved in order to be punished; negative attention for them was better than none at all. I have worked with husbands and wives who within the framework of their marriages have felt the chill of indifference. We suggest indifference or neutrality by what we do and do not do, as well as by what we say and do not say. It is conveyed by such means as tone of voice, posture, and facial expressions.

Physical and vocal clues that demonstrate concern and respect for the well-being of others communicate *empathy*. Whereas neutrality stimulates defensiveness, empathetic communication is particularly supportive. When another person's way of speaking or listening to us gives us the impression that they genuinely care about our feelings and ideas, we feel encouraged to communicate in open and trusting ways. We are going to consider this further in chapter 6, which is about listening.

Superiority and Equality

We sometimes feel belittled and act defensively when others communicate to us their feelings of *superiority*. Of course superiority does exist—people are not identical. Some can throw a baseball harder than others, some know more about history, some have more money, and so on. However, when little significance is attached to these differences, they seldom are perceived as threatening.

When communicators project feelings of *equality*, they do much to enrich the communication environment. The perception of equality assures us that our ideas and feelings will be treated with respect and importance. To illustrate: Teachers who enjoy impressing students with their "superior" knowledge often stimulate resistance. Other teachers, who are able to communicate that we are all equally important as human beings in spite of our differing backgrounds, abilities, training, and talents usually get a fair hearing from their students.

Certainty and Provisionalism

In this context, *certainty* refers to a closed-minded, I-am-always-right attitude. Certainty discourages communication. It is hard to talk to someone who is closed to new ideas. *Provisionalism*, the opposite of certainty, encourages communication. When a person reflects provisionalism, he or she communicates a willingness to be open, to experiment, to examine additional data and alternate viewpoints. You do not need to be without opinions to be provisional. People who demonstrate provisionalism frequently take strong stands, but in doing so they remain open for further data. Their attitude seems to be: "This is the way I feel now, but I am willing to learn more."

In review, we have considered six pairs of threatening and supportive behaviors. These categories were first articulated by

Jack Gibb in 1961. In the next few pages we will examine some of the ways we react when threatened.

Defensive Responses

Defensive responses often become so habitual that we fail to recognize them in ourselves and others; consequently, we sometimes fail to deal with them. This is not to suggest that defensive responses are completely undesirable. There are times when they are useful. However, they are habit forming, and overdependence on them can prevent us from dealing with their basic cause. Defensive reactions need to be considered because they are frequently disruptive to communication. John Powell calls them "human hiding places."[6] In this section we will examine some common mechanisms of defense.

Emotional Insulation

Emotional insulation occurs when we reduce emotional involvement in order to escape the pain it might incur. A person who has experienced hurt in a relationship sometimes withholds further emotional commitment to avoid similar hurts. Military corpsmen, doctors, nurses, and policemen, for example, often become emotionally insulated to reduce the pain of observing human suffering. When interpersonal partners experience emotional insulation, they fail to relate to one another as complete people.

Apathy

With *apathy* we escape failure and possible disappointment by not caring. A child who is threatened by a lesson may withdraw with listlessness and indifference. For example, a young boy wanted to play Little League baseball so intensely that the thought of failure frightened him. When asked why he did not try out for a team, he said, "I am not interested in that stuff any more, I have other things to do." When I am afraid you are going to reject me, or in some other way hurt me, I may respond by saying to myself, "Who needs her, I don't even like her anymore." Apathy prevents us from "taking our best shots."

Fantasy

With *fantasy* we escape from problems and unpleasant situations by retreating into the unreal world of our dreams. We escape the boredom of lectures by fantasizing instead of listening. We compensate for making a mistake by fantasizing about what we will do the next time around. When my employer treats me unfairly, I assuage the hurt by dreaming about how I will behave when I am the boss. Fantasies are sometimes entertaining, but frequently they are poor substitutes for constructive action. If I am afraid to say what I would like to say to you—and I consequently substitute fantasy for action—you may never know how I feel.

Dependency

Sometimes we escape problems by reverting to a childlike state of *dependency* on others. The wife who says, "Dear, I just don't know what to do about the children —I am going to leave it all up to you"; the husband who, afraid of making the wrong choice, says, "I don't care where we take my parents this weekend, you decide"; the committee member who says, "You are all so much brighter than I am, I am just going to depend on the rest of you to solve this problem"—all provide examples of dependency. Relationships often suffer when partners depend on the "tooth fairy" to make improvements in the relationship.

Identification

Sometimes we avoid responsibility by adopting the behavior of others with whom we strongly identify. Or, when we feel unsure, we may compensate by imitating someone else. *Identification* occurs in interpersonal relationships when we relate to one another by imitating popular models. Unfortunately, the models we learn from are sometimes poor models. Another negative aspect of identification is that we may get so involved in imitating someone else that we deny our own feelings and ideas.

Suppression

We are using *suppression* when we escape from unpleasant situations by denying their existence. You are supposed to study for a test tonight, but instead you go bowling with friends. Since you cannot enjoy the evening if you think about the test, you push the thought of it out of your mind. Suppression is particularly damaging to interpersonal relationships when partners suppress problems in the relationship itself and fail to face them squarely.

Compensation

Compensation is seen when we camouflage a perceived weakness by emphasizing a strength. The student, for example, who considers herself unfit for sports may work exceptionally hard at her hobby of electronics to compensate for what she considers a weakness. Compensation often results in meaningful achievement. But sometimes it is unhealthy. Parents who compensate for not loving their children by giving them frequent gifts provide one such example. The husband or wife who compensates for a poor marriage by working harder at his or her job might be better advised to address the problem in the marriage.

Projection

Projection occurs when we disown qualities in ourselves by ascribing or projecting them onto others. In other words, we tend to see in others what we see in ourselves. If I assume that the only way you could have received an A on the test is by cheating, it may be because this is the assumption I make about myself. The man who believes people are talking about him may think this because he enjoys gossiping himself. If in our relationships we insist on loading "our stuff" onto our partners, we don't get to know our partners as they really are, and we are prevented from seeing our own real problems.

Verbal Aggression

Verbal aggression occurs when we attack or hit back aggressively. It is often a smoke screen. We hide our fears behind it, hoping our outburst will obscure the elements of threat in our partners' communication. People manifest verbal aggression when, confronted with a threatening argument, they "fly off the handle," when they swear, when they make indiscriminate attacks on irrelevant points, and when they make derogatory personal remarks. Verbal aggression gets in the way of examining issues and solving problems.

Reaction Formation

When we utilize *reaction formation* as a defense mechanism, we mask uncomfortable feelings by acting in exaggerated ways that are opposite to the ways we really feel. Examples are the "Don Juan" who secretly is unsure of his manliness, the "life of the party" who really is shy and afraid of social groups, and the housewife who attends excessively to her housework in order to mask her resentment at having given up her career. The difficulty with reaction formation is that it nearly always results in extremes.

Rationalization

One of the most common forms of defense against negative feelings about self is *rationalization*. With rationalization we divest ourselves of responsibility and blame. We invent logical and acceptable explanations for our actions in order to justify our behavior. I rationalize when, instead of accepting responsibility for stubbing my toe on the living room chair, I blame my wife for moving the furniture around. Rationalizing is a dangerous habit because it prevents us from seeing ourselves clearly and accepting responsibility. When we blame others for our problems, the problems seldom get solved.

Displacement

Displacement occurs when we hold back hostile feelings until we can discharge them on subjects less dangerous than those who aroused them. A girl is reprimanded by her mother. Wanting to lash back but afraid to do so, she goes instead into her room and spanks her doll. A college student is the object of her teacher's sarcasm. Afraid to respond, she blows up instead that evening at her roommate for not having dinner ready.

Displacement can do considerable harm to the communication climate. If you are insulted by a customer and as a consequence go home and vent your feelings of rage on your wife, she is bewildered, hurt, and may very well react defensively.

This list could be much longer. It is intended as an introduction to some of the interesting ways we behave when threatened. Sometimes these reactions are useful; more often, they are counterproductive. They interfere with finding solutions to problems and they usually result in additional defensive reactions.

In Section A of this chapter, we have considered the reciprocal nature of defensiveness, some threatening and supportive behaviors, and some typical defensive reactions.

Key Ideas in Review

☐ **One way to promote communication is to provide an atmosphere in which people feel that it is safe to communicate.**

☐ **When people are threatened psychologically, they often respond by reacting defensively.**

☐ **Defensive responses usually damage the communication environment.**

☐ **Defensiveness is reciprocal.**

☐ **Six categories of threatening and supportive behaviors are evaluation and description, control and problem orientation, strategy and spontaneity, neutrality and empathy, superiority and equality, and certainty and provisionalism.**

☐ **Sometimes defensive reactions are useful.**

☐ **Generally, defensive responses obscure basic relationship problems and discourage the discovery of solutions.**

☐ **Some typical defensive reactions are emotional insulation, apathy, fantasy, dependency, identification, suppression, compensation, projection, verbal aggression, reaction formation, rationalization, and displacement.**

Section B

Person-to-Group Focus

A man that will fight may find a cudgel in every hedge.

John Clarke

In Section A of this chapter we discussed some threatening and supportive behaviors as they affect interpersonal communication. In Section B we are going to consider those same elements as they apply to person-to-group communication. We will briefly re-examine parts of the Gibb study, and we will consider the conversational mode as supportive behavior.

The Gibb Study Revisited

The end effect of perceived threat on communication is no different in the person-to-group situation from in the interpersonal situation. It substantially reduces chances for successful communication. Let us look at some of those threatening behaviors identified by Gibb and notice how they might be reflected by the public speaker. Keep in mind that these behaviors are listed separately here for convenience of study. In actual practice they intermix and appear in endless combinations. Also remember that these behaviors are threatening only if they are perceived as threatening. A great variety of elements attendant to the communi-cation situation intersect to determine how the speaker and the message will be perceived.

Evaluation

When people feel they are being judged or evaluated, they often react defensively. When public speakers threaten their listeners by appearing to be evaluative, the action is usually inadvertent or accidental. It most frequently happens when the audience feels that the speaker is "speaking down" to them. A home economist gave a cooking demonstration for a group of men, most of whom were amateur chefs. Unfortunately, the speaker proceeded as though her listeners had never seen the inside of a kitchen. Her opening remark was, "Do not be frightened, I am not going to do anything that will be too complicated for you." Her tone and manner, as well as what she said, sounded evaluative to some of her listeners. They reacted negatively. Well-meaning remarks such as, "I am not going into that part because you people would never be able to understand it" or "I am going to keep this simple so you get it" are sometimes interpreted as evaluative. Comparisons sometimes appear to be judgmental. "The people in my part of the country don't think the way you people do"; or "In my office, we always did it like this"; or "My classes at the college always picked this up a lot faster than you people seem to" are examples of comparisons that could sound evaluative. Listeners also often resent unflattering evaluations about such things as the facilities for speaking, the occasion, previous speakers, or the geographical area. Remember that a number of factors combine to determine how the audience perceives the speaker and the message. Remarks that are perceived as threatening in some situations may be perceived differently in other situations.

Control

People often react defensively to unnecessary and abusive *control*. Of course, speechmakers are expected to exercise enough control to maintain and direct the attention of the listeners. However, when control becomes excessive, listeners usually experience negative reactions.

The speaker who appears unwilling to let listeners think for themselves is sometimes perceived as being excessively controlling. We usually react more favorably to the speaker who presents the arguments and evidence and then lets us make up our own minds. We often resent those who would manipulate our thoughts and feelings.

Sometimes, in an effort to persuade, speakers select atypical evidence and deliberately ignore more relevant and compelling support. Audiences perceive this "card stacking" as unnecessary control, and they resent it. Sometimes speakers exhibit more obvious control by keeping the audience waiting or trying to hold the listeners long after the expected time period. During question and answer periods, speakers sometimes try to control the outcome by ignoring questions that might be challenging. Once again, we expect a certain amount of control from speakers; we resent unnecessary and unfair control.

Strategy

We perceive *strategy* when we suspect that the speaker is disguising her or his motives, methods, and feelings—when we feel the speaker is trying to trick us. Our defensive reactions to strategy are particularly strong because we resent being used. We often know that the speaker's purpose is to persuade, and expect the speaker to use the most effective techniques at his or her command. However, when we perceive the techniques to be dishonest, we react defensively.

The candidate who pretends to be one thing before one group and another thing before another group is often perceived as a strategist. The speaker who ostensibly is speaking on behalf of a charity but in reality is trying to promote personal business is a strategist, as is the person who compliments the audience by saying things obviously not meant. In short, just about anything the speaker says can be perceived as strategic and manipulative if the audience sees it as being insincere. To avoid being perceived as strategic then, speakers are advised to be honest with their listeners—to say only those things they really mean.

Neutrality

Once again, as it is used here, *neutrality* means *indifference*. People are threatened by indifference. When listeners feel the speaker doesn't really care about them, they are apt to react negatively. I once listened to a speech by a government official who was obviously giving the same speech he had given in another city a few days earlier. Several times he incorrectly identified the group he was addressing; he also got the name of the city wrong a few times. In retrospect, these do not appear to be grievous errors, but the negative effect they had at the time was amazing. After the speech, time after time people were heard to say, "But he doesn't know us—he doesn't know who we are."

Delivery, as well as content, often communicates indifference or neutrality. When the speaker mechanically "just goes through the motions," when he or she delivers a "canned" memorized speech, the audience often feels left out of the process. We will talk more about this later in the chapter when we discuss the conversational mode.

Superiority

When speakers display obvious feelings of *superiority*, listeners often feel "put down." A man whose job required that he make occasional public presentations once came to me for help. He was alarmed because on these occasions he often encountered hostility that he could not account for. Before long we were able to discover the cause of this unnecessary hostility. Someone had once advised him to proceed as though his listeners were completely ignorant of the subject. Sometimes this advice is good. If we overestimate the knowledge of the audience, our statements are often unclear. Un-

fortunately, this man went to extremes. He addressed his audiences as though they were small children and explained in painful detail ideas and concepts that they already knew. Without meaning to, he gave the impression that he felt superior to his listeners. They often reacted defensively. Frequently, speechmakers are experts in the subjects about which they speak. This is desirable. They must be careful, however, not to flaunt their expertise in such a way that listeners feel belittled.

Certainty

By *certainty*, Gibb meant the I-am-always-right, I-know-it-all attitude that sometimes appears in human communication. This attitude is threatening because it implies that those who see things differently must necessarily be wrong. Sometimes speakers who display certainty appear more interested in "winning" than in solving problems. Speechmakers communicate certainty when they fail to give credit where credit is due and when they admit no possibility of error. Such an attitude is unrealistic, and audiences know it. We want speakers to believe strongly in what they say, but we don't want them to have tunnel vision. The attitude should be, "I believe strongly in this, but I will consider new data as it turns up."

We have been noticing how speechmakers sometimes invite defensive responses from their listeners. Let us now turn to a method of speech delivery that is supportive and, consequently, very effective.

The Conversational Mode

The conversational mode is a style of speech delivery. It is usually the best style for our times. It is generally supportive, and in many respects the antithesis of the negative behaviors we have been discussing.

The Conversational Mode Described

This style is called the *conversational mode* because, like good conversation, it is natural, direct, spontaneous, and above all communicative. It is not pretentious, artificial, or "canned." As Charles Mudd and Malcolm Sillars point out, "Good delivery, even in formal situations, needs all the best qualities of good conversational speech."[7] The conversational mode is marked by physical and vocal directness. Speakers should not "recite"; instead, they should direct their thoughts and voices to each of their listeners. This facial and vocal directness helps listeners to feel that speakers are talking directly to them.

Good delivery is natural, direct, and communicative.

As the name implies, this style of speech delivery is natural, friendly, and sincere. As far as delivery is concerned, there is no essential difference between conversation and speechmaking. People mistrust speakers who put on one voice for the speaker's platform and another for private conversation. The fundamental quality of the conversational mode is a sense of communication. When the conversational mode is being utilized, listeners have the feeling that the speaker is talking with them, not reciting a performance at them.

As we noticed at the outset, the conversational style of delivery usually contributes to a cooperative and supportive atmosphere. Because it is not flowery or pretentious, listeners are less apt to feel threatened by perceptions of speaker superiority and evaluation. Because it is physically and vocally direct, listeners usually don't feel speaker indifference. Because it is natural, because the speaker is being what he or she really is, audiences are less likely to feel the threat of control and strategy. Research shows that speakers who use the conversational mode are more likely to be perceived as trustworthy and honest than are speakers who utilize oratorical styles of delivery. In short, this manner of delivery embodies the positive reverse of many of the negative behaviors we have discussed.

Most good speakers of modern times have achieved this conversational communicative style. Franklin D. Roosevelt was able to achieve this conversational quality while broadcasting on the radio. His famous Fireside Chats were outstanding demonstrations of the effectivenss of the conversational mode. When at their best, Gerald R. Ford and Jimmy Carter both demonstrated this conversational quality in the 1976 presidential contest. Although they displayed distinctly differing personalities, both candidates rejected the artificial, rhetorical flourishes that were characteristic of public speakers in the past.

Developing the Conversational Mode

Most students have little or no difficulty achieving the conversational mode. Developing it depends largely on understanding the role of the speaker in the person-to-group situation. One thing to understand is that, as far as delivery is concerned, there is no essential difference between communication in interpersonal settings and communication in person-to-group settings. We discussed this factor in chapter 1, but to amplify that material consider the following example:

On a warm, sunny day you and some of your classmates are seated on the grass near your classroom waiting for class to begin. You are chatting about the grading policy used in the class you are waiting for. When more class members arrive and join in the discussion, you stand up to get a better view. After a while you decide to share some ideas you have been thinking about in connection with grading. You ask your friends to hear you out, and you talk without interruption for several minutes.

Where in this example did conversation stop being conversation and start being a speech? When you got on your feet? No, it is possible to have a conversation while standing. It probably became a speech when the crowd let you speak without in-

terruption. Whenever it was, the point is that conversation differs from person-to-group speaking in degree only.

Another helpful thing to understand while working for the conversational mode is that a speech is not a performance or a show. As we observed in the last chapter in discussing stage fright, speakers should forget about themselves and concentrate on getting the message across to listeners. As Elizabeth Andersch and Lorin Staats observe, "If you concentrate on getting a message across to your listeners, you will instinctively avoid the so-called 'oratorical' style of delivery and rely on a more intimate, direct vocal approach."[8]

The soundness of this advice was once demonstrated by a man who was enrolled in an evening speech class. He had been criticized from time to time for being hesitant and indirect. One night during an informal but heated discussion, he delivered a spontaneous, direct, almost passionate appeal in support of a proposal to use city funds to establish a home for runaway children. The home was to provide counseling and temporary shelter. Later someone asked him how all of a sudden he had been able to achieve such directness. He replied that several years earlier his own daughter had run away. In the case of the impromptu appeal he had been so interested in convincing his listeners that he had forgotten about himself.

If you will concentrate on communicating your thoughts to your listeners and if you understand that in delivery there is no essential difference between communication in personal and public settings, you will have little difficulty in achieving the conversational mode.

Speech Rehearsal and the Conversational Mode

Speakers who use the conversational mode often spend considerable time in speech preparation. They plan, research, and rehearse their speeches. They rehearse, however, in ways that enable them to speak confidently, conversationally, and accurately without appearing to have memorized the material. Occasionally speakers complain that rehearsing is incompatible with the spontaneity that is associated with the conversational mode. The problem, however, is usually not too much rehearsal but the wrong kind of rehearsal. Speech rehearsal is personal. Methods will vary from speaker to speaker and from occasion to occasion. The following three suggestions, however, have proven immensely helpful to many people.

Let the speech grow over a period of time Whenever possible *begin the rehearsal early* so that the speech can become a part of you —so that you can become comfortable with it. When you are thoroughly familiar with its ideas, you become free to concentrate on your listeners and on communicating the ideas to them. Try to spread rehearsal time over several days. If you begin early enough, you can think about the ideas in the speech at odd moments during the day.

Simulate actual speech conditions Communication is contextual—it takes place in a specific situation. *Try to imagine that situation* as you rehearse the speech. Picture the room in which you will be speaking and pretend that the audience is in front of you. It is one thing to speak the speech to yourself while you are taking a shower in the morning and another thing to communicate the ideas of the speech to real people when you haven't thought about those people. A speech is a means by which you share ideas and feelings with others. Try to see those others as you rehearse your speech.

Don't memorize words This is the most important suggestion. Strive to *memorize the ideas* in the outline of the speech but avoid at all costs memorizing the words with which you will develop that outline. The purpose of each rehearsal is to fix ideas in memory and not to memorize words. If you express the ideas a little differently each time you rehearse, you are on the right track. Resist the temptation to memorize beautiful phrases. Unless you are an outstanding actor, memorized phrases will sound like memorized phrases. If you are thoroughly familiar with the ideas in your speech, the words will come as you react to your listeners and they react to you.

The conversational mode, then, is a supportive, effective style of speech delivery. With the right mental attitude you can achieve it with little difficulty. When rehearsing give the speech time to grow and try to simulate conditions as they will be when the speech is given. Try to fix thoughts in memory but be sure to avoid memorizing words.

In Section B of this chapter, we have considered some of the ways public speakers stimulate defensive responses and we have considered the conversational mode as a supportive style of speech delivery.

Key Ideas in Review

- ☐ When listeners feel threatened by speechmakers, they often react defensively.
- ☐ Some forms of threatening behavior have been identified as evaluation, control, strategy, neutrality, superiority, and certainty.
- ☐ The conversational mode is a style of speech delivery that is natural, conversational, direct, spontaneous, and communicative.
- ☐ The conversational mode is supportive because it is the antithesis of the negative behaviors previously identified.
- ☐ Two suggestions helpful in developing the conversational style are (a) remember that in delivery there is no essential difference between conversation and speechmaking, and (b) concentrate on the message rather than on self.
- ☐ When rehearsing, try to imagine conditions as they will be when the speech is given.
- ☐ Rehearse to fix ideas in memory, but don't memorize words.

Suggested Assignments

Integrated Assignments

These assignments are designed to help you practice the principles of person-to-group communication presented in Section B while at the same time you further explore the ideas presented in Section A.

Select one of the topics listed below and give a short, informal talk to the class. Each topic is designed to help you and your listeners think further about threatening and supportive behaviors. When you present your remarks, do your best to use the conversational style that we discussed in Section B.

Speech Topics

1. Select those threatening and supportive behaviors articulated by Gibb that you most frequently encounter in a current relationship. Explain how you support and threaten your partners and explain how they support and threaten you. Be specific, provide real examples.

2. Keep a diary for a few days. Record the threatening and supportive behaviors you encounter. Tell your audience about the behaviors you encountered most frequently. Describe how they affected communication.

3. Ask a friend to tell you what you do that threatens or supports him or her. Insist on examples. Report your findings to the class.

4. Describe a communication environment with which you are familiar. It can be at work, at home, or at school. Explain how the environment could be improved by replacing threat with support. Be specific and use examples.

5. Explain how speechmakers could elicit un-necessary, negative responses. Illustrate your ideas with examples.

6. Contrast the most threatening communication environment you know of with the most supportive environment you have encountered. Be specific about the elements in each environment. Give examples.

7. Explain what you would do as a parent, a teacher, or an employer to improve the communication climate in your home, in your classroom, or at your place of business.

8. Which of the common defense mechanisms do you use most often? Be specific. Provide examples.

9. Keep a defense mechanism log for a few days. Report on the defense mechanisms you encounter most frequently.

10. Describe speakers you have heard who have achieved the conversational mode. Explain what they seemed to do to accomplish this communicative style.

Auxiliary Assignments

Interpersonal Focus

1. The class is divided into groups of six. Each group is assigned one of the Gibb categories. After 30 minutes of discussion, each group will explain to the class its assigned category and provide the class with five real life examples illustrating the assigned behavior.

2. The class is divided into six groups. Each group is assigned one of the Gibb categories. Each group will prepare and deliver a role-playing scene illustrating the assigned category.

3. The class is divided into small groups. Group members discuss their own behaviors relative to the Gibb categories.

4. The class is divided into groups. Each group is assigned a number of the defense mechanisms that were discussed in the chapter. After 30 minutes of discussion each group reports on the assigned mechanisms and provides real life examples for each.

5. Keep a defense mechanism diary for a few days. In a general class discussion report on the defensive reactions you most frequently encountered in your own behavior.

Person-to-Group Focus

1. This exercise is helpful in developing the conversational mode of delivery. It requires the cooperation of the entire class. A student rises and goes before the class. Various members of the class raise their hands to ask questions. The speaker calls upon class members and answers their questions. Speakers should try to be as direct, conversational, and communicative as possible. Needless to say, questions should be simple and in good taste. This exercise can be repeated with profit throughout the course.

2. This exercise should not be considered a speech. Class members are given a list of topics of current interest. After a few moments they are asked to get up individually and comment on one of the topics. No one will be expected to give a speech. All that is requested is a personal, spontaneous, unre-hearsed reaction to one of the topics. The goal, of course, is for speakers to be as natural, as communicative, as conversational, as nonthreatening as possible while making comments. This exercise can profitably be repeated periodically throughout the course.

3. Prepare a short talk and deliver it to the class. Concentrate on being communicative and conversational. You will find it easier to be natural and conversational if you talk about

something you know well and are interested in. Suggested topics are as follows:

a. What you would like to be doing ten years from now.
b. The funniest (most exciting, most embarrassing, etc.) thing that ever happened to you.
c. The most influential class you have ever taken.
d. Your hobby.
e. Three things that you value highly.

4. Come to class prepared to share a short, one-paragraph news item you have clipped from a newspaper or magazine. Read the paragraph to the class and then chat about it informally with the class.

5. Think of times when you have been defensive because of a speaker's behavior or manner. In a general class discussion, share those experiences with the class.

Suggested Readings

Interpersonal Focus

Bach, George R., and Wyden, Peter. *The Intimate Enemy: How to Fight Fair in Love and Marriage.* New York: Avon Books, 1970. According to the author, most partners don't fight too much, they just don't fight constructively. A useful discussion about dealing with conflict.

Brammer, Laurence M. *The Helping Relationship: Process and Skills.* Englewood Cliffs, N. J.: Prentice-Hall, 1973. A very readable book about how help can be genuinely supportive. It presents specific skills, activities, and exercises.

Chapman, Arthur H. *Put-Offs and Come-Ons: Psychological Maneuvers and Stratagems.* New York: Putman, 1968. A fascinating book about the forces that bring people together and keep them apart. This book is full of illuminating everyday examples.

Person-to-Group Focus

Bradley, Bert. *Fundamentals of Speech Communication: The Credibility of Ideas.* Dubuque, Iowa: William C. Brown Co., 1974, pp. 206–50. This chapter on delivering the speech is very well documented. It refers to several studies that shed light on how speakers affect listeners.

Cobin, Martin. "Response to Eye-Contact." *Quarterly Journal of Speech* 48, no. 4 (December 1962): 415–418. This is one of the few experimental studies concerned with eye contact.

Note Directory

1. Jack R. Gibb, "Defensive Communication," *Journal of Communication* 11, no. 3 (September 1961): 141–48.

2. Carl R. Rogers, *On Becoming a Person: A Therapist's View of Psychotherapy* (Boston: Houghton Mifflin, 1961), pp. 130–31.

3. Everett L. Shostrom, *Man, the Manipulator: The Inner Journey From Manipulation to Actualization* (New York: Bantam Books, 1968).

4. Gibb, "Defensive Communication," pp. 141–48.

5. Carl R. Rogers, *Freedom to Learn: A View of What Education Might Become* (Columbus: Charles E. Merrill Publishing Co., 1969), pp. 231–37.

6. John J. Powell, *Why Am I Afraid to Tell You Who I Am?* (Niles, Ill.: Argus Communications, 1969), p. 103.

7. Charles S. Mudd and Malcolm O. Sillars, *Speech: Content and Communication* (San Francisco: Chandler Publishing Co., 1962), p. 17.

8. Elizabeth Andersch and Lorin Staats, *Speech for Everyday Use* (New York: Holt, Rinehart & Winston, 1960), p. 156.

Chapter Four

**The
Subject**

What we choose to talk about is important in both interpersonal and person-to-group settings. In Section A of this chapter we will discuss factors related to subject choice in interpersonal situations, and in Section B we will discuss factors related to subject choice in person-to-group situations.

Section A: Interpersonal Focus

We choose to talk about something: a discussion of subjects for interpersonal communication with emphasis on self-disclosure.

■ What we talk about ■ the rewards and risks of self-disclosure ■ guidelines for self-disclosure

Section B: Person-to-Group Focus

The speechmaker chooses a subject: a discussion of purpose and subject in person-to-group communication.

■ The subject ■ the topic ■ the purpose statements ■ places to look for speech subjects

Suggested Assignments

Section A

Interpersonal Focus

"The time has come," the Walrus said,
"to talk of many things:
of shoes—and ships—and sealing
wax—
of cabbages and kings."

Lewis Carroll

In a very funny essay entitled "The Waltz," the late Dorothy Parker referred to the difficulty of knowing what to talk about: "Look at him—what could you say to a thing like that? Did you go to the circus this year, What is your favorite kind of ice cream, How do you spell cat?"[1] Although most of us seldom think about it, the matter of what we talk about is often more serious than humorous. The topics we consistently select for discussion in our interpersonal relationships provide a barometer for gauging the state of those relationships.

An analysis of one's behavior in this area often reveals possibilities for choices and alternatives. Consequently, in Section A of this chapter we are going to discuss the kinds of things people talk about with their interpersonal partners. Because some topics require a certain amount of self-disclosure, we are also going to consider the risks and rewards of self-disclosure. Self-disclosure is simply the process of deliberately communicating something about oneself to someone else.

Interpersonal Topics

Let's begin by making a distinction between the subject and the topic. The term *subject* refers to a broad area. The term *topic* refers to a narrow slice or portion of that broad area. Education, for example, is a broad subject that could generate innumerable topics—the new reading program at our elementary school, my thoughts about modern methods of teaching reading, new federal legislation in the area of student financial aid, and athletic recruitment practices at our college, for instance. Obviously, subject and topic differ simply by degree, emphasis, and direction. In the next few pages we will discuss topics for interpersonal communication. We will consider the specific kinds of things that interpersonal partners talk about.

The topics we discuss with our interpersonal partners are, of course, infinitely varied. Surprisingly, however, most interpersonal topics can be grouped into three classifications: (1) general topics, (2) you/me topics, and (3) us topics.

As we discuss each category, please keep in mind the distinction between subject and topic. This will help you understand how, with a slight change in emphasis, a topic can move from one category to another.

General Topics

Often in interpersonal settings the talk is about things, people, events, and places that are not at the moment directly, intimately, or personally associated with any of the participants in the discussion. Topics of this nature are called general topics. Whenever the discussion is not about you or me or us, whenever it does not require us to reveal a great deal about ourselves as people the topic is usually general. *Examples:*

1. Tomorrow's assignment
2. The President's latest speech
3. The game that was on TV Sunday afternoon
4. Uncle Charley's operation
5. The boss
6. Fuel economy
7. The Equal Rights Amendment
8. The people who live next door
9. Mother's recipe for sauerkraut and dumplings

I can give you tomorrow's assignment, describe the President's last speech, tell some antecdotes about my boss, or give you my mother's sauerkraut recipe without directly revealing much about myself and without asking you to reveal much of yourself; the topics are general.

Since general topics are not as personal, they are not as threatening to most of us as other kinds of topics. Because they are usually nonthreatening, general topics are the focus of most of our everyday talk. Conversation about topics from this area can be entertaining, informative, and stimulating, or it can be dull, depending, of course, on how the topics are handled.

You/Me Topics

You/me topics are more personal than general topics because they center on a specific participant in the conversation. When we are talking about me, or when we are talking about you, the topic is a you/me topic. Such topics can include what one of the partners feels, what has happened to one of the partners, or what one of the partners thinks or wants. *Examples:*

1. My ideas about going into business
2. My desire to learn karate
3. My experiences in the army
4. Your anxieties about finishing college
5. Your fear of becoming pregnant
6. My fear of flying
7. My shame at failing freshman English
8. Your thoughts about disciplining children
9. Your ambition to lose ten pounds
10. Your thoughts about the President's latest speech.

Perhaps you noticed that the last example is similar to the second example given for general topics. This illustrates that interpersonal talk is sometimes mixed. Different types of topics often are introduced in a single conversation. For example, a general topic can quickly become a you/me topic. To illustrate: let's say that we are trying to recall together what the President said in his last speech. This topic is general. Next, the conversation takes a slight turn, and we start talking about what some of the critics said about the President's speech. Still a general topic. Finally, I tell you what I think about the President's proposals and you tell me how you feel about the President. Now we have turned to you/me topics. We are sharing our personal thoughts and feelings, and they have become predominant.

Perhaps you also noticed that in the last set of examples some of the topics were not very threatening, while others seemed a bit heavy. Because you/me topics usually require that we reveal something about ourselves, they are sometimes threatening for many of us. This is not always the case, however. It's not very threatening for me to tell you about my plans for going into business, nor is it threatening for you to tell me about your desire to lose ten pounds.

If all our conversations centered around you/me topics, our communication might become burdensome and overly serious. However, periodic, frank discussions centering on you/me topics are usually beneficial to relationships. After all, if I never deliberately communicate any of myself to you, you will need to be very good at guessing to get to know me well.

Us Topics

Us topics focus on you and me (your partner) together; they are concerned with our relationship. When we talk about problems in our relationship, our future together, or experiences we have shared, we are talking about an us topic. *Examples:*

1. Our feelings for each other
2. The things we do for each other that make us happy

3. How we should divide the household duties
4. What we might do together this weekend
5. The enjoyment we shared last summer
6. A problem we are having in our sexual relationship
7. How much time we should spend together
8. How we can do a better job of listening to each other
9. Whether we shall study together tonight

If people spend all their time talking about their relationships, some of the fun and spontaneity is apt to get lost. On the other hand, us topics usually demonstrate a degree of commitment to the relationship. As we noted in an earlier chapter, relationships usually don't just happen; they require some tending. An occasional discussion focused on one or more us topics usually is necessary for the health and growth of the relationship.

Now that you are aware of the three categories—general topics, you/me topics, and us topics—it should be emphasized that these classifications are merely rough guidelines. They do not make possible rigid, fixed distinctions. As we observed earlier, much of our conversation is mixed; all three types of topics can occur in a single conversation.

Analyzing the Topic Pattern

Of what use, then, are these classifications? For one thing, they provide a general clue to the state of intimacy a relationship has achieved. In a specific relationship if most of the talk is on general topics, the partners in that relationship either haven't begun to know each other very well or for some other reason don't choose to relate very personally. When a good deal of the talk is focused on you/me topics, partners have a good opportunity to get to know each other. When partners begin to consider us topics, they usually have achieved a degree of intimacy and are making a commitment one way or another to the relationship.

This is not to imply that one kind of topic necessarily is any better than any other. Whatever you and your partners are comfortable with is fine. Most healthy, growing relationships, however, eventually admit all three kinds of topics. Without general topics, our conversations lack breadth and may seem dull. Without us topics it is difficult to give direction to the relationship. Without you/me topics, it is difficult for partners to know one another well. If one kind of topic is missing from your interpersonal communication, you and your partner or partners may wish to explore the idea of adding the missing area to your repertoire.

One way to analyze the topic pattern in a specific relationship is to keep track of the kinds of things you and your partner talk about over a period of time. Another approach is to determine what kinds of occasions you and your partner select for discussing various types of topics. Do you talk about you/me topics only when you are angry and attacking or defending? Do you consider us topics only when outside circumstances force you to? Still another technique is to observe the kinds of things

Us topics are about you and your partner together—your relationship.

you usually talk about with various interpersonal partners. The answers to questions like these can be very helpful. For example, if you and your partner discover that you rarely discuss us topics, you may wish to schedule some discussions of this kind so that together you can better determine the direction of your relationship. If you find you are avoiding you/me topics, you may decide that you are not jointly sharing enough of yourselves and that your relationship would be richer if you knew each other better.

As we have observed, some kinds of topics are threatening because they require that we disclose important, often personal information about ourselves. This brings us to the subject of self-disclosure.

Self-Disclosure

Self-disclosure is the process of intentionally communicating to others something private and personal about yourself. To put it differently, self-disclosure is the act of revealing something about yourself that others wouldn't know if you didn't reveal it. Self-disclosure messages can be about your history, your thoughts, your feelings, or your desires. Because you/me messages and us messages usually call for self-disclosure, we are going to consider this process in the remaining pages of this section. Specifically, we are going to discuss the rewards and risks of self-disclosure and some guidelines for it.

To better understand the concept of self-disclosure as a form of communication, you should read this paragraph carefully. Self-disclosure is helpful on some occasions, and on some occasions it is not helpful. Self-disclosure is appropriate with some people, and with some people it is not. On occasions, some subjects are appropriate for self-disclosure and some subjects are not. Self-disclosure often facilitates relationship growth; however, too much of it too soon can be destructive. (Please read this paragraph again; doing so will help you to understand the pages that follow.)

The Rewards of Self-Disclosure

We are going to consider three rewards of self-disclosure.

Helps Others to Know Us Self-disclosure takes much of the guesswork out of relationships because it lets others know who we are. After all, if we tell others "where we are coming from" they don't need to guess. For example, if your roommate asks you what you want for lunch and you are noncommittal, he or she must guess, and there is a chance that the guess will be wrong. Suppose you want a cheeseburger. If you don't say so, you may end up with tuna salad. Admittedly, lunch is not a matter of great import. The example does, however, illustrate the process.

If you are disappointed, your partner may be disappointed because you are disappointed. The implications go on and on. Even if your roommate has something entirely different in mind for lunch, once you state your preference, she or he can at least act from a solid data base. More relationships run into trouble because people don't understand each other than because people do understand each other. As Kathleen and Rudolph Verderber put it, "The way you define yourself through your communication teaches others how they should act, react to, and communicate with you."[2]

Consider a more significant example. The traditional courtship period should be a time when two people get to know each other. Often this is not the case. Sometimes it works like this: I am afraid that if you get to know me you won't like me. Consequently, instead of showing you who I really am, I disguise myself. I show you only those things I think you will like. This course of action is eventually self-defeating. Sooner or later I will resent the masks I am wearing—masks take energy—and you will begin to see through them. I hope you will appreciate the real me, but wouldn't we have a better chance if we had honestly known each other from the start? As Sidney Jourard states, "When we are not truly known by the other people in our lives, we are misunderstood."[3]

Helps Us to Know Ourselves Self-disclosure also helps us to understand ourselves. Jourard and others have written that in order to know ourselves we must reveal ourselves to at least one other person. John Powell states that "It is only through sharing that a person comes to know himself."[4] There is nothing mystical about this. You have probably noticed that a good way to come to a better understanding of a subject is to attempt to teach it to someone else. When you explain to someone what you are thinking, feeling, or wanting, you come to understand those factors better yourself. The act of revealing yourself to others, then, is the act of revealing yourself to yourself.

A very successful counselor I know seldom gives advice to her clients. She is, however, a very good listener. She reports that, when her clients honestly explain themselves and their problems to her, they see themselves and their problems more clearly, and consequently solutions often become apparent. Many of us have had similar experiences when talking to our close friends. As we honestly communicate our thoughts, feelings, and desires, we often experience a clearer and deeper understanding of those elements.

Facilitates Relationship Growth Self-disclosure sometimes facilitates relationship growth. Indeed, some self-disclosure is usually necessary in order for relationships to begin. We usually start by exchanging names, occupations, marital status, future plans, etc. This fact is borne out by Leonard and Natalie Zunin,[5] Irwin Altman and Dalmas Taylor,[6] and others who have studied the process of initiating relationships. As we become more comfortable with one another, we communicate more personal data. If further growth and disclosure appear appropriate and mutually acceptable, we exchange even more intimate information. To a degree, disclosure and relationship growth seem to go hand in hand.

Two factors are involved here: One is need gratification; the other is trust. Voluntary relationships usually continue to the extent that the interpersonal needs of those involved are satisfied within the relationship. Needs are more likely to be gratified if they are known, and of course self-disclosure is the chief means of making them known.

William Schutz[7] has identified three interpersonal needs that are especially important to interpersonal relationships: inclusion, control, and affection. As we consider them individually, keep in mind that different people may satisfy these needs differently. Furthermore, an individual may satisfy the same need by differing means in different relationships. Finally, remember that we don't all experience these needs with the same degree of intensity. Some have a greater need for inclusion than do others, some have a greater need for control, some for affection.

Inclusion is the need to belong, to be accepted by others, to be part of a group. For some people this need is met by an occasional get-together with friends. Others need to belong to many groups and to be accepted by large numbers of people.

When partners in a relationship have different degrees of need for inclusion, conflicts can develop. Such conflicts are not inevitable, however. Satisfactory arrangements can be made when interpersonal associates respect one another's needs. For example, it is appropriate for one partner to seek inclusion and acceptance by many persons and groups while other parties to the relationship realize levels of inclusion more appropriate for them.

Control is the need to be in charge, to dominate, to direct one's environment. The need to control varies from person to person. At one extreme are people who seldom want to be in charge, who are not comfortable with responsibility or decision-making. At the other extreme are people who need to dominate on all occasions. Most of us live somewhere between these two extremes. If both partners are unusually submissive or need to be controlled, if neither wants to dominate or take charge, their relationship is apt to be frustrating in this regard. The opposite difficulty is more common. As Argyle states, "The commonest source of conflict in dyadic interaction is where each wants to dominate."[8] When people respect one another's needs, however, they can usually reach an agreement concerning who will be in control on what occasions. If both partners can exercise control appropriate to their needs, the relationship can be mutually satisfying in this regard.

Affection is the need for intimacy, the need to like and be liked, the need to love and be loved, the need to stroke and be stroked. As with the other needs discussed here, people vary in the ways they seek to gratify their need for affection. Some people prefer to have many close and affectionate friends while others prefer to share affection with only one or a few others. Some need almost constant reassurance and stroking while others are far more reserved. When differences of this kind exist in a specific relationship, they are extremely difficult to reconcile.

As Gail and Michele Myers state, "In the case of affection, a mixed group is not the best combination for productive interpersonal relationships. Aloof, cold people and warm people do not mix well. Each makes the other uncomfortable and hard to figure out. Neither is able to satisfy the other's needs."[9]

This has been a short look at three interpersonal needs that affect relationship growth. Human needs as they affect communication will be treated more extensively in chapter 8. We focus here on self-disclosure as it relates to relationship growth. Relationships are maintained to the extent that the interpersonal needs of the persons involved are satisfied within the relationships. It is difficult to satisfy needs if they are not known. Self-disclosure is important to relationship maintenance and growth because it is the chief means of making needs known.

Another element that connects self-disclosure and relationship growth is *trust*. We are closest to those who trust us and whom we trust with our thoughts and fears and feelings and hopes. Self-disclosure, of course, requires trust. Before significant self-disclosure can occur, we must believe that the other or others involved won't ridicule us or reject us or in other ways hurt us because of the disclosure. Furthermore, trust, like most interpersonal behaviors, is reciprocal. Trust begets trust: the more I trust you the more I am likely to disclose myself to you. The reverse is also true: the more I disclose without being hurt the more I am going to trust. The more I trust you the more you are apt to trust me. The more we trust each other the closer we feel together. The closer we feel together the more we are going to trust. The equation goes on and on.

We have observed that self-disclosure benefits us as an ingredient in relationship growth. Self-disclosure facilitates need gratification, which in turn promotes relationship growth. An atmosphere of trust is important for continuing relationships. Trust is encouraged by mutual self-disclosure, and self-disclosure is encouraged by mutual trust.

This is not to imply that self-disclosure is like a fertilizer that can be applied to relationships in order to force their growth. Too much of it too soon can be counterproductive. Self-disclosure must be appropriate, and everyone involved must be ready for it. We will talk more about this later in the chapter when we consider guidelines for self-disclosure. For now, remember that self-disclosure can help others to know us, it can help us to know ourselves, and it can facilitate relationship growth.

The Risks of Self-Disclosure

In spite of the benefits that sometimes accrue from self-disclosure, we frequently seek to avoid it. The risks are generally related to one or more of the following: cultural factors, psychological factors, and relationship factors.

Cultural Factors Our culture seems to reward the denial of self. The strong, silent hero and the long-suffering heroine popularized by motion pictures provide an illustration. Conversely, people who honestly reveal themselves to others are sometimes seen as foolish or naive. This is particularly true in the area of feelings. The expression of feelings is often perceived as a weakness. The prevailing stereotypes are especially hard on men. In his well-documented book *The Liberated Man*, Warren Farrell states, "Boys are unconsciously taught to be emotionally constipated. The self-fulfilling prophecy of stereotyped masculinity is flourishing by the time a child is 13 months old."[10] Farrell goes on to describe a man who failed to receive a promotion because once under trying circumstances he cried in the presence of other employees.

Psychological Factors Sometimes self-disclosure makes us psychologically vulnerable. When we communicate important personal information to another, we can't be sure how that person will respond. We are therefore vulnerable to a variety of negative as well as positive responses. We could, for example, be ridiculed, laughed at, or rejected. Another reason disclosure is sometimes psychologically threatening is that it often results in self-discovery. People are frequently afraid to find out about themselves. As Dan and Frank Millar point out, "They fear that if they fully disclose and understand themselves, then somehow they will discover themselves to be less than they wish and being less is intolerable.''[11]

Relationship Factors   Self-disclosure doesn't always enrich the relationship. It sometimes has the opposite effect. If you reveal something about yourself that your partner can't accept, the relationship can suffer. Furthermore, self-disclosure requires energy and emotional commitment from the receiver as well as the sender. When the receiver is not prepared to make this commitment, she or he often feels compromised or embarrassed by the sender's attempt at self-disclosure. This of course has a negative effect on the relationship.

Guidelines for Self-Disclosure

Self-disclosure is neither always risky nor always rewarding. Both the rewards and the risks are situational. What is appropriate disclosure in one circumstance can be inappropriate in another circumstance. Three situational factors appear to be particularly pertinent: the topic for disclosure, the state of the relationship, and the self-esteem of the discloser.

Obviously some topics are riskier than others. As we move from impersonal topics to topics with more intimate meaning for ourselves and our relationships, self-disclosure becomes riskier and, incidentally, often potentially more beneficial. Not much is at stake when we share our feelings about Saturday afternoon's game. Much more is involved when we share our feelings about one another.

The state of the relationship is also a factor. If partners have grown to under-stand and care about each other, if past disclosures have been successful and partners have grown to trust each other—then disclosure is more appropriate than if the relationship is new and untried.

The self-concept is another factor. People with a strong, positive sense of their own worth are usually more comfortable with self-disclosure than are those with more negative feelings about themselves. Those who value themselves highly are less apt to anticipate negative responses to their self-disclosing messages and to be disturbed by negative reactions than are those of us who are less secure.

The three factors we have just discussed are easily translated into guidelines for self-disclosure. They seem to suggest that self-disclosure should be gradual, selective, reciprocated, and timely.

Graduality   Too much self-disclosure too soon can "overload the circuit." If everyone concerned is not intellectually and emotionally ready, self-disclosure can be threatening. Partners should begin with relatively safe disclosures. As they become more comfortable with each other and as trust develops, more significant disclosure can occur.

Selectivity   Self-disclosure is sometimes beneficial but not inevitably so. Personal disclosures thrust upon casual acquaintances can prove embarrassing and threatening for those acquaintances. We should reserve highly personal self-disclosures for those with whom we have a mutual and continuing personal commitment.

Reciprocity   As we have observed before, self-disclosure requires energy and commitment from the receiver as well as from the sender. One sign of willingness to make this commitment occurs when your partner responds to your self-disclosure with self-disclosure of his or her own. Trusting behavior builds on trusting behavior. Self-disclosure works best when it is reciprocal.

Timeliness Since self-disclosure often requires physical and emotional energy, it must be suited to the occasion. An upset, tired, preoccupied, or even very festive partner might be able to respond to your plans for the summer or your preference in sport cars. However, on such occasions heavy disclosures might be more than your partner can accept. Disclosure, then, must be suited to the occasion. It must be timely, as well as gradual, selective, and reciprocal.

In Section A of this chapter we have discussed three kinds of interpersonal topics. Because some of them require self-disclosure, we also defined self-disclosure, talked about its rewards and risks, and considered some guidelines for its use.

Key Ideas in Review

☐ Interpersonal topics include three categories: general topics, you/me topics, and us topics.

☐ Topics can be moved from one category to another with the slightest change of emphasis.

☐ More than one kind of topic is often contained in a single conversation.

☐ An analysis of the kinds of topics they ordinarily use can provide interpersonal partners with valuable information.

☐ Self-disclosure is the process of deliberately communicating private and personal information about oneself to another.

☐ Self-disclosure frequently helps others to know us, often helps us to know ourselves, and sometimes promotes relationship growth.

☐ Self-disclosure sometimes involves cultural, psychological, or relationship risks.

☐ Self-disclosure should be gradual, selective, reciprocal, and timely.

Section B

Person-to-Group Focus

The wise man, before he speaks, will consider well what he speaks, to whom he speaks and where and when.

Ambrose

In Section A of this chapter, we discussed some factors relevant to the selection of subjects for interpersonal communication. In this section we are going to consider some factors relevant to subject choice for person-to-group speaking. Specifically, we will talk about the selection of a subject and topic, we will consider both the general and specific speech purpose, and, finally, we will note some places to look for speech subjects.

Before we begin, let's briefly define some of the terms we will be using. The term *subject* refers to a broad area—an area much too broad to be covered in one speech or several speeches. For example, crime, education, and recreation are three broad speech subjects. The term *topic* refers to the narrow portion of the subject that the speaker intends to present to a specific audience. In way of illustration, consider three topics that could be taken from the subject of recreation: how to select equipment for snow skiing, the pleasures of backpacking, and how to watch a football game.

The term *general purpose* refers to the overall objective you wish to serve with the speech. The general purposes of speech are usually to inform, to convince, to activate, or to entertain. The term *specific purpose* refers to the specific objective you have for your speech. It can be described as what you expect your listeners to understand, to believe, to do, or to feel as a result of the speech. *Examples:*

1. As a result of my speech, I want my listeners to believe that nuclear energy is safe.
2. I want the audience to understand how to make wheat bread.
3. I want my listeners to vote no on the new zoning ordinance.

Now that we have a general understanding of these terms, let's consider each area in more detail.

The Subject

As you will recall, the term *subject* refers to a broad area. Selecting a subject is often the first step in preparing a speech but not always. Sometimes the speech purpose comes first. There is no hard and fast rule. Circumstances usually suggest the starting point. In any event, both the subject and the purpose are important. We are going to begin by discussing the speech subject. Finding just the right subject is often a giant step toward success. Conversely, even experienced speakers have difficulty when the subject is inappropriate. Three factors are of paramount importance in subject selection: (1) the speaker, (2) the audience, and (3) the occasion.

The Speaker

Speakers should choose subjects that are suited to themselves, that is, subjects that they are interested in and know something about. If you are not truly interested in your subject, you will have difficulty generating the enthusiasm that in turn will stimulate audience interest. Furthermore, if you speak without genuine interest in your subject, your audience may think you are insincere.

Without thoroughly knowing your subject it will be difficult for you to speak with authority and confidence. This doesn't mean that you have to be a recognized expert on all aspects of the subject. Perhaps the purpose of your speech is merely to raise some questions, to report some interesting research, or to recount some personal experiences in connection with the subject. You don't need to be a definitive expert on the entire subject to discuss these topics. However, even topics such as these require that you have some personal involvement with, and knowledge of, the subject. You must be thoroughly familiar with the aspect of the subject you are going to present, even though that aspect might be very personal or narrow.

Keep in mind that person-to-group communication is communication from the mind and heart of the speaker to the minds and hearts of the listeners. This personal sharing, which makes all communication exciting, is impossible unless the speaker is personally involved with the subject matter. Without the speaker's personal knowledge of, and involvement with, the subject, the speech is nothing more than a plastic, mechanical recitation. Most listeners would rather hear you discuss a simple subject that you are interested in and know well than listen to you recite lines about a more significant subject that you know or care little about.

The Audience

Subjects must be suited to the audience as well as to the speaker. Person-to-group communication does not take place in a vacuum. It matters not whether the speaker is presenting a formal speech to a large audience or informal remarks to a small group—the speaker speaks to people. These people must be able to participate emotionally and intellectually in the speech subject. That is, speakers must select subjects their listeners can both find interesting and understand. For example, you would be ill advised to present a speech on how to spend retirement income to a group of teenagers; they just wouldn't be interested. Nor would you explain how to solve advanced problems in nuclear physics to people with no background in that area; they would have difficulty understanding.

When considering your audience in relation to a potential subject, you will find that the following questions are usually helpful:

1. What common interests and beliefs do the listeners hold?
2. What will be the audience mood and attitude relative to the subject?
3. What will the listeners be expecting of me?
4. What will be the probable age range within the audience?

5. What will be the socioeconomic background of the listeners?
6. What will be the educational level of this audience?

Of course circumstances may not permit a careful answer to each of these questions. However, to the extent that they can be answered, they provide insight into the nature of the audience. The overriding question should always be, "Why should this audience hear my speech on this subject?" If you can't find an affirmative answer to this question, perhaps a different subject is in order.

The Occasion

Subjects should be appropriate to the occasion as well as to the speaker and the audience. Speeches that are acceptable on some occasions won't work at all on other occasions. To illustrate: After three days of difficult meetings, an association of college counselors gathered for a farewell dinner. The purpose of the dinner was to provide an opportunity for unwinding. The first after-dinner speech was charming. It was light and quite short. The second speech was less successful. It was a serious rebuttal to one of the positions the convention had adopted. Technically the speech was excellent. If it had been given earlier in the conference it would have been well received. Unfortunately, in the atmosphere that prevailed at the farewell dinner, the speech was completely out of place.

The term *occasion*, as it is used here, also includes the concept of the time limit.

The subject should be suited to the speaker, the audience, and the occasion.

If you have been allocated only five minutes, you won't be able to present a history of the Second World War. On the other hand, if you have been asked to speak for 45 minutes, a few personal anecdotes won't fill the bill.

In review, speech subjects should be suited to the speaker, the audience, and the occasion. Students sometimes remark that these requirements are severely limiting. They needn't be. A specific dimension or portion of most subjects can be found to fit all three requirements.

================

The Topic

As we observed earlier, the topic is the narrow portion of the subject that the speaker intends to present to a specific audience. Some authorities make no distinction between the subject and the topic. We are using the term *topic* here to emphasize that the subject must be narrowed and adapted for specific audiences.

Often the subject is suggested by your job, your special competence, the audience, the occasion, or even the program chairman. In your speech class, for example, in order to serve certain course objectives your teacher may assign many of your subjects. However, even when circumstances predetermine the subject, the speaker retains the task of narrowing and adapting it by formulating a topic.

Once again, guidelines are (1) the speaker, (2) the audience, and (3) the occasion. To illustrate: let's assume that the subject is physical fitness.

The Speaker

If your hobby is yoga, you might consider explaining the history of yoga, or demonstrating some simple yoga techniques, or describing the benefits of practicing yoga. If you have been studying nutrition, you might decide to discuss fad diets or the effects of certain foods on health. If you are a jogger, you might decide to recount some personal experiences with jogging or to provide some suggestions for getting started. If you haven't had much success with your own fitness programs, you are still not out of the picture. An obviously overweight and underexercised man once gave a very funny speech on six ways to avoid exercise while overeating.

The Audience

If your audience is a group of professional women, you might present a simple exercise program that could be worked into a crowded daily schedule. For an audience of junior high school students you might emphasize the advisability of avoiding drugs. For a more general audience you could discuss several of the more general fitness problems most of us face, such as maintaining good nutrition in a world of processed foods, or dealing with stress.

The Occasion

If the occasion is a lighthearted meeting, you might relate a few humorous anecdotes concerning your attempts at physical fitness. On the other hand, if you are speaking at ceremonies honoring intramural competitors, you might wish to make some rather serious remarks concerning the contributions of intramural sports to the nation's health.

With ten minutes to speak, you probably would have time to demonstrate three helpful isometric exercises or to report on recent research into the value of skipping rope. With more time you could explain the relation between fitness factors and heart disease. Or perhaps you could outline a complete program for good nutrition.

Finally, let's combine several of these factors. Assume that you are a telecommunications major and that your subject will be television. Your audience is the campus advertising club, and you have 30 minutes to speak. You could decide to discuss the strategy behind several well-known television commercials. This is a topic that you have studied and know about, it is something that your audience will be interested in, and it is something you could present in 30 minutes. If you had only ten minutes to talk to this same group, you might limit yourself to a description of just one successful television commercial.

Now let's switch the audience and assume that you are speaking to a chapter of the Parent-Teacher Association instead of the advertising club. For this audience you might well decide to report on research into the effects of TV violence on juvenile behavior.

Finally, let's change one more factor. Let's assume that you are not a telecommunications major and that you don't know much about the technical side of television. You are, however, a parent. You are still speaking to the PTA and the subject is still TV. You may well decide to report on how your family successfully reconciled a conflict between TV-watching and homework.

In summary, the speech topic is the narrow aspect of a particular subject that the speaker presents to a specific audience. The subject should be narrowed with care. When selecting topics, speakers should consider themselves, the audience, and the occasion.

The Purpose Statements

It is difficult to separate the speech purpose from the speech subject. They grow together in the same soil. We often become aware of one before the other, however. Consider this example: you are president of your chapter of NOW. You have been asked to speak to a local chapter of the Republican Women's Club on the subject of equal employment opportunities for women. You have the subject. But what about your purpose? Should your purpose be to inform the listeners about past and present job discrimination? Should you try to convince them that pending legislation in the area should pass? Or should you try to activate them to write to their legislators? Consider a different example: you have been asked to give an educational speech to a study group. Your purpose is apparent: it is to inform. But what about your subject? Should it be history, which is your major; literature, which is your hobby; or landscaping, which is your job? The point is that the starting point is sometimes the subject and at other times the purpose. Both are important ingredients.

We considered the speech subject earlier. In the next few paragraphs we will discuss both the general and the specific speech purpose.

The purpose is the audience-centered goal you hope to reach with your speech—the response you expect to get from your listeners. The formulation of the purpose is a very important step. Statements of the purpose serve as guidelines with which to focus your energy as you prepare and deliver your speech. Without the purpose fixed clearly in mind, you are "spinning your wheels." When you get into your car to go someplace, you are more apt to get there if you know where you are going. The same reasoning applies to speaking.

General Purpose

The term *general purpose* refers to the overall audience-centered result you expect from your speech. Do you want your listeners to understand something, to do something, to be entertained? Do you have some other goal? The general purposes of speech are often considered to be to inform, to convince, to activate, to entertain.

To Inform When you speak to inform, you are transmitting information. Your goal is to secure understanding of that information. You want your listeners to know how to do something, how something appears, how it happens, how it's made, or how it's organized. Much of the speech we encounter in the classroom is informative. For example, when your economics teacher lectures on the causes of the last Great Depression, he or she is speaking to inform. The goal is for you to understand what caused the Great Depression.

To Convince When your purpose is to convince, you want more than simple understanding; you want agreement with or belief in certain things. A campus speaker once spoke on the discovery of America.

His purpose was to induce his listeners to agree that America was first discovered by Chinese sailors. Another speaker once spoke on extrasensory perception. Her goal was to have her listeners believe that some people have the ability to foresee the future. Both of these were speeches to convince. The speakers were seeking intellectual agreement.

To Activate Sometimes you want more than belief from your listeners. You want them to take specific action. When this is your purpose, you are speaking to activate. A candidate for office is not content to have the listeners believe that he or she is the best candidate; the goal is to have listeners actually cast the appropriate vote. Television salespersons want more than belief in

"Try to get in a personal word to the schizophrenics, urging them not to vote a split ticket."

their products; they want people actually to buy their products.

To Entertain   When your primary purpose is to entertain, your objective is to have your listeners enjoy themselves. A popular myth about speeches given to entertain is that they must be funny. Sometimes they are humorous, but often they are not. Speeches about interesting places, interesting people, and interesting events are often given simply to entertain. A student once described some unusual experiences she had had while serving with the Peace Corps in Sarawak. Her primary purpose was to entertain.

Combinations   Although one of the purposes is usually dominant, several purposes are often attendant to a single speech. Sometimes to inform we must also entertain. Frequently in order to activate we must inform and also convince. For example, consider the speaker who wants you to vote for a particular candidate. She or he may need to inform you concerning the candidate's background, convince you that the candidate is the best choice, and finally activate you to go to the polls and cast your vote for the candidate.

Even though more than one purpose may bear on a single speech, speakers should know the dominant purpose and keep it clearly in mind. When subordinate purposes get out of hand, they are apt to take over and to jeopardize the primary purpose. For example, the teacher who becomes enchanted with joke-telling may find that the point of the lesson has been lost in the process. The speaker who wants to teach us how to play chess may give us so many details about the history of the game that we fail to learn how to play it. Once the dominant purpose has been decided upon, all the speaker's energies should be marshalled to serve that purpose.

Of course, it is not enough to decide what you wish to accomplish in general. You must be more precise. You must do more, for example, than want to activate or to inform. You must decide exactly what you want your listeners to do or to understand.

Specific Purpose

As the term implies, your *specific purpose* is the particular listener goal you wish to achieve with your speech. It is advantageous to think clearly about the specific purpose. When speeches appear to be vaguely pointless or slightly out of focus, the speaker has usually failed to identify the specific purpose. Most speakers find it helpful to commit the specific purpose statement to paper. One way to begin the statement is with the words: As a result of my speech I want my audience to _____. Sample specific purpose statements:

1. General purpose: To inform. Specific purpose: As a result of my speech I want my listeners to know how to administer mouth-to-mouth resuscitation.

2. General purpose: To convince. Specific purpose: As a result of my speech I want my audience to believe that the general education requirements presently in force at our college are in the best interest of students.

3. General purpose: To activate. Specific purpose: As a result of my speech I want my audience to attend Saturday night's performance of *The Merchant of Venice,* which is being presented by the University Players.

4. General purpose: To entertain. Specific purpose: As a result of my speech I want my audience to be amused by my description of some of the customers who come into my father's garage.

In review, determining the general and specific speech purpose is an important step in speech preparation. Without careful attention to this step, the speaker is likely to waste time in preparation and the speech itself may lack focus.

Discovering Speech Subjects

Ordinarily, speakers have little difficulty finding appropriate subjects. Subjects are usually suggested by the occasion, the audience, the speaker's expertise or reputation, the program chairman, or, in the case of your speech class, by the nature of the assignment. Occasionally, however, these guideposts offer little help and the speaker must search for an appropriate subject.

Your Own Experience

One of the best places for speakers to look for speech subjects is within their own experience. Speaking from experience is by far the easiest way to learn to speak with confidence and authority. All of us have had experiences on which we can draw. We have grown through childhood, we have gone to school, we have related to other people, and we have hopes and abiding interests. Many of us are married and some of us have children. All these areas can provide countless ideas for speech subjects.

From the area of childhood, for example, a woman once spoke about her favorite Christmas. Other speeches from this area have included such subjects as experiences with Little League, childhood fears, the first night away from home, and divorce from the child's point of view.

Experiences in school have provided speeches on my favorite teacher, designated smoking areas in high schools, prayer in school, and improving the high school experience. College students often find speech subjects in the classes they take, such as history, literature, health education, drama.

Marriage has provided such topics as picking a mate, keeping the family budget, disciplining children, separate vacations for husbands and wives, and surviving divorce.

In short, we have all had experiences. With a little thought we can pull some interesting speech subjects from them.

Current Events

The present as well as the past can be a source for speech subjects. Daily occurrences, matters of controversy, matters of local and national interest can all be translated into speech subjects.

Day-to-day occurrences can often produce speech subjects. A student once gave a speech on traffic laws because he received what he considered an unfair traffic citation. Grading policies, automobile courtesy, apartment-hunting, job-hunting, applying for credit and dealing with telephone solicitors are a few subjects that were suggested by an event in the life of the speaker.

Attention to the news media can also generate speech subjects. It is almost impossible to glance through a newspaper or to watch a newscast without being confronted with several speech ideas. Speeches suggested by discussions in the media have reflected such subjects as gun control, abortion, legalized gambling, censorship, energy conversation, and crime.

In review, when the immediate circumstances surrounding the speech opportunity fail to suggest a subject, speakers can often find speech subjects by considering past experiences and by being alert to what is going on in the world around them.

In this chapter we discussed factors in the selection of speech subjects and topics, we considered the general and specific speech purpose, and we noted some places to look for speech subjects.

Key Ideas in Review

☐ Selecting the subject, the topic, and the speech purposes are vital steps in speech preparation.

☐ The term *speech subject* refers to a broad area.

☐ The term *speech topic* refers to the narrow aspect of the broad subject that the speaker wishes to present to a specific audience.

☐ When selecting subjects and topics speakers should consider themselves, the audience, and the occasion.

☐ The term *general purpose* refers to the general or overall listener response you expect to achieve with your speech.

☐ The general purposes of speech are usually to inform, to convince, to activate, and to entertain.

☐ The specific speech purpose is the precise, audience-centered objective you have set for your speech.

☐ Without a clearly defined specific purpose, the speaker is apt to waste time in preparation and the speech itself may appear to be out of focus.

☐ Speakers can often find speech subjects by reviewing their own experience and by being alert to what is going on in the world.

Suggested Assignments

Integrated Assignments

The assignments in this section are designed to help you further explore and experience the subject matter presented in Section A and Section B. Select one of the suggested topics and present an informal talk on it to the class. The topics will encourage you to think about the ideas presented in Section A of the chapter. As you prepare and deliver your presentation, try to utilize the principles we discussed in Section B. Even though the topics have been suggested, you will need to determine your general and specific purpose and to adapt your topic to the listeners. Try also to reflect the other aspects of good person-to-group communication that your class has thus far considered.

Speech Topics

1. From your own experience illustrate the three basic kinds of interpersonal topics presented in Section A of this chapter (general topics, you/me topics, us topics). Give several real examples of each.

2. Keep a log of the percentage of time you devote to each of the three kinds of topics in a specific relationship. Note on what sort of occasion you habitually discuss each kind of topic. With specific examples report your findings to the class.

3. According to the chapter, self-disclosure often takes the guesswork out of relationships. Illustrate this thesis by describing occasions on which you were misunderstood because you failed to disclose what you were really thinking, feeling, or wanting.

What was the result? How did you feel and how did your partner feel? Why did you fail to disclose?

4. Describe your own thoughts and feelings about self-disclosure. Illustrate your talk with specific, personal experiences, both positive and negative that you have had with self-disclosure.

5. Contrast specific environments you have encountered that encourage self-disclosure with environments that discourage self-disclosure. Be specific about the elements in each environment.

6. We noted in the chapter that our culture teaches some of us to perceive self-disclosure as a weakness. This is particularly true in the area of feelings and it often applies especially to men. Discuss this phenomenon. Use specific instances to illustrate the stereotypes involved.

7. The chapter mentioned three kinds of interpersonal needs: the need for inclusion, the need for control, and the need for affection. With real examples explain each of these needs. Please be specific.

8. Explain your own greatest interpersonal needs. With specific examples from real relationships, explain how you attempt to satisfy these needs.

9. Describe relationships you have observed or in which you have participated that tended (tend) to provide all partners with need gratification. Contrast those relationships with others in which some partners were (are) unable to satisfy basic interpersonal needs. In each case, what factors were involved? Why were partners able or unable to satisfy needs? What were the results?

10. Describe a number of relationships that would illustrate varying degrees of self-disclosure. Try to include relationships that admit almost no self-disclosure and relation-

ships that allow a high degree of self-disclosure.

Auxiliary Assignments

Interpersonal Focus

1. The class works in groups of four or five. Each member contributes to the group three or four examples of a general topic. The process is repeated with you/me and us topics. Each group will keep a master list of all the topics. At the end of the exercise, each group will share its list with the entire class.

2. The class is in groups of four or five. Each group member discloses to the other members of the group an important personal feeling, thought, or desire. The process is repeated until each member of the group has disclosed at least one thought, one feeling, and one desire. When all groups have finished, the class reconvenes to discuss the exercise. What was the easiest and what was the most difficult thing to disclose? How did it feel to disclose and how did it feel to listen to disclosure? Who in the group was helpful and who was threatening? Why?

3. The class is divided into groups. Each group will devise and present a role-playing scene that illustrates each of the three kinds of interpersonal topics.

4. The class is divided into four or six groups. Half the groups will each devise and present a role-playing scene designed to illustrate the advantages of self-disclosure. The other groups will each present a role-playing scene designed to illustrate the risks of self-disclosure.

5. Keep a diary for one week in which you record the interpersonal topics you discuss. At the end of the week analyze your diary. Write down your conclusions.

Person-to-Group Focus

1. Come to class prepared to participate in a discussion on speech subjects. Be prepared to list at least five subjects you would like someone in the class to consider during the term. As the discussion proceeds, class members should suggest topics for each subject that is presented.

2. Present at least five subjects to the class that you feel would be appropriate for you to speak on sometime during the term. Invite class reaction and note the degree of interest that is expressed in each subject.

3. List on paper ten subjects you feel you might suitably use for speeches during the term. For each subject list a topic, a general purpose, and a specific purpose.

4. Give a short, informal speech to the class. Try to pick a subject that you can cover from your own experience. Select a subject that is suited to you, the audience, and the time limit. Also try to reflect the other qualities of good person-to-group speech that your class has thus far considered. Before giving the speech, hand in a paper listing your general subject, your topic, the general purpose, and the specific purpose.

15–44. This chapter is a detailed but easy-to-read discussion of the speech subject and purpose. It contains a list of sample subject areas.

Suggested Readings

Interpersonal Focus

Jourard, Sidney M. *The Transparent Self.* Rev. ed. New York: Van Nostrand Reinhold Co., 1971. One of the best treatments of self-disclosure for the beginning student. Even though it was written for professionals, it is so easy to read and so provocative that it has been very popular with college students.

Miller, Sherod et al. *Alive and Aware: Improving Communication in Relationships.* Minneapolis: Interpersonal Communication Programs, 1975. This book provides a comprehensive, step-by-step explanation of the skills involved in self-disclosure.

Powell, John J. *Why Am I Afraid to Tell You Who I Am?* Niles, Ill.: Argus Communications, 1969. This short paperback is extremely easy to read. The author discusses why we are afraid to disclose ourselves and encourages the readers to be less defensive and more self-disclosing.

Person-to-Group Focus

Fletcher, Leon C. *How to Design and Deliver a Speech.* New York: Chandler Publishing Co., 1973, pp. 141–64. A good chapter on establishing a speech purpose.

Jeffrey, Robert C., and Peterson, Owen. *Speech: A Basic Text.* New York: Harper & Row Publishers, 1976, pp. 110–33. A good chapter on finding and narrowing speech subjects.

Mudd, Charles S., and Sillars, Malcolm O. *Speech: Content and Communication.* 3d ed. New York: Thomas Y. Crowell, 1975, pp.

Note Directory

1. Dorothy Parker, "The Waltz," in *The Portable Dorothy Parker* (New York: Viking Press, 1973), p. 51.

2. Kathleen S. Verderber and Rudolph F. Verderber, *Inter-Act: Using Interpersonal Communication Skills* (Belmont, Calif.: Wadsworth Publishing Co., 1977), p. 50.

3. Sidney M. Jourard, *The Transparent Self,* rev. ed. (New York: Van Nostrand Reinhold Co., 1971), p. iii.

4. John J. Powell, *Why Am I Afraid to Tell You Who I Am?* (Niles, Ill.: Argus Communications, 1969), p. 98.

5. Leonard Zunin and Natalie Zunin, *Contact: The First Four Minutes* (Los Angeles: Nash Publishing Corp., 1972), p. 6.

6. Irwin Altman and Dalmas A. Taylor, *Social Penetration: The Development of Interpersonal Relationships* (New York: Holt, Rinehart & Winston, 1973), p. 11.

7. William C. Schutz. *The Interpersonal Underworld* (Palo Alto, Calif.: Science and Behavior Books, 1966), pp. 18–20.

8. Michael Argyle, *Social Interaction* (New York: Atherton Press, 1970), p. 201.

9. Gail E. Myers and Michele T. Myers, *The Dynamics of Human Communication: A Laboratory Approach* (New York: McGraw-Hill Book Co., 1973), p. 278.

10. Warren Farrell, *The Liberated Man: Beyond Masculinity: Freeing Men and Their Relationships with Women* (New York: Random House, 1975), p. 31.

11. Dan P. Millar and Frank E. Millar, *Messages and Myths: Understanding Interpersonal Communication* (New York: Alfred Publishing Co., 1976), p. 148.

Chapter Five

**Perception
and
Structure**

Perception influences every aspect of
human behavior, including communication. In Section A of this chapter we will
consider the nature of human perception
and how knowledge of perception can be
used to improve interpersonal communication. In Section B we will note how
speakers in person-to-group situations
can structure the reports of their perceptions by utilizing patterns of organization
so that listeners can better perceive them.

Section A: Interpersonal Focus

Our perception structures our reality: a
discussion of human perception and how
it influences interpersonal communication.

■ Human perception is personal and
incomplete ■ controlling
factors ■ perception affects
communication

Section B: Person-to-Group Focus

The speaker guides audience perception
with speech structure: a discussion of
organization and its effects on
person-to-group communication.

■ Organizational patterns guide audience
perception ■ organizational patterns are
based on knowledge of perception ■ the
four-part deductive pattern ■ variations
of the basic pattern ■ outlining

Suggested Assignments

Section A

**Interpersonal
Focus**

*The universe as we know it is a joint
product of the observer and the
observed.*

R. D. Carmichael

In a very real sense, we all live in different
worlds. The world that each of us occupies
is the world that each of us perceives—and
we all perceive things somewhat differently. Our perceptions are unique because
each of us is equipped with personal perceptual machinery. Consequently, each
of us perceives the world in a unique and
personal way. This is a very important fact.
Since it is also difficult to grasp at first, let's
back up and say the same thing with different words.

The process of human perception can
be compared to the process of manufacturing a product. The sunset, the person, the
dining-room chair that exists in your perception is the product of your personal
manufacturing process. You use two kinds
of materials in this process: (1) the external
phenomena being perceived and (2) the
components of your individual perceptual
machinery. Several people, then, can observe the same phenomena and produce
differing products, because each person has
a unique perceptual apparatus. As Colin
Cherry states, "The stimuli received from
nature—the sights and sounds—are not
pictures of reality but are the evidence from

which we build our personal models, our
impressions, of reality."[1]

Because knowledge of human perception is important to improved communication, in Section A of this chapter we are
going to discuss several factors that affect
perception, and then talk about how knowledge of these factors can be used to improve human communication.

Factors That Affect Human Perception

The factors that affect perception are so
numerous that a complete list would be impractical in this chapter. We shall therefore
limit our discussion to five: the senses, experience, expectancy, selectivity, and language.

The Senses

Perception can be defined as the process of
collecting, organizing, and interpreting
sensory data into meaningful patterns. The
first step in the process of perception, collecting or "picking up" raw sensory data is
accomplished with the specialized organs
that we call senses. The sense organs provide among other things, skin sensitivity,
vision, scent detection, hearing, taste, the
sense of balance, and the sense of body
movement.

Our senses are truly phenomenal, and
yet at the same time they are limited. There
is a world of sensory data beyond our skins
that usually escapes our notice simply be-

cause our senses are unable to receive it. We are like radios that are tuned to receive a limited number of frequencies. Your dog, for example, can hear sounds that you can't hear. Humans cannot hear sounds below 20 cycles per second or above 20,000 cycles per second. Additionally, your dog can usually detect scents that you are unable to detect. Human vision is also limited. It is sensitive to only a narrow band of radiation, 1/17 of the total light spectrum.

Sensory sensitivity varies considerably from person to person. People are not stamped out by cookie cutters—our sense organs are not identical. Many people, for example, benefit from wearing eyeglasses. The lenses in the glasses should, of course, be individually prescribed because we don't all require the same kind of correction.

Just as vision varies from person to person so does the ability to hear. When you go to a concert, the chances are slim that you and the person sitting next to you are hearing exactly the same music. One reason for this is that you and your neighbor may well have different degrees of hearing acuity.

The same kind of thing applies to the other senses as well. You can experiment for yourself with the sense of taste by obtaining from your biology department a supply of PTC paper. PTC papers are thin strips of paper that have been treated with the chemical phenylthiocarbamide. Ask everyone in your class to taste one of the paper strips. Typically some members of your class will find the paper bitter, some will find it sour, some will find it sweet, some will find it salty, and some will find it

tasteless. These papers are often used to demonstrate that we don't all inherit identical "tasting machines."

It is not surprising, then, that you and others often disagree about how the food tastes, or whether or not the room is too chilly, or whether the new coat of paint is bright enough. Such differences in perception are inevitable. Let's try to remember this when in a few pages we talk about improving communication through knowledge of perception.

Experience

Once collected, the raw sensory data must be organized and interpreted before it becomes meaningful. Our past experience constitutes one factor in the processing of sensory data. For example, when someone talks to you, your auditory receptors receive the sounds. Your brain interprets these sounds as meaningful words. You hear, then, with your brain as well as with your ears. Your brain, however, could not translate the sounds of your native language until you had accumulated enough experience to give meaning to the various sound patterns, or words. The same would apply today were you to attempt to learn a new language.

Vision is accomplished similarly. As Kenneth Johnson points out, "We see with our experience as well as with our eyes. The I behind the eye does the seeing."[2] People who have suddenly gained their sight after a lifetime of blindness report that the visual patterns of the world are meaningless to them until time and experience bring significance to the hues and shapes that are so familiar to the rest of us.

The point is that people interpret the environment in terms of their background or experience. In 1977, 26 years after he created the role of the king in the musical *The King and I,* Yul Brynner appeared in a Broadway revival of the show. The "revived" king, he said, was an entirely new king. In response to questions he explained that the experience of living 26 additional years enabled him to perceive the role in a new way. People with specialized training illustrate the same point. The geologist is often able to see features in the landscape that the rest of us miss. An experienced football coach can look down the line of scrimmage and see subtleties of play that the inexperienced observer fails to detect. An auto mechanic can often listen to an engine and hear things the rest of us don't hear.

Further illustrations are provided by cultural differences. Each culture has its own point of view, its own way of looking at the world. We learn to perceive the way our particular, familiar culture perceives. The culture provides experiences that influence our perception. A public pinch on the bottom is perceived differently in Rome from the way it is perceived in most American cities. In some cultures for men to hold hands is considered natural. Such behavior is perceived as unnatural in our culture. In Japan elderly people are honored for their experience and wisdom and are considered valuable assets. Our culture often perceives the elderly as "used up," doddering, or useless.

Because of differing background and experience, no two people can be expected

to perceive the world in exactly the same way. People often say, "I call them as I see them." It probably would be more accurate to say, "I call them as my culture and experience have taught me to see them."

Expectancy

A factor closely related to experience is the psychological set of the perceiver. Because of past experience, we often expect to perceive certain things. Because of that expectation, we sometimes see those things even when they are not there. In other words, we tend to perceive what we expect to perceive. This fact has been demonstrated experimentally time and time again.

I once played a symphonic recording for a group of musicians. As a matter of fact,

I played the same recording twice. The musicians, however, didn't know they were hearing the same recording twice. They were told that the first rendition was done by the London Philharmonic Orchestra and that the second was done by a local college group. The listeners were asked to put their analysis of the two renditions (actually the same recording) in writing. Some of them wrote at length on the differences they heard. All felt the first rendition was superior to the second. They heard, of course, what they were expecting to hear. They had been programmed by the labels that were given to each recording.

The tendency for people to perceive what they expect to perceive is one of the reasons that stereotypes are so insidious. Stereotypes serve as labels. They program us to see certain characteristics in particular people. Because we are programmed, we tend to see the characteristics whether or not they exist.

In one study, Robert Rosenthal demonstrated the effect of expectation in the classroom.[3] Teachers were told that certain of their students had done well on an IQ test and were exceptionally promising. The teachers tended to see those students as being brighter, better adjusted, and more industrious than the other students. This phenomenon is sometimes referred to as the *halo effect.* When teachers expect that certain students will do well, they tend to perceive those students as doing well. The same applies, of course, to coaches, bank managers, policemen, and all the rest of us.

For years I have shown my classes the same abstract sketch. Half the students are told the drawing represents an advertisement for a costume ball. The other half are told it is an advertisement for a trained seal act. Each student is given three minutes to study the drawing. All students are then given a questionnaire concerning what they saw in the drawing. Those that thought they were looking at an advertisement for a trained seal act usually report seeing animals, fish, and other things associated with such acts. Those that thought they saw a sketch for a costume ball usually report seeing women, chandeliers, and musicians.

Human perception is powerfully affected by the psychological set or state of expectancy. You can prove this for yourself by reading the phrases in the triangles aloud (see Figure 5–1).

Most people read the phrases several

A place
in the
the sun

Springtime
in the
the Rockies

Barefoot
in the
the park

Figure 5.1

times before they notice that in each phrase the word *the* is used twice. If you saw them with just one *the,* you saw them that way because that's the way you expected them.

Experienced speakers often take advantage of the principle of expectancy when they organize their speeches. We will talk about this in Section B of this chapter. For now let's emphasize that, because people have differing expectations, they often perceive the same phenomena differently.

Selectivity

Human beings seem to be unable to attend to a wide spectrum of sensory input at one time. Consequently, we select the items to which we will direct our attention—our perception is selective. After summarizing much of the experimentation that has been done in the field, Magdalen Vernon reports, "He (the observer) can view only a small part of his surroundings at any one moment; and even when he scans them deliberately, there is much that he tends to overlook or to perceive incompletely or inaccurately."[4]

An interesting experiment was reported by G. H. Mowbray.[5] Subjects were required to locate places on a map by following directions, part of which were presented visually and part of which were presented orally. Both visual and oral directions were necessary for success. The experimenter found that when the two kinds of messages were presented simultaneously, the subjects comprehended one or the other—but not both.

In short, at any one time we are being bombarded with a variety of sensory stimuli. We are aware of only a small percentage of this stimuli because we must of necessity be selective. It is possible, then, for several people witnessing the same event to perceive different aspects of it because each has selected a different aspect to attend to. Law enforcement officers, for example, frequently report that eyewitnesses have disagreed; at the time of the event each witness was focusing on a different element in the event.

Several factors help determine the focus of our attention. As we observed earlier, past experience and expectancy tend to direct us in a particular direction. Our immediate needs and interests also influence our selection. We are more apt to notice restaurants when we are hungry than when we are not hungry. After a student decided to look for and buy a particular model of used car, he became amazed at the number of those cars on the road. The cars had been there all the time, of course. He didn't notice them before because he hadn't been interested.

We perceive what we are paying attention to. Because the range of our perceptual awareness is limited, we miss a great deal. What we do select and perceive in a situation is highly personal.

Language

Language is more than a tool that we use for reporting our perceptions; language actually helps to shape our perceptions. For example, names tend to influence our perception of the things named. Officials of a small community college once tried to pass a bond issue to finance a combined speech facility and little theater. The measure was identified as the Little Theater Bond. With this label voters perceived the proposed facility as a luxury, and the bond issue failed to pass. A year later the proposed building was called the Language Arts Learning Center, and the measure passed easily. Advertisers have long known the importance of selecting just the right names for products. Clothes for fat men don't sell as well as clothes for portly gentlemen.

The influences of language on perception are numerous and subtle. Benjamin Whorf sums up the matter in this fashion, "Every language is a vast pattern system, different from others, in which is culturally ordained the forms and categories by which the personality not only communicates, but analyzes nature, notices or neglects types of relationships and phenomena, channels his reasoning, and builds the house of his consciousness. . . . Each language performs this artificial chopping up of the continuous spread and flow of existence in a different way."[6] In short, language patterns tend to direct perception into habitual channels. We will talk more about the influences of language on perception in chapter 10.

Thus far we have noted that perception is personal, that individuals inevitably vary in the way they perceive the world. We have discussed how our senses, our past experience, our expectations, and our language influence perception. We have also observed that human perception is selective. Let's next consider how knowledge of these facts can be used to improve communication.

Improving Communication through Knowledge of Perception

Our perceptions are the personal, internal responses we have to external stimuli. We own our perceptions; they happen within us. Our unique perceptual equipment allows each of us to perceive the world in a unique way. When others perceive the world differently from you, it doesn't mean that you are wrong or that they are wrong;

In a sense, we each live in separate worlds.

it simply means that you are different from each other, and it's not wrong to be different.

Although we know these things about perception, we sometimes act as though we didn't know them. We often communicate as though our perceptions were external facts rather than personal, internal events. Think about it. We spend a lot of time talking about our perceptions. We often talk about them in a way that suggests a finality that is unrealistic. We say, "This room is cold" or "That movie stinks" instead of saying "I feel cold" or "That movie didn't appeal to me." The tendency to talk in this fashion is understandable. After all, our own perceptions are the only ones we have ever known firsthand. It is easy, therefore, for us to assume that the way we experience the world equals the way the world is.

Although understandable, this tendency has several negative effects on communication. When we assume that the only way to see something is the way we see it, our minds tend to become closed on the subject. We are not good listeners, and we are not receptive to new ideas. This attitude discourages others from wanting to talk with us. They feel that we will not give their ideas a fair hearing. It is not much fun to talk to someone with a closed mind. Most importantly, when we proceed as though our perceptions were the only legitimate perceptions, we imply to others that they have no right to their own perceptions. Such denial constitutes threatening behavior. As William Haney states, "A fundamental reason for defensive behavior appears to be the inability of so many people to acknowledge differences—differences between their perceptions and reality and

differences between their perceptions and those of others."[7]

Fortunately, we can learn to share our perceptions in a nonthreatening way. We can utilize knowledge about perception actually to improve communication.

Ownership Statements

You can use your knowledge of the perceptual process by presenting your perceptions in a way that accurately reflects the fact that your perceptions are taking place within you and that they are not immutable extensional facts. For example, the following two statements are not accurate: (1) the music is loud; (2) the game was dull. They suggest that the qualities referred to exist independent of the observer. They imply that the loudness and the dullness are inherent in the movie and the game and that everyone must find the music loud and the game dull. It would be more accurate to say: (1) I think the music is loud; (2) for me the game was dull. The second set of statements suggests that the experience being described is personal and internal.

Statements of this kind are called ownership statements because the speakers clearly indicate ownership of their own perceptions. Ownership statements in effect say, "These are my perceptions, I am proud of them, but I recognize there are other ways of perceiving and that you must have space for your own perceptions."

Just for practice, translate the following sentences into ownership statements:

1. He is a good guy.
2. She didn't say that.

3. Capital punishment doesn't deter crime.

A number of translations are possible. Here is one suggestion:

1. Based on my experience with him, he seems to me to be a good guy.
2. I don't recall hearing her say that.
3. From the data I have been able to gather, I have concluded that capital punishment does not deter crime.

For most of us, developing the habit of making ownership statements involves only a slight change in language habits. For many people, however, this slight change has been very rewarding. Ownership statements improve communication, primarily in three ways.

By Contributing to an Open Mind Our language habits condition our thinking. If we consistently talk about our perceptions as if they were the only ones possible, we condition ourselves to think that way. On the other hand, when we make ownership statements, we remind ourselves that perceptions other than ours are possible. This can result in better listening, which encourages others to communicate with us.

By Reducing Defensiveness Ownership statements are often supportive because they demonstrate respect for the perceptions of others. They imply permission for others to have perceptions separate from our own. When we say, "That is a lousy plan," we are implying the other person is wrong if he or she likes the plan. Evaluative

behavior of this kind is often threatening. But when we say, "I think, according to the data I have been able to get, that this is a lousy plan," we are admitting the possibility of a different perception.

By Contributing to Flexibility Ownership statements can help us avoid painting ourselves into "psychological corners." Face-saving seems to be involved here. Sometimes when we state our perceptions with a great deal of finality, it is difficult for us to admit we were wrong or that we have changed our minds. Strongly worded statements that report perceptions as though they were immutable facts seem to generate an emotional commitment to defend those statements regardless of any evidence that might turn up. This is particularly true in public discussions. It is easier for most of us to amend our perceptions when we have acknowledged from the first that additional perceptions are possible.

In short, the habit of making ownership statements can reduce defensiveness and contribute to openness and flexibility.

In this section we observed that human perception is personal, we noted some of the factors that affect perception, and we discussed the advantages of making ownership statements.

Key Ideas in Review

☐ Each of us perceives the world personally.

☐ We each possess unique perceptual equipment.

☐ Some factors that affect perception are the senses, experience, expectation, selectivity, and language.

☐ When we act as though our perceptions are the only ones possible, we discourage communication by appearing to be closed-minded and by implying that perceptions different from ours are ill advised.

☐ Ownership statements acknowledge that our perceptions are personal, internal events.

☐ Ownership statements can contribute to openness and flexibility and reduce defensiveness.

Section B

Person-to-Group Focus

Good order is the foundation of all good things.

Edmund Burke

In Section A we observed that, to make sense from the data provided by our sensory receptors, we need to organize that data into meaningful patterns. In order for listeners to make sense from the data provided by a speaker, they must impose on the speaker's remarks a structure that has meaning for them, the listeners. The speaker can help listeners find meaning by using recognizable patterns of organization. Speakers organize their messages, then, not only to aid themselves in preparation and delivery but most importantly to meet the perceptual needs of the listeners. Ideas are simply easier to understand and remember when they are presented in organized patterns. As Harold Barrett puts it, "Listeners want guidelines and direction; they find structure and arrangement helpful and disarrangement baffling."[8]

In this section we are going to talk about how speakers can guide listener perception by structuring speeches. Specifically, we will discuss the four-part deductive pattern of speech organization, consider some variations of the basic pattern, and, finally, talk about outlining. As we discuss the four-part pattern, we will note how various parts of the pattern reflect the elements of the perceptual process that we considered in Section A of this chapter.

The Four-Part Deductive Pattern of Speech Organization

Although there are many useful patterns of organization, the one most generally used and probably the most practical is the four-part deductive pattern. This pattern was developed by Corax of Sicily in the fifth century B.C. Corax was one of the most successful speakers and teachers of his time, and the formula he developed was based on practice and observation. Modern insight into the processes of perception would indicate that this pattern was also based on an intuitive understanding of human perception.

In this chapter we will concentrate on the four-part deductive pattern. Most other patterns are merely adaptations of this basic one. Once you have learned to use this pattern you will have little difficulty with the others. As the name implies, the four-part pattern has four basic parts: the introduction, the thesis statement, the body, and the conclusion. Furthermore, the various parts and subparts are woven together with transitional statements.

This pattern is based on the old adage: Tell them what you are going to tell them, tell them, tell them what you told them. With the introduction and thesis statement you tell them what you are going to tell them, in the body you tell them, and in the conclusion you tell them what you told them.

Organization helps both the speaker and the listener.

This pattern is also based on an understanding of the importance to perception of the anticipatory set. As we discuss the pattern, note that it provides that the listener be frequently reminded about what to expect. Let's talk now about each of the parts separately.

The Introduction

Speakers often utilize the introduction to gain attention, to establish personal credibility and rapport with the audience, and to stimulate listener interest in the speech subject. In other words, the purpose of the introduction is to put the audience in a mood for listening. The degree of emphasis given to the various functions of the introduction depends upon the speaker, the audience, and the occasion. If you are well known to your listeners, if they admire and respect you, if they have previous interest in the subject, your introduction can be very brief. On the other hand, if your listeners have no prior interest in the subject or knowledge of your qualifications, you may need to spend more time with the introduction. Before we discuss specific techniques appropriate for the introduction, let's consider some general guidelines.

Be Brief For reasons we have just discussed, some introductions will be longer than others. You should always get to the point as soon as possible, however. Introductions are intended to put audience members in the mood for listening. Rambling introductions often have the opposite effect.

Be Direct The worst possible time to have your eyes glued to your notecards is during the introduction. Before it is too late and they "tune you out," indicate to listeners by your manner that you intend to share ideas with them naturally, directly, and conversationally. Avoid giving them the idea that they are about to hear a mechanical, memorized recitation.

Provide a Reason for Listening In Section A we noted that people tend to focus on stimuli that coincide with their personal needs and interests. In the introduction, therefore, communicate to the listeners that you are going to provide them with something they will benefit from. In other words, give them a reason for listening.

Be Relevant   To secure attention is not enough. You must direct that attention toward the speech subject. Consequently, all material used in the introduction should be directly related to the central purpose of the speech. Don't, for example, confuse your listeners with a funny story that has nothing to do with your speech.

Don't Apologize   Remember the power of the anticipatory set. Don't condition your listeners to expect a poor speech by apologizing for your ability or your subject.

Prepare the Introduction Last   It is difficult to introduce something before you have learned what you are introducing. Most speakers, consequently, wait until the rest of the speech has been developed before preparing the introduction.

Theoretically, there are as many introductory techniques as there are speakers and speeches. You will be able to develop approaches of your own that fit your style, your subject, and your listeners. The techniques described below are some that have been useful to speakers in the past. They are seldom used alone. They are most useful when they are woven into the fabric of the introduction. Keep in mind that the purpose of the introduction is to put the audience in a mood for listening. To do this you may need to gain attention, you may need to establish your credentials, you may need to develop rapport with the listeners, and you may need to stimulate interest in

the subject. The following techniques may be helpful.

Use an Illustration   Practically everybody loves a story. Consequently, one of the most effective means of beginning a speech is to tell an illustrative story, real or fictional. It can be taken from history, from literature, or from real life. If the story is interesting and directly related to the speech subject, it can be an excellent device for getting attention and focusing it on the speech. Consider the following introduction:

Last Monday afternoon I looked out of my kitchen window and saw Sam Ward, my neighbor, on his hands and knees in front of the tree he had been trimming. As I watched, he got to his feet, took a few steps toward his back door, and then slumped to the ground again. By the time I reached him, he was on his feet. As I helped him into his house, he explained that while trimming the tree he had developed cramps in his legs and had felt dizzy. Sitting in his front room he seemed all right, but every time he got to his feet he became dizzy again. I took his pulse and found that his heart was palpitating wildly.

Sam spent two days in the hospital restoring his body's supply of potassium. Today he is fine. For high blood pressure he had been taking a diuretic prescribed by his physician. Unfortunately, the doctor had forgotten to tell him that diuretics deplete the body's store of potassium, and that potassium supplements should be taken with diuretics.

Sam's is not an isolated case. Too often people take drugs without being aware of their side effects. Because this is a potential problem for all of us, today I want to explain what health professionals and government officials are suggesting we do to avoid the dangerous side effects of prescription drugs.

Use a Quotation Another popular device for focusing interest is the quotation. This is easy because quotations are readily available from a variety of sources. The following introduction was developed with aid from a popular book of quotations.

> I would like to begin today by quoting one of our best-known and most respected presidents. Thomas Jefferson once said, "I am mortified to be told that, in America, the sale of a book can become a subject of inquiry, and of criminal inquiry too." I wonder what Jefferson would say if he were alive today. I think that he would be concerned, as many of us are, about recent court decisions affecting freedom of the press. Today I would like to share with you my concern about the state of the free press in America.

Ask a Rhetorical Question Sometimes you can focus attention on the subject of the speech by asking an interesting question. For this technique to be effective, the question must be truly stimulating. Avoid questions that can be quickly dismissed with a yes or a no. Consider this example.

> Good evening. I would like to begin tonight by asking you to think seriously about this question. How would you react if, in the course of a routine physical examination, your doctor told you that you faced the serious possibility of a debilitating illness but that in all probability this illness could be avoided with a small amount of sacrifice on your part? How would you feel when you heard the news? What would you do? Would you make the sacrifice necessary to

improve your chances for good health? These questions are being answered by millions of Americans each day. The Americans I am referring to are those who regularly smoke cigarettes. Their answers to these questions may very well determine their future happiness. So that you might better answer these questions yourself, or help a loved one answer them, this evening I want to describe some of the hazards involved in cigarette smoking.

Use a Humorous Anecdote Another popular introductory device is the humorous anecdote. Sometimes a funny story or a humorous description will get the speech started in fine style. A word of caution is in order, however. In order to work, the anecdote must really be humorous and it must be relevant. Keep in mind that it often takes an expert to make an audience laugh, and that what's funny in one situation may not be funny in another situation. If you begin with a joke that falls flat, both you and the audience will feel uncomfortable. The following story was used by a speaker who was beginning a lecture on the semantics of sexism. The audience was supportive, and the story worked. Perhaps you can think of some audiences that would not find this story amusing.

> I think the dictionary is very funny. The other day I was able to find 25 words in the dictionary to describe a woman who nags but not one word to describe a man who nags. A man who nags is called an efficiency expert. Let me tell you some other things about women, men, and language.

Refer to the Importance of the Subject Sometimes a reminder about the significance of the subject is enough to arouse audience interest. With this technique the speaker makes clear that the speech will provide something of benefit for the listener. In the following introduction the speaker uses the enticement of better appearance and improved health:

> Hi—with the kind of weather we are enjoying today, we don't need the calendar to tell us that spring is here and that summer will soon be upon us. Shortly it will be time to hit the beaches and the pools. This means that it's time right now for many of us to shed a few pounds so that we won't feel embarrassed in last year's swimsuit. Improved appearance, of course, is not the only good reason for losing weight. Doctors tell us that excessive weight is a serious health problem at any age. Some authorities think, for example, that children who are overweight run a high risk of developing obesity and high blood pressure as adults. Among other things, excessive weight is frequently blamed for heart and kidney disease, high blood pressure, arterial schlerosis, lassitude, and excessive fatigue. Because spring is traditionally a time for renewal, today I want to explain a simple, safe, reducing diet that really works. It worked for me and it has worked for several members of my family. Follow this diet for just a few weeks and you will be in better health, you will feel more vigorous, and of course, you will look better at the beach this summer.

Refer to the Audience and the Occasion   Sometimes speakers can establish rapport and develop interest by referring to the audience and the occasion. Such references should be simple, direct, and sincere. The president of the National Association of Student Financial Aid Administrators once began an address to a regional meeting of Financial Aid Administrators in this fashion.

> As I approached Cincinnati on the plane this morning, I thought to myself that financial aid workers are the only people I know who would come to Cincinnati during World Series time and go to a meeting. I think I understand your attention to duty. You have seen firsthand, as I have seen, how important our work is to the students we serve. Because of the present high cost of education many deserving students would be unable to experience post-secondary education were it not for your dedicated efforts. The meetings we will hold in the next few days may very well have impact not only on our students but also on the institutions they attend and ultimately on the future of this country. At this time I would like to report to you on recent federal legislation affecting student financial aid.

In review, speakers have found these introductory techniques useful. To them you will be able to add devices of your own that are particularly suited to you, your listeners, and the subject. Keep in mind that the purpose of the introduction is to put the audience in the mood for listening. Sometimes you will be able to accomplish this with a few sentences. On other occasions it will take longer.

The Thesis Statement

In the four-part deductive pattern of organization, the thesis statement follows the introduction. Sometimes it is considered part of the introduction. It doesn't make much difference whether you consider it to be a part of the introduction or a separate unit in the pattern. For a speech to be effective, the various parts of whatever pattern you are using must be developed as a unified whole. We are discussing the thesis statement separately here to emphasize its importance.

Your *thesis* is the central idea of your speech. The thesis statement is a clear, concise statement that informs the audience of this central idea.

Deciding on the central idea or thesis of the speech is one of the first steps in speech preparation. The thesis is the cornerstone of the entire speech. Everything the speaker does or says in the speech should be designed to support the thesis. If the speaker fails to keep the central idea clearly in mind, the speech is apt to wander or lack focus.

The thesis statement should be presented in clear, complete sentences. Usually it is presented in a single sentence. If more than one sentence is needed, they all should support a single idea, since each speech should deal with just one central idea. It should prepare the audience as accurately as possible for what to expect from your speech. As you have already surmised, the thesis statement takes advantage of the anticipatory set. As we observed in Section A, people are more apt to perceive what they are expecting to perceive. If you have alerted your listeners about what to look for with your thesis statement, they are more apt to find it.

The thesis statement, then, is a key part of the speech. It should be as specific as possible. "I wish to talk about baseball," for example, is much too broad. This statement doesn't inform the listeners about what aspect of baseball is going to be covered. The speaker could be planning to talk about baseball rules, famous players, signals used, or any number of other things. Consider the following thesis statements and decide for yourself which are satisfactory and which are unsatisfactory.

1. Today it is my hope to dispel three popular myths concerning waterbeds.
2. Air pollution
3. It is my hope today to convince you that mandatory auto safety checks should be instituted in our city.
4. Today let's look at two pros and two cons of capital punishment.
5. Today it is my hope to convince you that every student should take a speech course, and that we should all attend this week's production of *Our Town,* which is being presented by our drama department.
6. This talk will be devoted to a description of four aspects of safe weight reduction.

Statements 1, 3, 4, and 6 are probably satisfactory. They are fairly clear and specific. They give listeners a clear idea of what to listen for. The second statement is incomplete; it is not a complete sentence, and it does not give listeners a clear idea of what to listen for. The fifth statement is unacceptable because it presents two ideas—two thesis statements. It could serve two separate speeches.

Unlike the purpose statement, which we discussed in chapter 4, the thesis statement actually appears in the speech—it is for audience consumption. The specific purpose statement, you will recall, is a statement that the speaker formulates as an aid in the preparation and delivery of the speech. It sets forth what the speaker wants to accomplish with the audience as a result of the speech. A sample specific purpose statement is, "As a result of my speech I want my audience to know how to organize a term paper." A sample thesis statement for the same speech could be, "Today I would like to offer some tips about how to organize a term paper."

For any one speech your thesis statement will usually be similar to your purpose statement. *However, sometimes it is not similar.* Sometimes the speaker will temper the thesis statement in order to avoid initial audience resistance. Assume that you are going to speak on gun control. Your purpose statement could be, "As a result of my speech I want my listeners to vote for gun control legislation." If you are pretty sure your listeners agree with you about gun control, your thesis statement will be similar to your purpose statement. It could be, "Today I would like to explain some of the reasons that we should all vote for gun control."

On the other hand, if you suspect that your listeners are strongly opposed to gun control, you might wish to soften the thesis statement to avoid initial resistance. In this case your thesis statement could be, "Today let's consider the pros and cons of gun control"; or it could be, "Let's consider what some of the experts are saying about gun control." A third alternative could be, "Let's take a look at what has happened in some of the countries that have adopted gun control."

In summary, the thesis statement is a statement that prepares the audience for listening to your speech. It is usually quite similar to your purpose statement. However in some instances it is less direct than is the purpose statement. The thesis statement is for audience consumption. The purpose statement is for the speaker's use.

The Body

The body will constitute the primary portion of your speech. After you have prepared your listeners for your message (with the introduction and the thesis statement), you deliver that message in the body of the speech. To accomplish this, you divide your message into units and subunits. These are called main heads and subheads.

Main heads are subdivisions of the thesis. Each main head should support and be subordinate to the thesis. Subheads are subdivisions of the main heads and should be subordinate to the main heads they support. Simple main heads do not usually require subdivision, but when they are complicated, dividing them into subheads is sometimes in order.

This orderly approach helps speakers remember their ideas. It also, of course, helps listeners follow the speech. Remember what we said about selective perception. People have difficulty attending to more than one thing at once. It's easier for them to focus on a single idea at a time. For the speaker to wander haphazardly from one main head to another would confuse both speaker and listener. Furthermore, as George Miller points out, research into perception indicates that dividing material into related parts makes it not only easier to recall at a later time but also easier to follow.[9]

There is no hard and fast rule about the number of main heads a speech should contain. This depends, of course, on the subject matter and the time available. Many speakers, however, try to keep the number under five. Most people can't absorb much more than that at one sitting. William Brooks reports on research that tends to validate this conclusion.[10]

Main heads and subheads should be arranged in the manner that seems best suited to the speech material and to the particular speaking situation. The following organizational plans illustrate some of the many possible ways to arrange main heads.

A. *Geographical plan:* If you wanted to show how various geographical regions of the country are affected by unemployment, the body of your speech could look like this:

1. Unemployment in the East
2. Unemployment in the South
3. Unemployment in the central region
4. Unemployment in the West

B. *Chronological plan:* If you wanted to explain the recent history of unemployment, the body of your speech could be arranged in this fashion:

1. Unemployment in the fifties
2. Unemployment in the sixties
3. Unemployment in the seventies

C. *Situation to cause plan:* If your purpose was to show some of the causes of unemployment, the body of your speech could look like this:

1. The present unemployment situation in this country
2. The major causes of the present unemployment situation

D. *Situation to effect plan:* If you wanted to predict some future results of present-day unemployment, you could arrange your materials as follows:

1. The present unemployment situation in this country
2. Predicted effects if the present situation is allowed to continue

E. *Situation to cause to effect plan:* If you wanted to describe the present situation, discuss the causes, and predict the effects, you could combine the last two plans in this way:

1. The present unemployment situation
2. The causes of the present situation
3. Predicted effects

F. *Problem solution plan:* If your purpose was to analyze the unemployment problem and to offer solutions, you could arrange main heads in this manner:

1. Aspects of the present unemployment problem
2. Suggested solutions to the present problem

G. *Topical plan:* If you wished to talk about various kinds of unemployment, the body of the speech could look like this:

1. Unemployment and teenagers
2. Unemployment and unskilled adults
3. Unemployment and displaced workers

4. Unemployment and the handicapped

These examples have demonstrated only a few of the more widely used organizational patterns.

Before leaving the subject of main heads and subheads, let's consider some of the mistakes most commonly made in the arrangement of material.

Avoid Overlapping of Main Heads and Subheads In the following example B and D overlap.

Thesis: Today I would like to explain some of the advantages of backpacking.

A. Backpacking can be done by people of almost any age.
B. Backpacking is good for you.
C. Backpacking is inexpensive.
D. Backpacking is a healthy recreation.

Keep Subordinate Heads within the Scope of the Headings They Are Designed to Support In the following example the third main head does not support the thesis statement. The thesis statement indicates that the speaker is going to explain what to look for when buying a puppy. Main head C goes beyond the scope of that statement.

Thesis: I would like to point out some things you should look for when buying a puppy.

A. Characteristics of the breed
   1. Size
   2. Temperament

3. History
B. Health of the puppy
   1. Shots
   2. Appearance of coat
   3. Size and weight in comparison to litter mates
   4. Degree of alertness
C. How to housebreak the puppy
   1. Feed at regular intervals
   2. Take outside at regular intervals
   3. Provide newspapers or sandbox

Avoid Compound Main Heads and Subheads In this example main head A is compound.

Thesis: I want to present some of the advantages involved in making one's clothes.

A. You pay less and you have a better fit.
B. You can usually find the style you want.
C. You get a feeling of personal accomplishment.

In review, the body is the principle part of the speech. In the body, the speaker's material is grouped into units called main heads and subheads. The type of speech material and the specific speaking situation should determine the arrangement of the main heads and subheads.

The Conclusion

The last part of the four-part deductive pattern is the conclusion. Its primary purpose is to summarize, or to refresh the memory of the listeners about the content of the

"In conclusion, I will now read the second draft of this speech."

speech. This can be accomplished in many ways. You may restate the main point of the speech, or you may summarize each main head separately. Sometimes speakers summarize indirectly with a short anecdote or quotation that emphasizes the central idea of the speech.

The conclusion also gives the speaker a chance to end the speech gracefully—to "round it off." Sometimes, especially when the purpose has been to activate, the speaker will close with a short appeal to action. Ordinarily the various functions of the conclusion are accomplished concurrently.

At all costs, avoid introducing new ideas in the conclusion. Eliminate all material that is not directly related to ideas previously introduced.

Finally, although the speech should not end abruptly, avoid boring the listeners with long rambling conclusions. Nothing is more agonizing than a speaker who seems not to know how to sit down. Once your audience senses that the end is in sight, it is best not to disappoint them. In the following sample conclusion, the speaker summarizes, makes a final appeal, and ends gracefully with an apt quotation:

> Today by explaining the principles of aerobic exercise, by presenting some sample aerobic programs, and by discussing some of the many benefits available from regular aerobic exercise, I hope I have interested you in beginning your own aerobic exercise program. Remember, begin gradually but do begin. Join the thousands in our town who have found improved health and greater happiness through exercise. In the words of the eighteenth-century philosopher James Thompson, "Health is the vital principle of bliss, and exercise is the vital principle of health."

Thus far we have considered the basic parts of the four-part deductive pattern of organization. In way of review, consider the following outline.

   I. Introduction

      A. Gain attention.

      B. Establish rapport.

      C. Develop interest.

  II. Thesis (Make central idea clear to listeners.)

 III. Body

      A. First main head

         1. Subhead

         2. Subhead

B. Second main head

   1. Subhead

   2. Subhead

C. Third main head

   1. Subhead

   2. Subhead

IV. Conclusion

A. Summarize.

B. Round off.

C. Make a final appeal.

Transitions

Now that we have considered each part of the four-part deductive pattern, let's talk about transitions. Transitions tie the four separate parts of the speech together into a unified whole. They also redirect the wandering attention of the audience throughout the speech. They remind listeners where the speaker has been and where he is going next. They utilize the perceptual principle of the anticipatory set by telling listeners what to expect.

Transitions are simple connecting statements or phrases. In the four-part pattern, the first major transition comes between the introduction and the thesis statement. This connecting device is a phrase or a group of phrases that leads naturally and simply from the introduction to the thesis statement.

The second transition connects the thesis statement and the first main head. It reminds the listeners of the thesis and announces the first main head. The transition that joins the first main head to the second

main head summarizes the first and announces the second. The transition from the second main head to the third main head summarizes or briefly mentions the first two and announces the third, and so on throughout the speech. Formal transitions are not usually necessary between subheads or between subheads and main heads. Nor is a formal transition usually necessary between the last main head of the body and the conclusion, since the conclusion itself usually contains a summary of the main heads.

Think of transitions as signposts. They remind the audience where you have been and where you are going next. Please study the following diagram, which illustrates the use of transitions.

Diagram Illustrating the Use of Transitions

General purpose: To inform

Specific purpose: As a result of my speech I want my audience to know how to prepare for, plant, and care for a home vegetable garden.

Introduction

I. Remind audience that it will soon be "garden planting time."

II. Emphasize the economic, recreational, and nutritional benefits of home gardening.

First transition: "Four summers ago I tried my first garden. I have been at it ever since. Because gardening is so worthwhile, ⟶

Thesis

today I'm going to show you how you can grow your own vegetables at home."

Second transition: "The first step in home gardening is

Body

I. soil preparation." Explain how to prepare the soil for gardening.

Third transition: "Once the soil is prepared, we are ready for the second step which is

II. planting the seeds." Explain what seeds to plant, where to plant them, and how they should be planted.

Fourth transition: "After soil preparation and planting comes

III. maintenance." Explain how to cultivate, weed, and water.

Conclusion

I. Summarize the three main heads

II. Round off by wishing audience a "happy harvest."

Thus far we have noted that speakers organize material to aid themselves in speech preparation and delivery and to accommodate the perceptual needs of the listeners. We have discussed the four-part deductive pattern of speech organization and observed that this pattern utilizes basic principles of human perception.

Variations of the Basic Pattern

The four-part deductive pattern is the most widely used pattern of speech organization. We are probably well advised to master that pattern before attempting variations. Variations do, however, exist, and in this section we will briefly consider two varieties of the basic pattern.

The four-part pattern we have been discussing is a *deductive pattern* because it begins with a general statement (the thesis statement) and proceeds toward specific aspects of that statement (the main heads and subheads). In deductive discourse we always begin with a generality and then support it with specific details. A deductive pattern can be diagrammed (see Figure 5–2).

Induction works in the opposite way. We begin with specific details and from them develop a generalization or conclu-

Figure 5.2

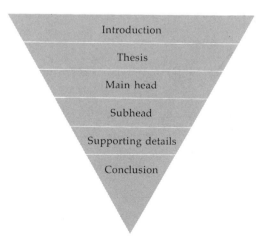

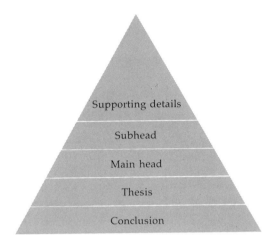

Figure 5.3

sion. Induction can be diagrammed (see Figure 5–3).

Remember that the four-part deductive pattern we have been discussing is based on deduction; the first variation we will discuss is based on induction.

The Inductive Pattern

With the inductive pattern the speaker begins with *specific data*. This data develops and leads to the announcement of the first point or main head (which doubles as an introduction). After announcing the first main head, the speaker offers specific details that will develop and lead to the announcement of the second main head. After announcing the second main head, the speaker presents details leading to the third main head, and so on throughout the speech. In the conclusion of the inductive speech, the speaker summarizes the main heads and states the thesis or central idea

that they have supported. Although the inductive pattern often lacks the clarity of the deductive pattern, in some situations it is more persuasive. The following sample outline illustrates the inductive pattern. For the sake of comparison and clarity, it will be followed by a deductive arrangement of the same material.

Sample Inductive Pattern

General purpose: To convince

Specific purpose: As a result of my speech I want my listeners to agree that San Diego is a good place in which to spend the spring vacation.

I. Body

   1. Golf courses
   2. Beaches
   3. Zoo
   4. Sea World Park
   5. Boating harbors

  A. Recreational facilities

   1. Shakespearean festival
   2. Starlight opera
   3. Orr's Gallery of Art
   4. Timken Gallery
   5. Reuben H. Fleet Space Theater

  B. Cultural opportunities

II. Conclusion with thesis statement

  A. Summary of main heads: San Diego offers many opportunities for both recreational and cultural experiences.

  B. Statement of thesis: San Diego is an

outstanding place in which to spend the spring vacation.

C. Final appeal: I am a resident of San Diego, I look forward to seeing you there this spring vacation.

Sample Deductive Pattern

General purpose: To convince

Specific purpose: As a result of my speech I want my listeners to agree that San Diego is a good place in which to spend spring vacation.

I. Introduction
   A. Easter vacation is near.
   B. San Diego is close by.
   C. I am a resident of San Diego.

II. Thesis: Because Easter vacation is approaching and because San Diego is so near, today I hope to interest you in spending at least part of your spring vacation in San Diego.

III. Body
   A. Recreational facilities
      1. Golf courses
      2. Beaches
      3. Zoo
      4. Sea World Park
      5. Boating harbors
   B. Cultural opportunities
      1. Shakespearean festival
      2. Starlight opera
      3. Orr's Gallery of Art
      4. Timken Gallery
      5. Reuben H. Fleet Space Theater

IV. Conclusion
   A. Its many recreational and cultural facilities make San Diego unique as a vacation city.
   B. I hope you will spend at least part of your spring vacation in San Diego.

The Semiinductive Pattern

The semiinductive pattern of speech organization can be almost any combination of the strictly inductive and the strictly deductive patterns. The usual procedure, however, is to develop the introduction and the thesis in the deductive pattern. After stating the thesis, the speaker postpones the announcement of the first main head until it has been fully developed with specific supporting details. After developing the first main head, the speaker announces it and proceeds with material to develop the second main head. When it is developed, it is announced, and so on throughout the body of the speech. The conclusion is handled in the deductive pattern. In other words, the introduction, the thesis, and the conclusion are handled deductively and the body inductively. The following sample outline will serve as an illustration:

Sample Semiinductive Pattern

General purpose: To convince

Specific purpose: As a result of my speech I want my listeners to agree that San Diego is a good place in which to spend a spring vacation.

I. Introduction

   A. Easter vacation is near.

   B. San Diego is close by.

   C. I am a resident of San Diego.

II. Thesis: Because Easter vacation is approaching and because San Diego is so near, today I hope to interest you in spending at least part of your spring vacation in San Diego.

III. Body

     1. Golf courses

     2. Beaches

     3. Zoo

     4. Sea World Park

     5. Boating harbors

   A. Recreational facilities

     1. Shakespearean festival

     2. Starlight opera

     3. Orr's Gallery of Art

     4. Timken's Gallery

     5. Reuben H. Fleet Space Theater

   B. Cultural opportunities

IV. Conclusion

   A. Its many recreational and cultural facilities make San Diego unique as a vacation city.

   B. I hope you will spend at least part of your spring vacation in San Diego.

In this section, we have considered two variations of the basic four-part deductive pattern. It should be emphasized that most persons are well advised to master the deductive pattern thoroughly before attempting the variations. The deductive pattern is usually clearer and easier to handle for both speakers and listeners.

Outlining

Outlines, like nuclear energy or automobiles, can be either constructive or destructive depending on how they are used. If the speaker reads from the outline as though it were a manuscript, if the outline becomes a crutch and a substitute for active thought in front of the audience, then it is an obstacle to communication. If used properly, the outline can be a useful tool. It can provide an overview of the speech and a visual check on the arrangement of material. It also serves as a working plan during speech rehearsal. The outline is a map or a plan—a blueprint from which your speech will emerge.

There are many systems for outlining. Each seems to have advantages and disadvantages. Speakers are urged to use the method that best meets their own needs and the needs of the occasion. Most outlines, however, contain (1) a statement of the general purpose, (2) a statement of the specific purpose, (3) an introduction, written in full or outlined, (4) the body, outlined, and (5) a conclusion, written in full or outlined.

Outlining needn't be difficult. The following simple principles are usually helpful.

Use a Consistent System of Notation

The main divisions of the speech can be indicated by Roman numerals: I for the introduction, II for the thesis, III for the body, and IV for the conclusion. The main heads can be indicated by capital letters. The subpoints can be identified by Arabic numerals. Supporting details can be indicated by lower-case letters. Consider the following:

I.

   A.

      1.

         a.
         b.

Use More Than One Subpoint

Never have a single subpoint. The subpoint indicates that you have divided a main point. Division means more than one. If you can identify only one subpoint, you should develop the point as a whole without dividing it.

**Use Headings That Are
Expressed in Parallel Form**

All headings of the same rank should be expressed in similar form. If A is a complete sentence, B should be a complete sentence; if A is a noun, B should be a noun; if 1 is an infinitive phrase, 2 and 3 should be infinitive phrases; and so forth. In the following example C is not parallel with A and B.

A. Poverty in the cities
B. Poverty in the rural areas
C. Viewing poverty in suburbia

Use Headings That Do Not Overlap

In the following example B and D overlap.

A. Reading is informative.
B. Reading is relaxing.
C. Reading is inspirational.
D. Reading reduces tensions.

**Use Subheadings That Stay within
the Limits of the Headings They Support**

Main heads and subheads should fit the scope of the headings they describe. In the following example the third subhead goes beyond the scope of the main head.

A. Advertising provides useful services.
   1. Advertising advises people of new products.
   2. Advertising tells people where they can find products.
   3. Advertising is inexpensive.

Use Headings That Express a Single Point

Main heads and subheads should not be compound. In the following example, the third main head is compound. It expresses more than one thought.

A. Capital punishment does not deter crime.
B. Capital punishment is administered unfairly.
C. Capital punishment is contrary to Judeo-Christian tradition and it often excites criminal elements.

Use Enough Headings to Develop Your Central Idea

Be sure you use enough main heads and subheads to do what your thesis statement says you are going to do.

These few basic principles are helpful for most outlining. Your teacher may wish to provide further refinements to help you overcome specific problems. As a final review, consider the following sample outlines.

Sample Complete Sentence Outline

General purpose: To activate

Specific purpose: As a result of my speech I want my listeners to vote for Nancy Martin for student body president.

I. Introduction: Winston Churchill once said, "Democracy is the worst possible form of government except all others." In a short time each of us will have the chance to make democracy work on this campus. In just five days we will have an opportunity to vote for next year's student body officers. These elections are always important. This year they are particularly important. Our next representatives will have an opportunity to represent us on such important matters as proposed changes in the grading policy and proposed changes in general education requirements. These policies affect every student at this college. To be well represented we need to elect well-qualified people. Today I would like to speak to you about one such person.

II. Thesis: I would like to use the time allotted to me to tell you why I am going to vote for Nancy Martin for student body president.

III. Body

  A. Nancy Martin has an outstanding scholastic record.

    1. Nancy maintained a 4.0 grade average while in high school.

    2. Nancy has maintained a 3.2 average in college while pursuing a difficult English major.

  B. Nancy has participated in a variety of extracurricular activities.

    1. In high school she demonstrated a broad range of interests.

      a. Nancy worked on the school paper during each of her high school years.

      b. As a junior and senior she was a member of the high school marching band.

    2. In college Nancy has continued to pursue a variety of activities.

      a. Nancy was editor of the college paper this semester.

      b. Nancy has been a strong member of the college debate team for the last two years.

  C. Nancy Martin has demonstrated leadership qualities.

1. Nancy served as chairperson of a committee that last year revised the associated student body constitution.
2. Nancy organized last semester's highly successful drive for blood donors on this campus.

IV. Conclusion: Next week as you go to the polls to cast your vote thoughtfully in this important election, I hope you will recall what I have told you about Nancy's scholastic record, her wide participation in extracurricular activities, and her proven leadership ability. Three fine candidates are running for the office of president. I think an objective look at the record will convince you that Nancy is the best qualified. Vote for Nancy Martin.

Sample Combination Complete Sentence and Key Phrase Outline

General purpose: To activate

Specific purpose: As a result of my speech I want my listeners to vote for Nancy Martin for student body president.

I. Introduction: Winston Churchill once said, "Democracy is the worst possible form of government except all others." In a short time each of us will have a chance to make democracy work on this campus. In just five days we will have an opportunity to vote for next year's student body officers. These elections are always important. This year they are particularly important. Our next representatives will have an opportunity to represent us on such important matters as proposed changes in the grading policy and proposed changes in general education requirements. These policies affect every student at this college. To be well represented we need to elect well-qualified people. Today I would like to speak to you about one such person.

II. Thesis: I would like to use the time allotted to me to tell you why I am going to vote for Nancy Martin for student body president.

III. Body

A. Scholastic record
  1. Record in high school
  2. Record in college

B. Extracurricular experience
  1. High school experience
    a. Journalism
    b. Marching band
  2. College experience
    a. Journalism
    b. Debate team

C. Leadership qualities
  1. Chairperson—constitution revision committee
  2. Leader of campus drive for blood donors

IV. Conclusion: Next week as you go to the polls to cast your vote thoughtfully in this important election, I hope you will recall what I have told you about Nancy's scholastic record, her wide participation in extracurricular activities, and her proven leadership ability. Three fine candidates are running for the office of president. I think an objective look at the record will convince you that Nancy is the best qualified. Vote for Nancy Martin.

Sample Key Phrase Outline

General purpose: To activate

Specific purpose: As a result of my speech I want my listeners to vote for Nancy Martin for student body president.

I. Introduction

   A. Elections next week

   B. Importance of elections

      1. Grading policy

      2. General education requirements

II. Thesis: I would like to use the time allotted to me to tell you why I am going to vote for Nancy Martin for student body president.

III. Body

   A. Scholastic record

      1. Record in high school

      2. Record in college

   B. Extracurricular experience

      1. High school experience

         a. Journalism

         b. Marching band

      2. College experience

         a. Journalism

         b. Debate team

   C. Leadership qualities

      1. Chairperson—constitution revision committee

      2. Leader of campus drive for blood donors

IV. Conclusion

   A. Remember the record

      1. Scholastic record

      2. Extracurricular experience

      3. Leadership qualities

   B. Vote for best qualified—Nancy

Key Ideas in Review

□ Organization aids the speaker in preparing and delivering the speech.

□ Organization aids the listener in perceiving the speech.

□ The basic four-part deductive pattern of speech organization consists of an introduction, a thesis statement, a body, and a conclusion.

□ Transitions unify the speech and aid the listener in reviewing what the speaker has considered and anticipating what the speaker is going to consider.

□ The four-part deductive pattern utilizes the principle of the anticipatory set by providing that the listener be frequently informed of what to expect.

□ The four-part deductive pattern accommodates the phenomenon of perception selectivity by providing that material be grouped into small units.

□ Outlines can aid the speaker by demonstrating an overview of the speech, by showing relationships, and by providing a plan for speech rehearsal and delivery.

□ Most speech outlines contain a general purpose statement, a specific purpose statement, an introduction (written in full or outlined), a thesis statement, a body (outlined), and a conclusion (written in full or outlined).

□ Outlining requires a consistent system of notation: parallel formations, avoidance of single subheads, overlapping, compound or insufficient headings, and subheadings that go beyond the limits of the headings they are designed to support.

Suggested Assignments

Integrated Assignments

The assignments in this section are designed to help you further explore and experience the subject matter presented in both Sections A and B. Prepare and present an organized speech, using the four-part deductive pattern of organization with transitions. Develop a written outline to help you plan and rehearse the speech. In addition to organization, try to demonstrate all the elements of good communication your class has considered thus far. Select or adapt your topics from the following suggestions.

Speech Topics

1. In Section A we considered several elements that affect human perception. Select one of those elements and explain it to the class. Illustrate your speech with specific examples and instances.

2. Select a controversial issue of local, national, or international interest. Present at least two perceptions or viewpoints concerning the issue. The purpose of your speech will be to demonstrate how an issue can be perceived in more than one way.

3. Think how your perception of a particular matter has changed over the years. You could consider such subjects as college, marriage, your parents, yourself, or your job. Explain to the class how your perception has changed and what caused it to change. Be specific. Use examples.

4. Interview a number of people about their view of some controversial issue. Report to the class on the different perceptions you encoun-

tered. Perhaps you will be able to correlate the differences with such factors as age, sex, occupation.

5. Try to recall disagreements and misunderstandings you have had with others that occurred because you and they perceived a matter differently. Describe those incidents to the class. Try to explain the factors of perception that were involved.

6. Show an abstract painting, a photograph of a person, a collage of unrelated items, or a proverb or a quotation to a number of persons. Question each person concerning his or her perception of the items shown. Report your findings to the class.

7. For several days keep a diary in which you record misunderstandings and disagreements you observe that are caused by differing perceptions. Report your observations to the class.

8. For several days try to use ownership statements when communicating your perceptions to others. Explain your experience to the class. Was it difficult? How did you feel? What effect did it have on communication? On your thinking?

Auxiliary Assignments

Interpersonal Focus

1. For this exercise the class is divided into pairs. Each pair will select for discussion a controversial issue about which they disagree. One partner presents to the other an idea about the issue. Before the second partner can present a counter idea, he or she must rephrase and explain the first partner's idea. This must be done to the first partner's satisfaction. Once the first partner is satisfied that his or her perception has been understood, the roles are reversed. The exercise should proceed in this way for 30 to 40 minutes. This is a little frustrating at first, but soon you will get the knack of trying to view an issue while standing in someone else's "perceptual shoes."

2. The class is divided into five groups. Each group will be assigned one perceptual factor—that is, the senses, experience, expectancy, selectivity, and language. Each group will be responsible for preparing and presenting a demonstration of its assigned factor.

3. The class is divided into groups of four or five. Each group will prepare and present a short dramatic scene to the class. The scene should involve everyone in the group and contain lots of action. After each scene is presented, class members will write down their perceptions of what happened. Finally, the papers will be read and discussed.

4. The class is divided into four or six groups. Half the groups will prepare and present role-playing scenes illustrating how disputes arise from people perceiving the world differently. The other groups will prepare and present role-playing scenes illustrating the use of ownership statements.

5. The class is divided into groups. Each group selects two or three controversial issues for discussion. As the discussion takes place, each group member will strive to use ownership statements when reporting his or her perceptions.

Person-to-Group Focus

1. Prepare and deliver a short speech on a topic that is appropriate to you and your listeners. Use the four-part deductive pattern of speech organization. Try also to utilize all the factors of good communication your class has considered thus far. Prepare an outline of your speech. After the speech, invite the class to comment on the organization of your speech.

2. Using the four-part deductive pattern of organization, give a speech on organization. Show how one topic could be organized deductively, inductively, and semiinductively.

3. Prepare an outline for at least four different speech topics.

4. Report to the class on a speech or a lecture you have heard outside of class. Comment on its organization.

5. Divide the class into groups. Working together, each group will develop a speech outline. Once the outline is developed, the group will "scramble" the outline and present it to the rest of the class. Class members will try to reconstruct the scrambled outline in proper order.

Suggested Readings

Interpersonal Focus

Sereno, Kenneth K., and Bodaken, Edward. *Trans-Per: Understanding Human Communication.* Boston: Houghton Mifflin, 1975, pp. 21–39. This chapter provides an easy-to-read overview of perception as it applies to communication.

Vernon, Magdalen D. *The Psychology of Perception.* Baltimore: Penguin Books, 1962. A comprehensive review of experimentation in human perception. It is well documented but not difficult to read.

Weintraub, Daniel J., and Walker, Edward T. *Perception.* Belmont, Calif.: Brooks/Cole Publishing Co., 1966. This short, easy-to-read paperback provides a good background for beginning students. The major theories of perception are presented.

Person-to-Group Focus

Bradley, Bert. *Fundamentals of Speech Communication: The Credibility of Ideas.* Dubuque, Iowa: William C. Brown Co., 1974, pp. 82–111. An excellent chapter on structuring the speech. With ample documentation, the author considers the effect of organizational variables on listeners.

Pomeroy, Ralph S. *Speaking from Experience: A Rhetoric for Extemporaneous Speaking.* New York: Harper & Row Publishers, 1977, pp. 130–59. An easy-to-read, up-to-date chapter on organization and outlining. It discusses how pattern-recognition relates to human attention and speech organization.

Note Directory

1. Colin Cherry, *On Human Communication: A Review, A Survey, and A Criticism* (Cambridge: M.I.T. Press, 1957), p. 62.

2. Kenneth G. Johnson, *General Semantics; An Outline Survey* (San Francisco: International Society for General Semantics, 1972), p. 5.

3. Robert Rosenthal, "Self-Fulfilling Prophecy," *Readings in Psychology Today* (Del Mar, Calif.: CRM Books, 1967), pp. 466–71.

4. Magdalen D. Vernon, *The Psychology of Perception* (Baltimore: Penguin Books, 1963), p. 217.

5. G. H. Mowbray, "The Perception of Short Phrases Presented Simultaneously For Visual and Auditory Reception," *Quarterly Journal of Experimental Psychology,* 6 (1954): 86–92.

6. Benjamin Whorf, "Language, Mind, and Reality," *ETC* 9, no. 3 (Spring 1952): 167–88.

7. William V. Haney, *Communication and Organizational Behavior: Text and Cases,* 3d ed. (Homewood, Ill.: Richard D. Irwin, 1973), p. 64.

8. Harold Barrett, *Practical Uses of Speech Communication* (New York: Holt, Rinehart & Winston, 1977), p. 41.

9. George Miller, "Information and Memory," *Contemporary Readings in General Psychology*, ed. Robert Daniel (Boston: Houghton Mifflin, 1959), pp. 106–08.

10. William D. Brooks, *Speech Communication* (Dubuque, Iowa: William C. Brown Co., 1971), pp. 34–35.

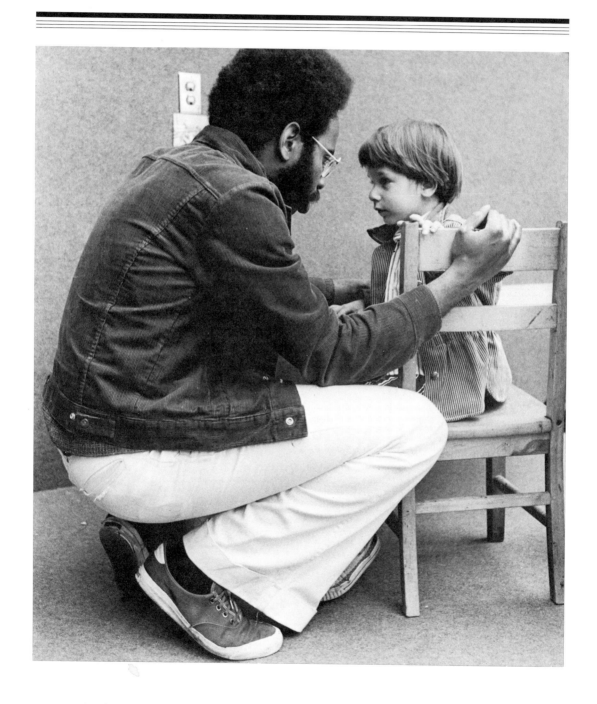

Chapter Six

Listening

Regardless of the setting, listening is an essential element of communication. In Section A of this chapter we will consider ways of improving listening in interpersonal situations, and in Section B we will consider ways of improving listening in person-to-group situations.

Section A: Interpersonal Focus

Listening encourages communication: a discussion of listening and its effects on interpersonal communication.

■ Active listening described ■ the benefits of active listening ■ negative listening games

Section B: Person-to-Group Focus

When we listen, we learn: a discussion of factors that influence how people listen to speeches.

■ The importance of data-listening ■ positive data-listening practices ■ negative data-listening practices

Suggested Assignments

Section A

Interpersonal Focus

A good listener is not only popular everywhere, but after awhile he knows something.

Wilson Mizner

This chapter is not about hearing; it is about listening. Hearing is to listening what seeing is to reading. Hearing and listening are not synonymous. Hearing is merely one step in the process of listening. Listening involves organizing and interpreting what is heard.

Until recently, listening was the most neglected of communication skills. This was unfortunate and in retrospect even illogical. Without listening there is no verbal communication. Conversely, listening improvement is one of the surest steps toward improved communication. Modern research reveals that, without training, most of us are pretty poor listeners. Fortunately, research also demonstrates that listening can be improved just as surely as any other skill.

Because the skill of listening is so important to communication and because listening can be improved, in this chapter we are going to be concerned with some factors in listening improvement. In Section A we will deal with interpersonal listening and in Section B we will talk about data-listening, or listening to speeches. Specifically, in this section we will discuss *active listening,* a method of listening that is particularly use-ful in interpersonal situations. We will talk about what is meant by active listening, when it is appropriate, and what benefits it offers. Finally, we will consider some of the negative listening games that people engage in.

Active Listening

The method of listening often referred to as active listening was first articulated by the noted therapist Carl Rogers. Subsequently, Rogers, Thomas Gordon, and many others demonstrated that active listening needn't be confined to professional therapeutic relationships. It has proven to be immensely valuable in the everyday lives of ordinary people.

Active Listening Described

The active listener behaves nonthreateningly while trying to understand another's message from that person's frame of reference or viewpoint. Additionally, she or he checks on the accuracy of the understanding by offering feedback from time to time. Let us examine the various parts of the process separately.

Indicate Willingness to Listen The first step in active listening is to indicate willingness to listen. This can often be done with a short phrase, such as: "I am interested," "Tell me about it," "What is on your mind?" "Want to talk? Shoot," "I am listening," "I would like to hear about it." Thomas Gordon[1] refers to these short phrases as *door openers*. Speakers some-times need the encouragement these simple phrases provide. Of course, we also indicate our willingness to listen by nonverbal means. Facial expression, gesture, and posture can reveal interest or lack of interest in the other person. One of the best ways to show willingness to listen is to stop talking. When we give in to the temptation to lecture, to analyze, to moralize, or to question, we effectively take the floor from the other person and interfere with his or her attempt to communicate.

Avoid Threat   The active listener must also take care to avoid threat. As we noted in chapter 2, one of the quickest ways to discourage communication is to be threatening. Threat tends to "turn off" the speaker. When one is threatened, one often reacts by counterattacking or withdrawing. Either of these reactions impedes comfortable, honest, self-disclosing communication. In speaker-listener situations the most common source of threat for the speaker comes from the listener's tendency to evaluate or judge. As Rogers puts it, "I would like to propose, as a hypothesis for consideration, that the major barrier to mutual interpersonal communication is our very natural tendency to judge, to evaluate, to approve or disapprove, the statement of the other person or the other group."[2]

This doesn't mean that listeners should never have opinions or form judgments. It does mean that when we are too quick to judge, when we react before we have sensed the matter from the other's viewpoint, when we evaluate while the speaker still feels unsafe and unsure, we are likely to threaten and discourage the speaker.

For times when evaluation is appropriate, keep in mind that, as we observed in the last chapter, evaluative remarks are usually less threatening when they are communicated as ownership statements. You will recall that with ownership statements we acknowledge that our perceptions are simply our perceptions and not extensional facts.

Although evaluation is a common stumbling block, listeners can also threaten speakers by any of the other means discussed in chapter 2. For example, we are often threatening when we attempt to control the conversation, or when we are manipulative, indifferent, superior, or closed-minded. Any of these behaviors can intimidate the speaker and shut down communication.

Sense the Speaker's Point of View   The active listener tries to enter into the speaker's frame of reference in order to get an understanding of the message as it is understood by the speaker. When our sole objective as listeners is to grasp the matter as it is perceived by the speaker, we are less likely to distort the message with our own filters.

This process is difficult, and it requires courage. To view the world as it is viewed by another, we must momentarily set aside our own defenses, prejudices, and feelings. This is risky. We might discover, for example, that our own perceptions should be amended.

When it can be achieved, this process is rewarding for both listener and speaker. It feels good to be in touch with someone else's world in this manner. And, of course, it feels good to sense that someone else is trying to understand our special world.

√ **Offer Feedback** The active listener checks listening accuracy by occasionally reporting to the speaker what has been heard. This reporting is called *reflection* or *feedback*. The listener usually begins these reports with such phrases as: "I want to be sure I have this right," "As I hear it, you are saying that . . . ," or "Let me be sure I am understanding you," "Do I understand you to say . . . ," or "As I get it, you feel that. . . ."

Feedback is necessary because words do not transfer meaning directly. To understand this statement better, pretend that you have a glass of water in your right hand and an empty glass in your left hand. To transfer the water from the glass in your right hand to the glass in your left hand, you simply pour it directly from the full glass into the empty one. This is not the way human communication works. Words do not transfer meaning directly from one mind into another mind. The process of translation is always involved. It works like this: (1) You have some meaning in you that you would like to transfer to another person. (2) You think of some words that might express that meaning. (3) You send your words to the other person. (4) The other person puts his or her meaning on your words. If the other person has the same meaning for your words that you had for them, you have successfully communicated. Often, however, the listener's meanings are different from the speaker's meanings. We will discuss the many reasons for this in chapter 10. For now it is enough to note that misunderstandings frequently occur because speakers and listeners place different meanings on words and events. In

way of example, consider the following dialogue:

Tim: I have a meeting in the morning. Set the alarm early.

Sue: What time?

Tim: Eight o'clock.

Sue: O.K.

Tim is going to miss his meeting. To him the question "What time?" meant at what time is the meeting. To Sue it meant for what time shall I set the alarm. Let's help Tim and Sue by inserting a little feedback.

Tim: I have a meeting in the morning. Set the alarm early.

Sue: What time?

Tim: Eight o'clock.

Sue: You want the alarm set at eight, right?

Tim: No, the meeting is at eight—set the alarm for six-forty-five.

Sue: O.K.

Feedback does more than help participants discover communication breakdowns. It also serves to encourage the speaker by reassuring him or her that the listener is trying to understand.

Before experimenting with feedback, consider the following suggestions:

Avoid excessive feedback. It turns the conversation into a kind of quiz show. Too much feedback can threaten and discourage the speaker.

Use feedback only when it is important to communication. In most routine conversation feedback is unnecessary. Consider the following:

Oscar: Hi, Harold, beautiful morning.

Harold: As I understand it, Oscar, you are saying that this is a beautiful morning.

This, of course, is a ridiculous application of feedback. Reserve feedback for those occasions when it is important to either you or the speaker that the speaker be understood fully and accurately.

Put feedback in your own words. In that way you tell the speaker that you have thought about her or his message.

Report the speaker's feelings as well as ideas. It is important for speakers to know that listeners understand what they are feeling as well as what they are thinking.

Report with ownership statements. There is a big difference between saying, "This is what I heard" and "This is what you said." Don't put words in the speaker's mouth. Phrase feedback in a way that says, "Here is what I think you said. Am I right?"

If the speaker corrects your feedback, *accept the speaker's version of the message.* The speaker is the authority on what he or she meant to say.

By observing these suggestions and practicing a little, you will soon become adept in the use of feedback. Feedback is a valuable listening tool.

Thus far, we have noted that active listening consists of communicating willingness to listen, avoiding threat, attempting to understand the message from the speaker's viewpoint, and utilizing feedback. Unfortunately, these components by themselves are not enough. To be effective they must be motivated by genuine desire to understand the other person and by be-

lief that others are worthwhile and worth listening to. Otherwise, active listening becomes mechanical and manipulative. However, when properly motivated, active listening produces many benefits.

The Benefits of Active Listening

Active listening affects the speaker, the listener, and the relationship they share.

Reducing Communication Breakdowns   As we noted earlier, communication failures sometimes occur because the speaker and the listener interpret the same words differently. Active listening reduces this kind of breakdown. When the listener's sole objective is to understand the speaker's viewpoint and when the listener utilizes feedback, differences in interpretation are usually clarified before damage is done.

Stimulating Communication   If there is a magic formula for promoting communication, it is active listening. Because active listening is nonthreatening, it makes us feel that communication is safe. It implies acceptance. The feeling that someone is listening and trying to understand encourages communication. Active listening is a turn-on. Conversely, experience has shown that people stop talking to one another as the quality of listening declines.

Promoting Positive Feelings of Self-Worth   Because active listening implies acceptance, it helps people feel better about themselves. When we listen to someone without judging, when we try to understand the world as it is viewed by another, we imply to that person that he or she is important and worthwhile. On the other hand, when we sense that no one is listening to us, we feel isolated, cut off, and unimportant. According to Rollo May[3] these feelings of alienation may be the most serious psychological problem of the twentieth century.

Reducing Hostility When we are upset, when we are angry or have complaints, it often reassures us to know that our feelings are being respected and that our views are being heard. When someone not only responds to our hostility nonthreateningly but also listens to understand our concerns, we usually feel better. Conversely, when hostility is met with hostility, it usually escalates. Persons experienced in handling complaints report that people are often satisfied merely to have their views heard and understood.

Helping People to Understand One Another Better Active listening enriches our lives by bringing us into closer touch with those around us. Listening is the chief means we have for knowing other people. Active listening encourages others to talk with us, and it helps us to know their worlds. It is surprising how close we can become and how much we can learn about others simply by listening.

Occasions for Active Listening

In spite of its many rewards, however, active listening is not always appropriate. Obviously active listening takes time, energy, and commitment. It cannot, there-

fore, be practiced on every occasion. When active listening is used for trivial, routine, unimportant situations, communication becomes awkward and stilted. Active listening is most appropriate on occasions when you and another person want to communicate fully and accurately. It works best when people are committed. Following are some occasions for which active listening is typically appropriate:

1. When information or directions important to one or both persons are being communicated.
2. When complaints are being communicated.
3. When intimate perceptions important to one or both persons are being communicated.
4. When interpersonal partners are discussing significant aspects of their relationship.
5. When persons are setting procedures and making plans for doing something together.
6. When persons are entering into agreements.
7. When one person has a problem he or she is trying to clarify.
8. When a person has need for emotional support.

This list is merely suggestive. You can probably think of many other occasions appropriate for active listening.

To review, we have discussed the characteristics of, the benefits derived from, and occasions appropriate for active listening. Next let's turn our attention to some activities that are destructive to active listening.

Negative Listening Games

Listening would improve if people would simply stop doing some of the things they do when they are supposed to be listening. In this section we will sample activities that tend to interfere with listening.

Rehearsal

Sometimes we are so anxious to say the right thing that we silently rehearse our messages while pretending to listen to the other person. To the extent that we are concentrating on our own rehearsal, we are not listening to the speaker. Much of what passes for conversation is flawed by rehearsal. Ralph Webb refers to discussions of this kind as *duologues*. In his book[4] duologues are compared to two television sets tuned to different channels and facing each other.

Rehearsal can occur in a variety of situations. Students sometimes miss important points in the lecture or discussion because they are mentally preparing a question or comment. Teachers often fail to hear their students for the same reason. In social situations, we are often so anxious to make a favorable impression that we fervently rehearse while others deliver what they have fervently rehearsed. Arguments are frequently unnecessarily prolonged because the persons involved don't hear one another. While we are arguing, most of us usually spend far more time rehearsing than we spend listening.

Earlier we noted that listening requires courage. It also requires self-confidence. In order to listen we must have confidence in our ability to make appropriate responses without an inordinate amount of rehearsal. We must be willing to hear the other person out before preparing our reply. To review what we have said about rehearsal, stop reading for a moment and think about the last time you missed something someone said because you were mentally preparing your own remarks.

Hidden Agendas

An agenda is the official list of items to be discussed at a meeting or convention. For most formal public meetings, the agenda is printed and distributed in advance. For informal meetings, the agenda is usually not printed although it is ordinarily understood. Frequently it is announced by the chairperson or the secretary of the group. When people get together for other reasons, they often have implied or understood agendas. You agree with a friend to have coffee and go over possible test questions before class tomorrow. The implied agenda is to prepare for the test. You meet with some friends on Saturday morning to shoot some baskets. The agenda, which is generally understood, is to relax by playing a little basketball.

Sometimes, in addition to the public or understood agenda, people have hidden agendas. The term *hidden agenda* refers to the personal, private motivation that sometimes governs our behavior. In other words, hidden agendas are the personal, undisclosed reasons we have for doing things.

In way of example, consider this hypothetical illustration. The city council is meeting to decide on next year's city budget. Their official task or agenda is to develop and adopt a budget that will best serve the needs of the community. But each council person also has a hidden agenda. Lucille Brown, the chairperson of the council, is planning to run for the state legislature next year. She wants to run on a program of tax reform. Her hidden agenda is to keep expenditures down regardless of the items involved. George Halfacre is still angry because a motion he presented at the last meeting was defeated. His hidden agenda is to make those who voted against him look foolish. Fred Herrara has had a

rough day at work. He is exhausted and his ulcer is bothering him. His hidden agenda is to get the meeting over as soon as possible. Harry Davis has been divorced for three years. He is strongly attracted to Lucille Brown. His hidden agenda is to impress Chairperson Brown. Dorothy Hill, the fifth member of the council, is absent from the meeting. Reportedly, she is ill. Her real motivation for being absent is to avoid taking a stand on certain budget items.

If this illustration is slightly exaggerated, it doesn't miss the mark by much. People do the things they do in response to personally felt needs. These needs sometimes emerge as hidden agendas, which often interfere with objective listening. For example, it is unlikely that the council members in our illustration will be receptive to messages that conflict with their hidden agendas.

Consider a different example. Ray is meeting with his boss to discuss several plans for reorganizing the office. He feels that it would look good on his record if his plans for reorganization were implemented. Although ostensibly he is helping to decide what would be best for the office, his real or hidden agenda is to promote himself by getting his own plan adopted. Consequently, it will be difficult for Ray to listen objectively to arguments in favor of other plans.

Win-Lose Listening

Win-lose listening involves a specific hidden agenda. It is so frequently encountered and so damaging to communication that we are going to discuss it separately. When we

Section A: Interpersonal Focus 135

are engaged in win-lose listening, the hidden agenda is to win, to dominate, to come out on top. John Stewart and Gary D'Angelo describe this kind of listening as follows:

> Usually, a severe win/lose confrontation is characterized by self-serving listening, i.e. listening that prepares you to tear down your opponent's argument, listening that avoids sharing information, and listening that helps you make the other person's ideas seem inferior to yours. In other words, the primary objective is to win while the other loses—to communicate that "I am right and you are wrong"; "I am strong and you are weak"; "I am smart and you are dumb"; "I am likeable and you aren't."[5]

But how can one win a conversation? Interpersonal encounters are not like games in which there must be a winner and a loser. Of course they are not, but we often act as if they were. The need to win, to control, to dominate is so great in some people that they turn every interpersonal transaction into a contest. I once attended a meeting between a department chairperson and

At times, everyone is talking and no one is listening.

a college dean. The purpose of the meeting was to review the chairperson's proposed departmental budget. I was amazed to find that the only item of controversy was a small $75 expenditure. As the discussion progressed, it became apparent that the money was not the issue. The issue was who would dominate. The welfare of the students and the college were forgotten. The only issue was who would be the winner.

Win-lose attitudes are terribly destructive to communication. It is impossible to see things from the other person's point of view when your primary objective is to "put down" the other person. Indeed, persons with strong win-lose attitudes often find it threatening to listen empathetically. This is especially true if the "other" is occupying a subordinate role. Some executives feel diminished by listening to employees, some teachers find it difficult to listen to students, and some parents find it difficult to listen to children. This is unfortunate because parents can learn from children, teachers can learn from students, and executives can learn from employees. After 30 years of work in the field of human communication, I have concluded that the need to win, to dominate, to control is one of the chief obstacles to empathetic listening.

What is the answer to this problem? The answer is to realize that not all human transactions need be contests. In many situations we must have winners and losers, but in many interpersonal situations it is possible for everyone to be a winner. A *win-win* attitude promotes good listening because the objective is to serve everyone's best interest. Consider a typical interpersonal situation: Bernice and Harry are making plans for this summer's vacation. Bernice would like to go to a metropolitan area to see some theater and do some shopping. Harry wants to go to the mountains so that he can fish. If they approach this problem with a win-win attitude, they will do their best to understand one another so they can develop vacation plans satisfying for both of them. Such an objective is entirely possible. Unfortunately this solution won't occur to them if they approach the matter with a win-lose attitude. With win-lose attitudes, the motive is to produce winners and losers.

Stereotyping

Walter Lippmann once described stereotypes as little boxes we carry around in our heads. Each little box is equipped with ready-made characteristics. When we meet someone, we plug them into a box and automatically apply the ready-made characteristics. We do all of this without bothering really to know the person we are stereotyping. Stereotyping affects listening because sometimes, instead of hearing what people say, we hear what our stereotype of them tells us they are saying. Stereotypes program us to expect certain things from certain people. Unfortunately, when we "know" what people are going to say, we stop listening. As Webb puts it, "If the speaker is a union member, the head of a large corporation, a college professor, an interior decorator, a Democrat, a German, a Jew, a newspaper reporter, over 30, under 30, male, or female, we make some assumptions about him or her, about the message he or she will present, and about attitudes and opinions just because of his or her group identification."[6]

In way of illustration, a friend of mine appointed to an advisory committee by the Secretary of Health, Education, and Welfare was the first woman to serve on that committee. She was eminently qualified and had lots of good ideas. Unfortunately, for some time her ideas were greeted with polite smiles and a quick dismissal. By trial and error she learned that her ideas were more acceptable when they were presented by one of the men present. All that has changed now, but for at least a year the stereotype those men had of her interfered with their ability to listen to her.

We have talked about some common obstacles to improved listening. We mentioned rehearsal, the hidden agenda, win-lose listening, and stereotyping. This list could be much longer. It was presented merely to suggest the kinds of things we do that interfere with listening.

In Section A of this chapter we discussed the characteristics of active listening, the advantages of active listening, and occasions that are appropriate for active listening. We also considered some activities that commonly interfere with listening.

Key Ideas in Review

☐ Hearing and listening are not synonymous.

☐ Listening involves organizing and interpreting what has been heard.

☐ Listening can be improved.

☐ Active listening involves communicating willingness to listen, being nonthreatening, entering into the other's frame of reference, and offering feedback.

☐ Active listening must be rooted in genuine respect for the opinions of others.

☐ Active listening reduces certain kinds of communication breakdowns, stimulates communication, promotes positive feelings of self-worth, reduces hostility, and helps people better understand one another.

☐ Active listening is sometimes inappropriate.

☐ Practices that interfere with listening are rehearsal, pursuing hidden agendas, win-lose listening, and stereotyping.

Section B

**Person-to-Group
Focus**

*We have two ears and only one tongue
in order that we may hear more and
speak less.*

Diogenes

In Section A our focus was on listening in interpersonal settings. In this section we will consider data-listening—listening to speeches and lectures. Obviously, these two areas are not mutually exclusive. Much of what we said about listening in interpersonal situations can be applied to listening to speeches and much of what we will say about listening to speeches can be applied to interpersonal settings. Nevertheless, each of these basic listening situations presents the listener with its own unique set of problems. For example, when listening to speeches, listeners usually don't have the opportunity to interrupt and ask for clarification. Also, person-to-group situations usually require that listening be sustained for relatively long periods of time. There are, of course, many other differences.

An early study by Paul Rankin[7] concluded that adults spend 70 percent of their waking hours engaged in some kind of communication activity. The study further concluded that 45 percent of that time is spent in listening. A more recent study by Verderber and Elder involving college students reported that students spend 50 percent of their time listening.[8] Much of this is data-listening.

Unfortunately, practice alone doesn't seem to make perfect in this area. Extensive studies at the University of Minnesota demonstrate that, immediately after hearing a short talk, the average person can recall only about 50 percent of the important points in the message.[9] Similar studies at some other colleges and universities confirm that, without training in listening, the average person functions at an efficiency level of 50 percent or less in data-listening situations.[10]

Fortunately, in the last two decades the question of how to improve listening has received considerable attention. That data-listening is subject to deliberate improvement is now widely accepted. For example, Ralph Nichols reports from the University of Minnesota an average improvement of 25 percent in listening classes there. The educational division of the Xerox corporation developed a short, programmed listening course, which they offered for sale to private industry, governmental agencies, and educational institutions. Some of the groups they have studied reported gains as high as 50 percent after a short training period.[11]

My own experience with listening instruction convinces me that practically anyone who is willing to try can, with the right program, effect significant data-listening improvement. Furthermore, improvement is sustained as long as the subject continues to apply improved listening techniques.

In the remainder of this chapter we will discuss certain of those techniques. Specifically, we will consider some positive listening practices and note some negative practices.

Positive Listening Practices

Your speech class provides an ideal environment in which to practice the skills that follow. Every classroom speech offers an opportunity for listening improvement. Additionally, as you strive to overcome listening problems, you will become more aware of what you can do to help audiences listen when it is your turn to speak.

Be Prepared

Listening, like most everything else, is easier when we are ready for it.

Physical Readiness   One aspect of listening preparedness is physical conditioning. The statement "I was just too tired to listen" is often a legitimate complaint. Listening is not passive; it requires energy. Concentrated listening is characterized by a slight rise in body temperature and a general increase in metabolism. That students do better in school when they are rested has been demonstrated time and time again. One way to prepare for listening, then, is to get some rest. Just as you would hope to be well rested before beginning a strenuous hike, you should be well rested before beginning a difficult listening assignment.

Mental Readiness   We should also be prepared mentally for listening. One step in such preparation is to discover a reason for listening. In the last chapter while considering perception, we noted that people select and attend to stimuli that coincide with their personal needs and interests. If before

Listening requires energy.

the listening experience you can discover a personal reason for listening, you will be better prepared to listen. Experience has shown that even a small reason is better than none. In short, one step toward mental preparation is to ask, "What can I get for myself from this speech?"

Another step in mental preparedness is to realize that you are responsible for your own listening. Remarks such as, "She must not be very good, I can't remember a thing she said," or "He didn't hold my attention," indicate that some people hold the speaker totally responsible for the listener's listening. This idea is fallacious. When the speaker is flawed, good listeners merely work harder at their end of the line. Your listening takes place within you; it is your responsibility. Acceptance of that responsibility is part of being prepared to listen.

Listen from the Start

Another positive listening practice is to "get to work on time." Postponing listening until the speaker is well into the message may be unfortunate for the listener. Often points in the speech are meaningless unless their antecedents have been understood. Nichols and Lewis report on studies which conclude that "Students begin their listening too late, thus missing much that would aid in comprehension of the entire lecture."[12]

Stay with the Speech

One of the main reasons for poor listening is that listeners can think much faster than speakers can speak. In this country people speak at around 120–140 words per minute. We know from using electronic speech compressors that people are capable of listening to speech at a much faster rate. Therefore, in most listening situations we have some spare thinking time. When we spend this spare time in daydreaming, we often miss portions of the speaker's message.

Superior listeners use any of several techniques to use the extra time construc-

tively. We are going to consider three such techniques. These help to occupy the mind in such a way that the listener stays with the speech and away from daydreams. Of course, to be overly concerned with these activities is as harmful as daydreaming. Think of them as short exercises that from time to time will direct your attention to the speaker's message.

Look for Main Points, Subpoints, and Supporting Details   If you will work at picking out the speaker's main points, supporting points, and supporting details, you will stay in tune with the speech. The ability to detect central ideas, subpoints, and supporting materials is enhanced by knowledge of traditional organizational patterns. We discussed these patterns in the last chapter. To review: with deductive development, the speaker states a general point and then supports it with specific details. With the inductive method, the speaker begins with supporting details and works up to the statement of the point. The semiinductive method is a combination of these two. When using the semiinductive method the speaker sometimes states a point before developing it and at other times develops the point before stating it. Most speeches fall more or less into one of these patterns.

We are well advised to remember, however, that speakers often leave huge gaps in these traditional patterns. Sometimes speakers forget to state the point they are going to develop or have developed, sometimes they state points without supplying any supportive materials, and on other occasions they present irrelevant supporting details. Armed with a knowledge of traditional compositional patterns, good listeners are able to fill in the gaps and organize the speaker's remarks while the speaker is speaking. Listening in this fashion helps the listener maintain contact with the speech and become aware of the speaker's central idea and main points.

Evaluate Evidence Another activity that promotes continuing attention to the speech is the evaluation of evidence. Ask such questions as, "Is the speaker using enough evidence?" "Is the evidence relevant?" "Is it timely?" and "Is the source of the evidence appropriate?"

To look for evidence that would tend to disprove your own views is extremely helpful. This is called *looking for negative evidence*. Most of us tend to shut out arguments and evidence that are threatening to our own ideas. By actually searching for such evidence, we help to keep our minds open. Most college debaters are trained in this activity. As they listen to their opponents, they search for every possible valid argument against their own position. Only by doing this can they defend themselves when their time to speak arrives. All listeners can profit from this habit of listening first and arguing second.

Recapitulate By frequently reviewing the speaker's main points, you tend to fix them in your mind and at the same time remain engaged with the speech. Dwelling on minor points would interfere with listening. Simply go over major points quickly. It helps you stay on track. To learn this technique, begin by reviewing short, uncomplicated material and gradually work toward more difficult material. By using

this training method, many students have learned to summarize hour lectures with little difficulty.

Suspend Judgment

Another useful practice to develop is hearing the speaker through. When we make premature judgments, we stop listening. If we judge the speech to be unimportant, we stop listening and start doing something more interesting, such as daydreaming. If we judge the speaker to be wrong, we are apt to start arguing mentally. We rehearse rebuttals and questions. If we judge that we already know what the speaker is going to say, we are likely to hear our stereotype of the message instead of the message itself. Listening improves as we develop the abil-

"What I do is believe ¹/₅ of what the convicted perjurers say, ²/₅ of what the suspected perjurers say, and ³/₅ of what anyone else says."

ity to withhold judgment and to hear the speaker out.

In review, four positive listening practices are: be prepared, listen from the beginning, stay actively engaged with the speaker, and suspend judgment.

Negative Listening Practices

Now that we have considered some positive listening practices, let's look at some practices that should be avoided.

Preoccupation with the Speaker

Sometimes we become distracted by the speaker's appearance, voice, accent, dress, or mannerisms. When we become preoccupied with the speaker, we often miss portions of the speaker's message. Using the speaker's peculiarities or inadequacies as an excuse for not listening is one of the most common negative listening habits. Consider the nature of listening. Your listening takes place within you. You are responsible for your own listening. Acceptance of this fact is helpful in overcoming distractions provided by the speaker.

Preoccupation with Personal Problems

Our pressing personal problems often successfully compete with the speaker for our attention. To overcome this obstacle, we must learn to deal with our problems one at a time. For example, before going into class,

say to yourself in effect, "I have problems A and B, and I also have the problem of listening to my instructor for the next hour. I am going to leave A and B out here and for the next hour concentrate on the lecture. When I come out, A and B will be waiting for me and I will contend with them at that time." With a little effort, this habit can be cultivated. It usually results in improved listening.

Preoccupation with Impediments in the Environment

Yielding easily to distractions provided by the listening environment is yet another negative listening practice. Poor listeners often simply give up too soon. Noise from the streets outside, an inadequate public address system, a draft from the air conditioner—all become excuses for not listening. Several investigators report that good listeners characteristically take action to overcome difficulties of this kind. If they can't hear the speaker, they move closer; if noise is coming in through the window, they close the window, and so forth. Once again, listening belongs to the listener. Your listening is your responsibility. When you accept this responsibility, you are more likely to overcome difficulties in the listening environment.

Overstimulation

General semanticists make a distinction between symbol responses and signal responses. *Symbol responses* are the more delayed, thoughtful responses. They require some thinking. *Signal responses,* on the other hand, are immediate, uncritical, "knee jerk" responses. Someone pricks you with a pin and you yell. You don't stop to think about it. This is a signal response. Unfortunately, we sometimes experience signal responses while listening. Most of us have at least some psychological sore spots. When with a word or an argument a speaker violates one of these, our reaction is often immediate and highly emotional. Mentally, we may argue with the speaker, formulate replies, belittle the speaker, or reinforce our own position. While engaged in activities of this kind, we are not listening.

S. I. Hayakawa states, "It happens, however, that as the result of miseducation, bad training, frightening experiences in childhood, traditional beliefs, propaganda, and other influences in our lives, all of us have what might be termed 'areas of insanity' or, perhaps better, 'areas of infantilism' in which we are at the mercy of ingrained inappropriate semantic reactions."[13] The tendency to become overstimulated is a common listening problem. To overcome it we must develop the habit of delaying responses until the speaker is finished. This is easier said than done, but it can be accomplished. Much overstimulation in listening is simply self-indulgence. As Wayne Dyer emphasizes in his popular book *Your Erroneous Zones,* "Feelings are not just emotions that happen to you. Feelings are reactions you choose to have."[14]

In review, overstimulation, preoccupation with impediments in the listening environment, preoccupation with personal problems, and preoccupation with the speaker are often factors in poor listening.

In Section B of this chapter, we discussed four positive listening practices and four negative listening practices.

Key Ideas in Review

☐ Studies suggest that, without training, the average person will listen to a ten-minute speech at an efficiency level of 50 percent or less.

☐ The ability to listen to speeches is subject to deliberate improvement.

☐ Listeners should prepare for listening by becoming rested, by accepting responsibility for listening, and by finding a personal motive for listening.

☐ Listeners should listen from the beginning of the speech.

☐ Because listeners can think faster than speakers can speak, listeners have extra listening time and consequently tend to daydream.

☐ Techniques for staying actively engaged with the speech are to look for central ideas and supporting points, to evaluate evidence, and to review frequently.

☐ Listening improves as we develop the habit of suspending judgment until the speaker has finished.

☐ When we become preoccupied with characteristics of the speaker, with our personal problems, or with distractions in the listening environment, we often miss the message.

☐ When we become overstimulated emotionally, we often stop listening.

Suggested Assignments

Integrated Assignments

The assignments in this section are designed to help you further explore and experience the ideas presented in Section A, while utilizing and practicing the person-to-group skills your class has thus far considered. Prepare and deliver a speech. Try to incorporate all the skills you have learned thus far. Select or adapt your speech topic from one of the following.

Speech Topics

1. We noted that listeners often discourage communication by threatening speakers. Explain how listeners are sometimes threatening. With specific examples illustrate how listeners can be evaluative, controlling, indifferent, manipulative, superior, or closed-minded. Be sure to use specific real examples.

2. Communication often breaks down because people have different meanings for the same words. Why do people interpret the same words differently? Think about the matter. Illustrate some of the factors that cause people to interpret words differently.

3. Think about some of the misunderstandings you have experienced or observed that occurred because people interpreted words differently. Describe those experiences.

4. Describe some instances in your life when someone has helped you by really listening. How did it feel and what were the results?

5. Describe some occasion in your life when you wanted to be listened to but were not. How did it feel? What were the results?

6. At appropriate times, try the skills of active listening. Explain these experiences to the class.

7. In Section A we discussed six suggestions for offering feedback. Explain and illustrate these suggestions. Please use specific examples.

8. In Section A we noted five benefits that are associated with active listening. With specific examples, illustrate these benefits.

9. With specific examples, illustrate occasions appropriate for active listening.

10. We discussed four negative listening games. Describe your own experience with these games. Illustrate your speech with specific instances.

11. Analyze your own patterns of interpersonal listening. Report to the class on your strengths and weaknesses. Illustrate your speech with specific examples.

Auxiliary Assignments

Interpersonal Focus

1. This is similar to an exercise we considered in a previous chapter. It is designed to provide the experience of understanding another from that person's viewpoint. The class is divided into groups of four. To begin the exercise two persons in each group serve as observers. The other two serve as participants. The participants select for discussion a controversial issue about which they disagree. As they discuss the issue, each partner can speak only after he or she has first restated the ideas and feelings of the other to that partner's satisfaction. After 20 minutes observers report and change roles with the participants. The process is repeated.

2. In a class discussion, each member of the class reports on the most effective listener and

the most ineffective listener he or she has encountered.

3. The class is divided into small groups. Each group selects two or three matters of current interest for discussion. During the discussion each member tries to utilize the skills of active listening. After 30 minutes discussion stops and members talk about how well the skills of active listening were implemented within the group.

4. The class is divided into five groups. Each group devises and presents a role-playing scene. One group will demonstrate the appropriate use of active listening, another will demonstrate win-lose listening, and still another will demonstrate the hidden agenda. Each of the other two groups will demonstrate either rehearsal or stereotyping.

Person-to-Group Focus

1. As you listen to each classroom speech, try to utilize the skills of data-listening we discussed in this chapter. At the conclusion of each speech be prepared to answer the following questions:

   a. What techniques did the speaker use in the introduction?
   b. What was the speaker's thesis?
   c. What were the main heads and the subheads?
   d. How adequate were the transitions?
   e. How adequate was the supporting evidence?
   f. What techniques did the speaker use in the conclusion?

2. Analyze your own adequacy in connection with data-listening. Give a speech to the class in which you explain your strengths and weaknesses and your plans for improvement. Be specific, use examples. Try to use all the skills of person-to-group speech you have learned thus far.

3. Think about speakers you have heard that were easy to listen to and speakers that were difficult to listen to. In a speech to the class, explain what some speakers did to make listening easy for you and what some did to make listening difficult. Try to use all the skills of effective speech you have learned thus far.

4. For a few days keep a record of all the time you spend engaged in data-listening. In a class discussion report your findings to the class.

Suggested Readings

Interpersonal Focus

Barker, Larry L. *Listening Behavior.* Englewood Cliffs, N.J.: Prentice-Hall, 1971. A helpful book that includes a set of suggestions for improving listening skills. Listening problems, feedback, and listening to biased communications are also discussed. Good for the beginning student.

Rogers, Carl R. *Client Centered Therapy: Its Current Practice, Implications and Theory.* Boston: Houghton Mifflin, 1951. Rogers is a pioneer in the area of therapeutic listening. Throughout the book, elements of active listening are illustrated. A very helpful and readable book.

Weaver, Carl H. *Human Listening: Processes and Behavior.* Indianapolis: Bobbs-Merrill, 1972. A challenging but rewarding book. It is divided into three areas: (1) listening behavior in the communication process, (2) process involved in selecting and understanding aural stimuli, (3) suggestions for improvement.

Person-to-Group Focus

Capps, Randall, and O'Connor, Regis. *Fundamentals of Effective Speech Communication.* Cambridge, Mass.: Winthrop Publishing Co., 1978, pp. 136–46. A short, easy-to-read chapter about listening to speeches. It contains exercises.

Holtzman, Paul D. *The Psychology of Speakers' Audiences.* Glenview, Ill.: Scott, Foresman, 1970. A fine book for students who are interested in listening as it is related to person-to-group communication. The author reports on factors in audience listening. Concise and readable.

Nichols, Ralph G., and Stevens, Leonard A. *Are You Listening?* New York: McGraw-Hill Book Co., 1957. A popular, early book on listening. Its primary focus is on listening accurately for information.

tion (Dubuque, Iowa: William C. Brown Co., 1954), pp. 3–4.

11. Xerox Learning Systems, *Effective Listening-Validation Report* (New York: Xerox Corp., 1963), pp. 1–3.

12. Nichols and Lewis, *Listening and Speaking,* p. 17.

13. Samuel I. Hayakawa, *Language in Thought and Action,* 2d ed. (New York: Harcourt Brace Jovanovich, 1964), p. 207.

14. Wayne W. Dyer, *Your Erroneous Zones* (New York: Funk & Wagnalls Publishing Co., 1976), p. 10.

Note Directory

1. Thomas Gordon, *Parent Effectiveness Training: The No-Lose Program for Raising Responsible Children* (New York: Peter H. Wyden, 1970), pp. 47–49.

2. Carl R. Rogers, *On Becoming a Person: A Therapist's View of Psychotherapy* (Boston: Houghton Mifflin, 1961), pp. 130–31.

3. Rollo May, *Man's Search for Himself* (New York: W. W. Norton & Co., 1953), pp. 13–40.

4. Ralph L. Webb, *Interpersonal Speech Communication: Principles and Practices* (Englewood Cliffs, N.J.: Prentice-Hall, 1975), p. 127.

5. John R. Stewart and Gary D'Angelo, *Together: Communicating Interpersonally* (Reading, Mass.: Addison-Wesley Publishing Co., 1975), p. 183.

6. Webb, *Interpersonal Speech Communication,* pp. 142–43.

7. Paul T. Rankin, "Listening Ability," *Chicago Schools Journal* 12 (June 1930): 417–20.

8. Kathleen S. Verderber and Rudolph F. Verderber, *Inter-Act: Using Interpersonal Communication Skills* (Belmont, Calif.: Wadsworth Publishing Co., 1977), p. 61.

9. Ralph G. Nichols and Leonard A. Stevens, *Are You Listening?* (New York: McGraw-Hill Book Co., 1957), p. 61.

10. Ralph G. Nichols and Thomas R. Lewis, *Listening and Speaking: A Guide to Effective Oral Communica-*

Chapter Seven

**Abstraction
and
Support**

We can frequently use knowledge of the abstraction process to improve communication. In Section A of this chapter we will note how we can utilize knowledge of abstraction in interpersonal situations. In Section B we will discuss how speakers in person-to-group situations can apply the abstraction concept by utilizing specific supporting materials.

Section A: Interpersonal Focus

Awareness of abstraction affects interpersonal communication: a discussion of the abstraction concept and its implications for interpersonal communication.

■ The abstraction process ■ the abstraction ladder ■ interpersonal uses for the concept

Section B: Person-to-Group Focus

The speechmaker utilizes the abstraction ladder: a discussion of how the speaker uses the abstraction concept by employing supporting materials.

■ Moving up and down the ladder
■ types of supporting materials ■ sources of supporting materials

Suggested Assignments

Section A

Interpersonal Focus

The more territory a map covers, the less it can say about that territory.

Kenneth Johnson

Abstraction has been defined as "the process of leaving out details."[1] For example, all maps are abstractions because all maps leave something out. Maps are representations of territories and not the territories they represent. Consequently, some aspect of the territory is always missing from the map. A map of your campus, for example, might include all the buildings but leave out all the fire hydrants. Consequently, it is an abstraction.

Furthermore, some maps are more abstract than others. A map of your city might designate your campus with a dot or an X. The city map shows the location of your campus but leaves out its details. A map of the state might show your city but leave out the campus entirely. Some maps leave out more details than do others.

The printed topographic or road maps that help us navigate our country's streets and highways are not the only maps in common use. We create verbal maps whenever we talk, whenever we describe our perceptions, our experiences, our thoughts, and our feelings. These maps are also abstractions because they always leave something out. We can't say everything about anything. As Irving Lee states, "We must conclude that just as no map can have

in it 'all' the features of the territory it represents, so, too, no verbal utterance can give 'all' the characteristics or details of whatever it is used to represent."[2]

For example, if you were to attempt a complete description of such a simple thing as a wildflower, you would need to describe every "microportion" of the flower both inside and out. You would need to describe its molecular and chemical structures, as well as its outward beauty and scent; its invisible submicroscopic aspects, as well as the aspects available to human observation. You would have to describe the flower's relationship with every other object in the universe. And finally, you would need to report on how the flower exists in the perception of all other perceiving creatures. Were you by some miracle to finish all this, the flower would have changed while you were observing and describing it and you would need to start all over. To repeat, we can't say everything about anything.

In short, our maps, whether they be printed or oral, are abstractions because they inevitably leave out some details. Furthermore, some maps leave out more details than do others. Because knowledge of abstraction is important to improved communication, in Section A of this chapter we will discuss the process of abstraction, the abstraction ladder, and some of the benefits of abstraction awareness.

The Abstraction Process

Inherent in the process of abstraction are the twin ideas that something is taken away and at the same time something is left behind. When you abstract gold from the river bottom, you take away the gold and leave the baser materials. When you abstract a magazine article, you write down (take away) the main points and leave behind some details.

Perception as Abstraction

As we suggested in chapter 5, human perceptions are abstractions. We simply cannot attend to all the stimuli that bombard us at any one time. We must select a narrow aspect of any event on which to focus our attention. This attention is further limited by such factors as the quality of our sensory receptors, past experience, expectations, and language. (For a review of the factors that limit perception, see chapter 5). We abstract when we perceive, then, because we take something in while we are leaving something out.

Place yourself in this example. In a busy used-car lot, there is much upon which you can focus your attention. There is a warm sun overhead, noise from the nearby freeway, music from the public address system, and the sounds of engines running and men working in the maintenance section. There is the odor of gasoline and of exhaust fumes. There are also people nearby and, of course, a large number of cars. You decide to look at the maroon 1977 Triumph sports car in the fourth row. You have abstracted from all the competing stimuli and focused your attention on that car. Since you can't perceive the entire car at once, you must abstract some more. The left rear tire captures your attention because it appears to be badly worn. As you examine the tire, you abstract even further; your impressions filter through your sensory receptors, your past experience, your expectations, your needs, and other such factors. Others examining the same tire will abstract somewhat differently, because each of us possesses unique perceptual filters.

Communication as Abstraction

We also abstract when we communicate. Furthermore, we can communicate about anything on several different levels of abstraction. Let's illustrate by assuming you are going to talk to someone about that left rear tire on the Triumph sports car. Before you begin, however, let's note some things about the tire. It exists on several levels below the level of your talking about it to someone else.

Human perceptions are abstractions.

The Submicroscopic Level   The basic level is submicroscopic. We cannot experience it with the senses or even with mechanical extensions of the senses. This basic level is called the *event level* or *process level*. It exists only as an event or process. Modern science tells us that at its core all matter is a swirling, ever-moving "mad dance" of atoms, electrons, and other submicroscopic elements. We can't sense this level; we can only infer it.

The Microscopic Level The next level is microscopic. At this level you can perceive with X rays, microscopes, and other extensions of the senses characteristics of the tire you couldn't perceive with the senses alone. You can, for example, observe the tiniest fibers in the tire.

The Observational Level The next level for our tire is observational. This we can experience with our unaided senses. It embraces all the tire's characteristics that are susceptible to unaided human perception. Note that in moving from one level to another we have abstracted, we have left behind certain details. When we moved from the basic process level to the microscopic level, we left behind those details that humans can't experience even with microscopes or similar instruments.

The Personal Perception Level The next level of the tire's existence will be provided by you. You have already abstracted from the numerous stimuli in the car lot by focusing your attention on the left rear tire of the maroon Triumph. As you experience the tire, you will abstract still further. You will select and process details with your personal perceptual equipment. The tire that exists on this level is the tire that exists in your personal perception.

First Verbal Level To experience further levels of abstraction you will need to communicate about the tire to someone else. When talking to friends, for example, you could describe the left rear tire. This talk would be an abstraction, a verbal map of the internal experience you have had. Verbal equivalents always leave something out. Your reference to the left rear tire would communicate some of the details of your perceptual experience with the tire and exclude some others. No one can share your perception completely. To put it differently: Your description of the tire is a verbal map of your perception of the tire. Your perception of the tire, in turn, is a subjective map of the tire itself. The tire itself exists on different levels. Each succeeding level and map leaves out more and more details.

Higher Verbal Levels Verbal abstraction can reach an enormous number of levels. You could refer to the left rear tire in a general reference to the tires on the Triumph. This abstraction would leave out details specific to the left rear tire and it would include only details common to all the tires on the car. You could become more abstract by referring to used automobile tires in general. This abstraction would leave out details specific to the tires on the Triumph and would include only details common to all used automobile tires. You could achieve another degree of abstraction by referring to tires in general. This abstraction would

Figure 7.1. Read from the bottom up.

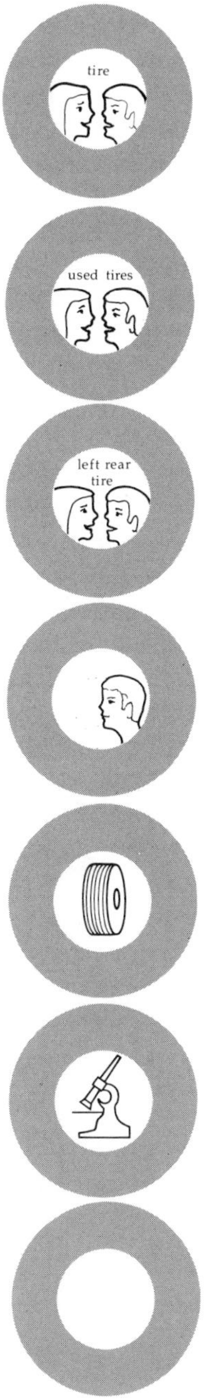

Higher verbal level — Includes only details common to all tires—leaves out details specific to individual tires.

Higher verbal level — Includes only details common to all used tires—leaves out all details specific to the left rear tire.

First verbal level — Includes only details of your personal perception of the left rear tire that were successfully communicated by you—leaves out all other details.

Personal perception level — Includes only details of the left rear tire that were processed by your personal perceptual equipment—leaves out all other details.

Observational level — Includes only details of the left rear tire that can be experienced with unaided human senses—leaves out those additional details that were a part of the first two levels.

Microscopic level — Includes details of the left rear tire that can be experienced with instruments—leaves out details that cannot be experienced even with instruments.

Submicroscopic level — Dance of submicroscopic elements that comprise the basic core of the left rear tire.

leave out special characteristics belonging to used-passenger-car tires and would include only characteristics that all tires— truck, tractor, car, used, and new—share in common.

The point is that, as we think and communicate about things, we abstract. That is, we include and leave out varying degrees of detail. To review and clarify this point, study the diagram (Figure 7.1), reading from the bottom up.

Thus far we have noted that abstraction involves leaving out some details while including others and that human perception and communication involve the process of abstraction. Furthermore, communication occurs on several levels of abstraction. To understand further and to apply the concept of abstraction, let's turn our attention to a device known as the abstraction ladder.

Verbal levels
{
7. thing
6. live thing
5. live plant thing
4. live tree
3. live oak tree
2. live California oak tree
1. live California oak tree in my backyard
}

Silent levels
{
4. the live California oak tree in my backyard that exists in the perception of the beholder
3. the live California oak tree in my backyard that can be observed with the unaided senses
2. the microscopic live California oak tree in my backyard that can be observed only with a microscope or some other extension of the senses
1. the submicroscopic process that is the live California oak tree in my backyard
}

The Abstraction Ladder

An abstraction ladder is a device to illustrate the various verbal levels at which we can talk about something. It is simply a list of items in the order of their specificity. The following abstraction ladder is based on a California oak tree that exists in my backyard. Note, as you read from the top down, that each succeeding item becomes more specific. All of 6 is included in 7, but not all of 7 is included in 6; all of 5 is included in 6, but not all of 6 is included in 5, and so on down the list. Also observe, as you read from the bottom up, that each succeeding level both refers to a broader territory and leaves out more details of the specific oak tree in my yard.

Often when constructing abstraction ladders we don't bother to put in the silent levels. We include them here to emphasize that the reference point for all levels was the tree that exists on the silent levels.

Abstraction ladders are used as training devices. Working with them helps us to develop an increased awareness of abstraction. If you decide to construct some abstraction ladders, keep in mind these simple suggestions:

1. List items in the order of their specificity. As you go down the ladder, make each succeeding entry more

specific. As you go up the ladder, have each item refer to a broader area but include fewer details of the item at the bottom.

2. Don't mix "apples and oranges." For example, the following ladder is actually two ladders. It develops two topics, recreation and protective materials.

> recreation
>
> outdoor recreation
>
> summertime outdoor recreation
>
> sunbathing
>
> protection while sunbathing
>
> commercially prepared sun protection
>
> suntan lotion
>
> suntan lotion containing coconut oil

3. Develop an abstraction ladder either by starting from the bottom and working up or by starting from the top and working down.

4. Remember that the bottom line of a ladder is not a definition of the term that appears on the top line. It is a specific instance of whatever appears on the top line.

5. You can develop a great number of different ladders from the same bottom or top lines.

Constructing abstraction ladders can help us develop a keener awareness of the process of abstraction. Here is a simple abstraction exercise. Following is a "scrambled" abstraction ladder. Take a few moments and put it in a proper order.

> four-wheeled motor-driven transportation
>
> mechanical transportation
>
> 1977 automobile
>
> the 1977 maroon Triumph sports car we were looking at earlier in the chapter
>
> transportation
>
> motor-driven transportation
>
> automobile

Right, unscrambled it looks like this:

> transportation
>
> mechanical transportation
>
> motor-driven transportation
>
> four-wheeled motor-driven transportation
>
> automobile
>
> 1977 automobile
>
> the 1977 maroon Triumph sports car we were looking at earlier in the chapter

One of the most difficult abstraction exercises is to select a highly abstract word or phrase such as, "the establishment" or "the American way" and from it develop a ladder all the way down to a specific life event. Following is a sample ladder for "the American way."

> the American way
>
> the American custom of celebrating national holidays
>
> the American custom of celebrating the Fourth of July

George Smith's customary observance of the Fourth of July

George Smith playing softball and barbecuing hamburgers with his family at El Monte Park in Lakeside, California, on the Fourth of July

Needless to say, an almost infinite number of ladders could be developed from this term.

Sometimes when we attempt this exercise, instead of becoming more specific we merely substitute words that are as abstract as the one or ones we started with. We do this because we frequently use high-level abstractions without having a clear idea of what they point to in the extensional world. When we use words in this vague, indefinite way, we are merely making meaningless noise—albeit sometimes pleasant noise. This is not to imply that we should avoid high-level abstractions. This is to say that the words we use should represent something for us. As the Latin poet Virgil observed, "He utters empty words, he utters sounds without mind."

Sometimes we use words that don't point to anything except our own feelings. Often when we say things like, "She is an establishment type" or "He is a real American," we are simply expressing approval or disapproval. Most of us would be hard put to define objectively an establishment type or a true American. It is all right to use high-level abstractions of this kind as long as we realize that the words are pointing to us, reflecting our feelings, and that they do not reflect objective facts. The test is not whether a word is of a high or a low level, or whether it points to an internal state or

an external event. The test is do we understand what details the word is pointing to.

In review, an abstraction ladder is a device for illustrating the various levels of abstraction at which we can communicate about anything. It is frequently used as a training device for increasing awareness of abstraction. Its use sometimes reveals that we use words without having a clear idea of what they represent.

Benefits of Abstraction Awareness

Consciousness of abstraction is often beneficial. In the remaining pages of this section, we will discuss five ways that it helps us.

Flexibility of Mind

Sometimes we are tempted to act as if we know all about a subject or as if we had said all there was to say. This is a dangerous tendency. As Gordon Allport says, "The surest way to lose truth is to pretend that one already wholly possesses it."[3] When we are conscious of abstracting, we realize that we can never know or say *all* about anything. When we realize that every map leaves out some details, we are less likely to develop a closed mind.

More Interesting Communication

The most effective sleeping pill ever created is the communicator who gets stuck at the top of the ladder, who never descends from higher level abstractions to concrete details and examples. Almost equally as dull is the person who pours out endless details and never generalizes or reaches a conclusion from them. The term *dead-level abstracting* is used in connection with people who are unable to move from one level of abstraction to another. When you are conscious of abstracting, you can make a real effort to avoid getting stuck on one level. The most interesting communicators are those who move freely up and down the ladder by supporting high-level generalizations with specific examples and by using low-level specifics to reach higher level conclusions.

Greater Clarity

By now you realize that high-level abstractions refer to more items than do low-level abstractions. The word *tree* refers to all trees. The words *California oak tree* refer only to California oak trees. The words *California oak tree in my yard* refer to a single tree. The higher the level of abstraction, then, the greater the chances for misunderstanding. Generally, we should try to use the lowest level consistent with what we want to express. "Pick me up a book at the library" is not as specific as "Get me a good mystery at the library." "Pick me up an anthology of Sherlock Holmes stories at the library" is even more specific.

> book
>
> good mystery book
>
> Sherlock Holmes anthology

"It's just a mild hyperinsulism due to islet cell hyperplasia with a touch of hepatic insufficiency and glycogen depletion. In other words, watch your diet."

Suspicion of High-Level Abstractions

When we become conscious of the abstracting process, we usually become somewhat suspicious of high-level abstractions. Although high-level abstractions are necessary and useful, a certain amount of skepticism about their use is probably healthy. High-level abstractions are sometimes used to mislead and confuse. When a speaker says, "I pledge to support humanitarian programs and to vote against those programs that are not consistent with the traditions of this great state," we really don't know what he or she is talking about. We don't know what programs the speaker is going to support.

I once attended a hearing at which a committee was recommending that a new position be created on a college campus.

The committee presented a proposed job description for the position. The job description was stated in very high-level abstractions. It was quite impressive, but it did not specify what a person in the position would actually do. One member of the audience was highly suspicious of the high-level abstractions. He repeatedly asked the committee to translate them into specific details about day-to-day responsibilities. For example, one of the stated responsibilities of the new position was, "Maintain and supervise a substitution system." When this statement was reduced to the "bottom line," it seemed to mean that, when someone was absent, the new employee would instruct a secretary to call a substitute from a standard list of substitutes provided by the personnel office. Someone in the audience estimated that this would take all of fifteen minutes a year. By the time the meeting was adjourned, it was apparent that the new position was probably not justified. This seemed to be a case in which high-level abstractions were used to lull and confuse the listener. Good listeners consistently ask themselves: What does that mean? What is the bottom line?

Aid in Problem-Solving

Sometimes we have difficulty solving problems because we state them and think about them in vague, high-level terms. Often when we bring problems down the ladder to more specific levels, they become easier to deal with. Consider the following example:

George and I don't get along anymore.

George and I argue.

George and I argue about the kids.

George and I argue about the kids when he comes home from work tired and I tell him how the kids have been behaving.

This abstraction ladder was based on an actual counseling session. The woman entered the session with a vague notion that she and her husband no longer "got along." She left realizing that the only serious disagreements occurred when he came home from work tired and she "dumped" the problems of the children on him. The problem became more manageable when it was stated more specifically.

A man once began an interview with a campus dean with, "I don't like what you people are doing over here." Eventually it became apparent that the man was upset about one assignment that one instructor had given him. Seen in this perspective, the matter didn't seem so serious. Through conscious abstraction we can often see our problems more clearly. This is frequently a significant step in solving those problems.

To review: Awareness of abstraction often contributes to a more open mind, more interesting communication, and greater clarity of communication. It also suggests a healthy suspicion of high-level abstractions and helps in problem-solving.

In this chapter we discussed the process of abstraction, the abstraction ladder, and several benefits of abstraction awareness.

Key Ideas in Review

☐ Abstraction is the process of selecting some details and leaving out others.

☐ We abstract when we perceive because we never perceive *all;* we experience some details and leave out others.

☐ Printed maps are abstractions because they include some details and leave out others.

☐ Some maps leave out more details than do others.

☐ Our verbal maps are abstractions because we can never say everything about anything. We inevitably communicate some details and leave out others.

☐ Some verbal maps leave out more details than do others; that is, we talk about things on different levels of abstraction.

☐ An abstraction ladder is a device that illustrates the various levels at which we can talk about something.

☐ Abstraction ladders are used as training devices to increase awareness of abstraction.

☐ Consciousness of abstraction contributes to a more open mind, clearer and more interesting communication, a suspicion of high-level abstractions, and problem-solving.

Section B
Person-to-Group
Focus

*I come from a state that raises corn
and cotton and cockleburs and
Democrats, and frothy eloquence
neither convinces nor satisfies me. I am
from Missouri. You have got to
show me.*

Willard D. Fandiver

In Section A we observed that the more territory a map covers the less detail it contains. Because high-level abstractions refer to broad areas, they lack detail and consequently are usually somewhat vague and difficult to understand. Because they are not concrete, they often do not command immediate attention. As James McBurney and Ernest Wrage point out, "Specific instances, items and cases are usually clearer and more interesting than general statements."[4]

In this section of the chapter, we are going to discuss how speakers can reinforce their high-level abstractions with lower level details and materials. In other words, we are going to talk about how speakers can support their generalizations with specific, concrete supporting materials. Just as the builder has certain materials with which to fill in the framework of the building, so the speaker has certain materials with which to fill in the framework (outline) of the speech. These are called *supporting materials*. It is with these materials that the speaker explains, proves, and holds attention. They tend to make high-level abstractions more

tangible and concrete. Their absence from a speech requires the listeners to understand and accept the speaker's generalizations and conclusions on faith. The listeners don't have the benefit of the supporting details that led the speaker to reach those generalizations and conclusions in the first place. In this section of the chapter we are going to consider some general suggestions for using supporting materials, some types of supporting materials, and some places to look for supporting materials.

General Suggestions for Using Supporting Materials

Later in the chapter when we talk about the various types of supporting materials, we will note suggestions specific to each type. At this time, let's consider some overall suggestions for using supporting materials.

Use Supporting Materials throughout the Speech

Supporting materials can be used in the introduction, with the main heads and subheads, and in the conclusion. Remember, supporting materials are used to hold attention, to explain, and to prove. Therefore, use them whenever you want to make an idea more interesting, more understandable, or more believable. Just as you distribute seasonings throughout the sauce, use supporting materials throughout the speech.

Use a Variety of Supporting Materials

Supporting materials usually work best when the various kinds are used in combinations. A speech developed entirely with one kind of supporting material—say, statistics—is apt to be dull. It may also be unconvincing. For example, a story about one alcoholic teenager does not prove that most teenagers are alcoholics. If you use a story or an illustration for proof, you must demonstrate that your illustration is representative. You can best do this by using it in conjunction with other types of supporting materials, such as statistics and authoritative quotations.

Use Supporting Materials Deductively

Although supporting materials can be used inductively, it is usually easier for listeners to appreciate the relation between the supporting material and the point it supports when that point is apparent at the outset. When the speaker presents the material before stating the point, she or he can confuse the listeners about the point to come. Listeners are apt to wonder what it is all about and what it is leading up to, rather than to concentrate on the material itself. On the other hand, when you state the point at the outset, you utilize the principle of the anticipatory set. Consider the following formula:

1. *State the point*

State the point you want to develop with the material—the point you want to clarify, to make more interesting, to prove.

2. *Present the supporting material*

After you have revealed the point, present the material to support it.

3. *Apply the material to the point*

Unless the relation between the material and the point is exceptionally obvious, remind your listeners that your material does in fact support your point. Because they have not been thinking about your speech to the extent that you have, they may need help in understanding how the material supports the point. Sometimes, by the time the speaker has presented long and complicated material, the listeners have forgotten the point. Often then, they may need a reminder concerning the relation between the material and the point.

Use Relevant Material

Be sure your material is directly related to the point it is designed to support. For example, you couldn't illustrate the effects of drunk driving with a story about an accident that was caused by faulty brakes.

Use Timely Material

Sometimes materials don't work because they are out-of-date. For example, major league baseball attendance figures gathered in 1973 don't do much to prove that baseball is the number one spectator sport today. An example showing how someone began a business in 1920 does not illustrate how one would start a business today; conditions have changed significantly.

In review, use supporting materials throughout the speech, use a variety of materials, use materials deductively, use materials that are relevant, and use materials that are timely.

Types of Supporting Materials

There are innumerable kinds of supporting materials, which people have classified differently over the years. We are going to consider eight forms of supporting materials: the detailed illustration, the specific instance, the hypothetical illustration, statistics, comparisons, quotations, visual aids, and audio aids.

The Detailed Illustration

A detailed illustration is an example that is given in detail. It is the narration of an event or an incident. Because it has a strong story element, the detailed illustration is an excellent way to hold attention while developing a point. People usually perk up when they sense a story coming. The detailed illustration can be taken from everyday life or from history. In the following example, notice that the speaker first states the point, then gives the example, and then reminds the listeners of the point.

> Another rule to follow when hunting is never shoot until you have a completely clear and unobstructed shot. I learned the importance of this rule at an early age. I was deer hunting with my best friend, Ralph Davies. I was eighteen and he was a year younger. We were hunting in the hills behind Angels Camp, an old California gold town in the foothills of the Sierras. We knew the country well because we had been raised in the area. This was the first time, however, either of us had been deer hunting without our fathers. We had come out that morning because Ralph's father had spotted a buck in the area a day earlier. We were resting after climbing a steep rise through heavy undergrowth. Suddenly I heard a rustling in the brush not thirty yards away. By straining I could make out a vague form behind some manzanita. I was exhilarated at the thought of getting my first buck. Certainly the form I could barely see had to be the buck Ralph's father had spotted earlier. I raised my rifle and fired at what I guessed to be the upper front quarter of the buck. Ralph reached the spot before I did. I will never forget his scream. I had shot a man. His face was contorted with pain and a thin circle of red was forming on the left shoulder of his mackinaw.
>
> I won't tell you about the horrors of the next few hours and days, of the blind dash through the woods for help, the wait at the hospital, the questions from authorities. Fortunately, the man was not hurt seriously. He was back at his job within a few days. However, it was several years before I picked up my rifle again. When I did return to the woods, I was a wiser and safer hunter. I sincerely hope you will profit from my experience. Never squeeze the trigger until you have a clear and unobstructed view of the target.

When using the detailed illustration, keep in mind the general suggestions for using supporting materials that we considered earlier. Be sure the illustration is timely and relevant and that you make clear the relation between your illustration and the point it is supporting. Additionally, try to resist the temptation to overgeneralize from your illustration. If you wish to generalize, use the illustration in combination with such other materials as quotations and statistics. A detailed illustration shows that something happened once. Statistics can suggest that it happened that way several times.

The Specific Instance

The specific instance is a brief example containing very little detail. Because specific instances are short and underdeveloped, they are usually used in series. They are frequently combined with a detailed illustration. Their use in series tends to show that whatever they are illustrating has general application. Consider the following:

> In addition to serving us as companions, dogs have performed valuable work over the years. For example, the Alsatian, or German shepherd, has served in war and in police work and is invaluable as a guide dog for the blind. The Newfoundland is a powerful swimmer and is used extensively in water rescue work. The Swiss mountain dog weighs over 100 pounds and was developed for pulling cheese around Alpine villages. The dalmatian was developed in Yugoslavia and has been used over the centuries as a companion and guard for horses. The collie has been a valuable shepherd and farm dog. Today the smooth-haired collie is used extensively as a guide dog for blind children. The bloodhound is used for tracking, the Labrador for retrieving, and even

the stylish Afghan hound was used over 4,000 years ago as a hunter in its native Afghanistan. We could go on and on, but I suspect the point is apparent. Dogs have performed valuable work over the centuries.

Once again, be sure that your instances are relevant and timely and that their relation to the point they are intended to support is clear.

The Hypothetical Illustration

Detailed illustrations and specific instances describe real events. The hypothetical illustration, on the other hand, is an imaginary example. Sometimes when for some reason you can't use an actual example, you can create one to illustrate your point. The hypothetical example is not used to deceive listeners; it is openly presented as fiction. It is used to show how something has happened, may have happened, or might happen. In the following sample the speaker illustrates one advantage of federally sponsored student financial aid with a hypothetical example.

> Federally sponsored student financial aid often enables students to attend college and become self-reliant, who otherwise would be unable to. To illustrate this point, let me utilize a hypothetical but typical example. This fiction is a composite of many real examples I have encountered in my work with financial aid. Nancy was married two weeks after she graduated from high school and was divorced at twenty-one. She has a five-year-old daughter named Marsha. She receives no support from her former husband and, in fact, doesn't know where he is.

Her parents are separated and neither can afford to help her. In three weeks Nancy will receive a B.A. degree from Western Hills College. She has already obtained an elementary teaching position for next fall. She made it through with the help of the college day-care center for Marsha, and a financial aid package consisting of a college work–study job, a grant in aid, and for the last two years a federally subsidized student loan. Although Nancy was created for this speech from my experience with financial aid, she is typical of thousands of students who are attending college today with the help of student financial aid.

Even though hypothetical illustrations are fictional, present them as though they could happen. Make them plausible and consistent with reality. On the other hand, never mislead your listeners by pretending such an illustration is anything more than hypothetical. This could lead to mistrust and doubt. Present hypothetical illustrations with enough detail to make them interesting and realistic.

Statistics

Statistics are numbers that can help the speaker develop a point of view. Because statistics are actually distilled examples, they are useful in broadening the application of specific illustrations. In the following example, the speaker uses statistics to help establish the conclusion that television programming contains violence.

I have heard a lot about television violence lately, and so I decided to do a little research of my own. For the first time in recent mem-

ory, I devoted an entire evening to television-watching last week. With paper and pencil in hand, I watched television last Thursday evening from eight o'clock to eleven. To substantiate my findings, I asked John and Mary Demaris, who are members of this class, to watch the same programs that I watched. As they will verify, their observations coincide with mine. As a result of my experiment, I am forced to agree with those who say that television does present considerable violence. In the course of three hours I witnessed six people killed in a bomb explosion, five fatal shootings, two automobile fatalities, and one stabbing. That is 14 violent deaths in three hours. In addition to the fatalities, I witnessed two near-fatal automobile accidents, four fistfights, and a man being severely mauled by an African lion. Friends, that is more violence than I want to encounter firsthand in my entire life. I was a party to 16 separate acts of violence in the space of three hours without leaving my living room. If you will sit down and watch television for three hours on any one night, I think you will agree with me that television does present considerable violence.

Whenever possible, show how your statistics were gathered and by whom. People have grown suspicious of statistics, and it is helpful to show that they have been gathered responsibly. Be sure your statistics are relevant and up-to-date. Because listeners have difficulty keeping track of numbers, you will sometimes need to explain what your statistics mean and how they relate to your point. Finally, try not to use too many statistics at any one place in your speech. It is difficult for an audience to absorb too many at one time.

Comparisons

There are two kinds of comparisons, literal and figurative. The *literal comparison* deals with two phenomena that are essentially alike—one restaurant compared to another restaurant, one country to another country, one baseball team to another baseball team. The *figurative comparison* compares phenomena that are essentially different—a man to a mountain, a country to a ship, a woman to a flower. We can sometimes make the unknown clear by comparing it to something that is known, or the questionable more acceptable by comparing it to something that is already accepted. The following is a figurative comparison.

Still another factor affecting your happiness is your outlook or point of view. Let me illustrate by telling you about two buckets. Two water buckets were talking one day. One said, "I am so discouraged, no matter how many times I come up from the well full, I always go down again empty." The other bucket replied, "Really, I am very happy, because no matter how many times I go down the well empty, I always come up from the well full." Friends, we are like those buckets. We can choose to accentuate the positive or we can choose to accentuate the negative.

The following is a literal comparison.

Finally, I am going to recommend an Italian restaurant. I believe Leno's is the best in the area. Let me compare it to Ralph's, since most of you are familiar with Ralph's. The food is good at both places; however, Leno's has a much greater variety. At Ralph's about all you can get is some kind of pasta. In addition to pasta, Leno's offers a number of veal and fish entrees. Leno's is slightly more expensive, but the atmosphere more than makes up for the difference in price. Ralph's is so large and crowded it is always noisy. Sometimes at Ralph's I get the feeling they want me to hurry so they can seat someone else. It is just the opposite at Leno's. Leno's is smaller and very quiet. Every customer gets individual attention. They actually encourage you to take your time and to enjoy the food. Really, considering the menu, the prices, the service, and the atmosphere, I strongly recommend Leno's for Italian food.

When using comparisons, keep in mind the general suggestions for using supporting materials. Additionally, be sure your comparisons are appropriate for your listeners. It does you little good to compare guavas to papayas if your audience is not familiar with either guavas or papayas.

Quotations

Quotations are a widely used form of support. They can come from practically any source—prose or poetry, history or literature, newspapers or magazines, conversations or even other speeches. Quotations give the weight of authority to an opinion or express an idea in a particularly pleasing manner. Consider the following:

> Let me emphasize, ladies and gentlemen, that our greatest contribution to the world has not been our armed forces or our great economic wealth. Our greatest contribution has been the hope we have provided for the spirit of humankind. To emphasize that idea, I would like to share with you some words that are inscribed on the walls of the Kennedy Center in our nation's capital: "I am certain that after the dust of centuries has passed over our cities, we, too, will be remembered not for victories or defeats in battle or in politics, but for our contribution to the human spirit." These words are a reminder to all of us that our greatest strength is not material but spiritual.

If you imply that you are using an exact quotation, be sure that it is exact. If you are paraphrasing, say so. Remember that the source of the quotation must be acceptable to the audience. Sometimes your listeners won't be familiar enough with your subject to appreciate the qualifications of the source you are quoting. If so, it is wise to explain the qualifications.

Visual Aids

Visual aids encourage listeners to become involved with their eyes as well as their ears. As we noted in chapter 1, human communication is multichanneled. The channels most frequently used are air waves (by auditory receptors) and light waves (by visual receptors). In other words, audience members usually see as well as hear the speaker. When a visual message reinforces and supports the auditory message, communication is considerably enhanced. For example, one study using instructional films with and without verbal exposition found that learning associated solely with listening was significantly less than learning associated with simultaneous viewing and listening.[5] Visual aids are anything the speaker uses for support that the listeners can see. They include pictures, charts, graphs, maps, models, chalkboards, objects, movies, slide projections.

Visual materials offer several advantages.

They Have Interest Value Visual aids stimulate listener interest. We are attracted to the definite, the specific, the tangible. We tend to lose interest in the vague, the abstract, the general. Visual aids have definite size, shape, and color. Thus they tend to make concrete the abstraction that is language.

They Promote Clarity Understanding is increased when messages are carried on more than one channel. When visual and audi-

Visual aids promote clarity.

tory messages complement one another, the chances for successful communication are improved. The adage about a picture being worth a thousand words is often true. We are more likely to understand when the speaker can show us as well as tell us.

They Promote Speaker Confidence Many speakers feel more comfortable when they have a visual aid to work with. The physical activity in holding, pointing to, manipulating, and explaining visual materials provides a useful outlet for excess nervous energy. As reminders of material to be covered and as memory aids, visual aids contribute to speaker confidence.

Although visual aids offer many advantages, they must be used properly for their value to be realized. The following guidelines apply to most visual aids.

Practice with the visual aid. Even though you have used an object many times, you will have to practice handling it in order to use it effectively in a speech. Such simple matters as getting the slide projections in order, finding illustrations in a book, or

having an extension cord available are apt to turn out better when you have practiced with the visual aid.

Control the attention the aid receives. Try to keep the visual aid out of sight until its use is appropriate. An aid in full view of the audience throughout the speech is apt to distract listeners. You can keep models and other objects in a container. Stack large charts, posters, and similar visual materials with their blank sides to the audience until you use them. Avoid passing objects among listeners during the speech. They invite competition. Instead of reinforcing the speaker's message, they often detract from it.

Maintain contact with the audience while using the aid. In the manipulation of visual aids, pauses are sometimes inevitable and even desirable. When pauses are long, however, listeners often become disinterested. Plan, then, for purposeful commentary during awkward pauses. Above all maintain eye contact with your listeners while using the aid. Resist the temptation to talk to the aid. Don't be like the proverbial absentminded professor who spends the entire hour with back to the class talking to the board. Practicing with your visual aids will improve your skill at maintaining vocal and visual contact while using them.

Be sure everyone can see the visual material. Visual aids must be large enough and placed well enough for everyone to see them. A visual aid too small to be seen comfortably is worse than no aid at all. People become annoyed and lose interest when they are unable to see important material. Be sure your material is placed so that everyone in the audience can see it. For example, don't place material on a low table that viewers in the back can't see. Don't stand between the audience and the visual aid. When writing or sketching on the board, move from side to side occasionally to allow everyone a clear view. Write and draw with large, broad strokes. Keep drawings simple and don't worry about artistic results. The idea is to illustrate a point in your speech, not to impress the audience with your artistic talent.

Use appropriate visual aids. In chapter 10 we will note that speakers must select words to which their listeners can attach appropriate meanings. The same can be said for visual material. Select visual support with an eye to what audience members already know about the subject. For example, if you were giving a speech about advanced engine designs to a group of skilled mechanics or engineers, you could use a more sophisticated model or diagram than you could use with a more general audience. Materials that are too complex or too elementary for a particular audience discourage listening.

Audio Aids

With the increasing availability of records, tapes, and recorders, audio aids are becoming more important to speakers. Short musical selections, recorded poetry, and excerpts from recorded interviews are examples of audio aids that can be used in speeches.

When using audio aids, we must take care to avoid substituting recorded material for the speech or for large portions of the speech. The speaker who "sits back" and merely plays a record may lose contact with the audience and the sense of immediacy. The speaker should use recorded materials solely to emphasize and to illustrate points in the speech. Many of the precautions we noted in connection with visual aids also apply to audio aids. Be sure the equipment is properly adjusted and ready to go before you start the speech. Be sure the volume is set at a comfortable level for everyone. Use material that is appropriate for your speech and for your audience.

Thus far we have considered several basic forms of supporting material and some suggestions for their use. Let's turn our attention now to the problem of finding supporting material.

Sources of Supporting Materials

Once we have developed an awareness of supporting materials, it is difficult to go through a day without recognizing a variety of useful materials. Some people carry a notebook for the purpose of recording useful materials they encounter. When you are searching for material to use in a particular speech, it is wise to employ all four of the following methods.

Think

One of the first steps in finding supporting materials is to sit down and think. Think about books you have read, courses you have taken, and experiences you have had that would relate to the subject of your speech. Materials that grow out of your own experience are often the most compelling. Don't be like the student who once gave a rather bookish speech on secondary education. In spite of his having spent four years in high school, he didn't once mention his own experience. He took his entire speech from a national magazine.

Look

It is remarkable how many different kinds of supporting material you can gather simply by observing. If you are giving a speech on swimming pool construction, go watch a pool being built. If you are going to talk about prospects for this year's basketball team, go watch the team work out. If you plan to give a speech about the city council, sit in on a meeting or two.

Listen

Listening is one of the most efficient means of gathering supporting materials. Whether it be in front of the television set, in an informal chat with friends, or in a formal interview, listening is the best means for utilizing the rich experience of others. If you are planning a speech about why students attend college, raise the question among some friends and then sit back and listen. If you are talking about modern methods of home construction, interview a building contractor. If your speech is on law enforcement, talk to several law enforcement officers. By listening you can obtain quotations, illustrations, instances, and many other kinds of supporting materials.

Read

Reading is one of the most important steps in securing supporting material. Books, newspapers, magazines, dictionaries, encyclopedias, and pamphlets are all potential sources of materials for the speaker. The library, of course, is the greatest repository for printed materials. In addition to the usual library tools, such as the *Reader's Guide to Periodic Literature* and the card catalog, libraries have many special resources. The numerous special dictionaries and encyclopedias on a wide variety of subjects are usually very helpful to the person searching for speech materials.

In short, speakers can find supporting material by thinking, observing, listening, and reading.

In this section of the chapter, we have considered some general suggestions for using supporting material, some forms of supporting material, and some methods of finding supporting materials.

Key Ideas in Review

☐ Speakers use specific supporting materials to make their abstract generalizations more understandable and meaningful.

☐ Specific supporting material tends to hold attention, clarify, and prove.

☐ In general, use supporting materials throughout the speech, use a variety of materials, use materials deductively, use materials that are relevant, and use materials that are timely.

☐ Eight forms of supporting material are the detailed illustration, the specific instance, the hypothetical illustration, statistics, comparisons, quotations, visual aids, and audio aids.

☐ Speakers can locate supporting material by thinking, observing, listening, and reading.

Suggested Assignments

Integrated Assignments

The assignments in this section are designed to help you better understand the ideas presented in Section A of this chapter, while you are utilizing the ideas presented in Section B. Prepare and deliver a well-organized speech. Use supporting materials throughout the speech. Try to reflect the characteristics of good speech your class has thus far considered. Select or adapt your topic from the following list. Be sure to use supporting materials throughout your speech.

Speech Topics

1. Select a high-level abstraction such as *beauty*, *freedom*, or *power*. Explain the abstraction in concrete terms and with specific supporting materials. Make it as meaningful as possible.

2. Select a well-known proverb such as "Haste makes waste" or "The early bird catches the worm." Use specific supporting materials either to prove or to disprove the wisdom of the proverb.

3. Analyze and compare different speeches and editorials for levels of abstraction. Present your findings to the class.

4. Sometimes people use high-level abstractions to mask ignorance or deliberately to confuse and mislead. Sometimes people will use high-level abstractions to impress. Explain and illustrate these reasons for using high-level abstractions.

5. Make a list of five or six commonly used high-level abstractions. Show the list to several persons and ask each one what the words mean. Report and interpret the results.

6. Explain misunderstandings you have observed which occurred because communicators used high-level abstractions without supporting them with lower level abstractions.

7. Illustrate occasions on which the use of high-level abstractions would be desirable.

8. The concept represented by the abstraction ladder is useful in solving personal problems. Explain and illustrate this fact.

9. Consciousness of abstraction reinforces the idea that we can't know or say everything about anything. Explain and illustrate what happens to people when they forget this.

Auxiliary Assignments

Interpersonal Focus

1. Divide into groups of four or five. Each group develops a complex abstraction ladder. After the ladder is developed, it should be "scrambled." A member of each group then reads the scrambled ladder to the class and class members try to put it in order.

2. Divide into groups of four or five. Each group selects a high-level abstraction from the following list: intelligence, love, good student, establishment, communist, justice, and beauty. Each group will develop an abstraction ladder with the selected term as the top line. Completed ladders will be read to the class. It is sometimes interesting when more than one group picks the same term.

3. Divide into groups and have each group develop a role-playing scene illustrating how the abstraction ladder can be used in problem-solving.

4. In groups of four or five, recall several real-life examples of persons using high-level abstractions to mislead deliberately. Groups then share examples with the class.

Person-to-Group Focus

1. Listen to or read a speech. Write a short paper analyzing the speech for supporting materials.

2. This exercise does not require you to give a complete speech. Come to class prepared to state a single point and develop it with as many kinds of supporting materials as possible. So that you can concentrate on supporting materials, don't bother with an introduction, main heads, a conclusion, or transitions. Simply state the point and support it.

3. Class members are assigned a specific kind of supporting material so that all types of supporting materials will be demonstrated. State a single point and develop it with the kind of material you were assigned.

4. Give a fully developed, well-organized speech on any appropriate subject. Use supporting materials throughout.

Suggested Readings

Interpersonal Focus

Bois, Joseph Samuel. *The Art of Awareness: A Textbook on General Semantics*. Dubuque, Iowa: William C. Brown Co., 1966, pp. 61–97. A challenging and provocative book for the serious student.

Bonah, R. Brent, and Shively, Sheila, eds. *The Language Lens*. Englewood Cliffs, N.J.: Prentice-Hall, 1974, pp. 356–86. This is an interesting treatment of abstraction. It contains an explanation of abstraction plus excerpts from literature which illustrate the concept.

Myers, Gail E., and Myers, Michele T. *The Dynamics of Human Communication: A Laboratory Approach*. New York: McGraw-Hill Book Co., 1973, pp. 66–69. A short, easy-to-read explanation of abstraction.

Person-to-Group Focus

Anastasi, Thomas E. *Communicating for Results*. Menlo Park, Calif.: Cummings Publishing Co., 1972, pp. 99–117. A good, easy-to-read chapter on using various kinds of visual aids.

McCabe, Bernard P., and Bender, Coleman C. *Speaking Is a Practical Matter*. 2d ed. Boston: Holbrook Press, 1973, pp. 113–23, 134–65. A comprehensive presentation of supporting materials, including separate chapters on visual aids, types of materials, and selecting materials for specific situations.

Note Directory

1. Wendell Johnson, *People in Quandaries: The Semantics of Personal Adjustment* (New York: Harper & Row Publishers, 1946), p. 151.

2. Irving J. Lee, *Language Habits in Human Affairs: An Introduction to General Semantics* (New York: Harper & Row Publishers, 1941), p. 59.

3. Gordon W. Allport, *Becoming: Basic Considerations for a Psychology of Personality* (New Haven: Yale University Press, 1955), p. 17.

4. James H. McBurney and Ernest J. Wrage, *Guide to Good Speech*, 4th ed. (Englewood Cliffs, N.J.: Prentice-Hall, 1975), p. 144.

5. Robert T. Oliver et al., *Communicative Speaking and Listening*, 4th ed. (New York: Holt, Rinehart & Winston, 1968), p. 151.

Chapter Eight

Valuing

The values we hold and the values held by others have an influence on communication. In Section A of this chapter we will consider the nature of values and how our personal values affect our communication with others. In Section B we will discuss how values held by audience members can influence person-to-group communication.

Section A: Interpersonal Focus

We have values: a discussion of human valuing and how it affects interpersonal communication.

■ Values described ■ values are acquired ■ values affect communication

Section B: Person-to-Group Focus

Audiences have values: a discussion of how the speechmaker can encourage belief by adapting to the values of the audience.

■ Adapting to audience values ■ analyzing the audience

Suggested Assignments

Section A
Interpersonal
Focus

*The greatest gift is the power to
estimate correctly the value of things.*

François de la Rochefoucauld

Considerable interest has been expressed recently in the question of values. Both young and old are searching for meaningful personal values and are questioning some of the traditional values that served an earlier time. This concern is understandable. Just a few generations ago it was possible for one to be born, to live, and to die without moving more than 50 miles from the birthplace. Other countries and cultures with different values were remote curiosities. Change was present, but it was usually slow. It was possible in this simpler life to live comfortably without questioning the values provided by one's parents and community.

Today's world is different. Changes occur at an astonishing pace. Modern communication brings a variety of cultures and subcultures as close as the living-room television set. Jet planes span continents and oceans in a matter of hours. We are bombarded with conflicting value proposals from religious groups, parents, educators, politicians, advertisers, traditionalists, and reformers. The home, the church, the stable community—once traditional value sources —are being challenged and radically altered. Is it any wonder, then, that many people are striving for a clearer under-

standing concerning the nature and worth of their own values?

We are concerned with values in this book because values are general guides to behavior. Communication, of course, is a form of behavior. Your values and the values of others influence communication situations. Your values affect what you talk about, what you say, how you say it, and how you react to what others say. A clearer understanding of your values will help you to understand better why you communicate the way you do. In this section of the chapter we will consider the nature of values, how values are acquired, and some of the ways in which values affect communication.

The Nature of Values

Values are the ideas and feelings we have about the worth and importance of things. They are relatively persistent conceptions of worth, desirability, good, and bad. Alvin Toffler defines a value as, "an attitude for or against an event or phenomenon, based on a belief that it benefits or penalizes some individual, group, or institution."[1] Toffler's is just one of many possible theoretical definitions. We use the term *value* in many ways. This is neither surprising nor undesirable. Values are multidimensional phenomena. To put it simply, values have many characteristics. There are many kinds of values and there are several ways of classifying values. In the next few paragraphs let's look at some general value characteristics and then at some of the ways in which values have been classified.

General Characteristics

Degrees of Awareness Some values exist on the conscious level and others exist below it. That is, you are aware of some of your values and are able to think and talk about them. You may also have values about which you are not aware. These "unconscious" values also influence your behavior. For example, Barry might not be aware that he values respect from others, but the fact that he strives for good grades, that he wants to excel at athletics, and that he wants a nice-looking car *may* be rooted in his valuing of respect.

Direction The direction dimension of a value moves over a continuum ranging from absolute desirability to absolute undesirability. In other words, you can value something either positively or negatively. You can feel that it is absolutely desirable or partially desirable. You can feel that it is partially undesirable or absolutely undesirable. You can also, of course, be neutral about the thing. Furthermore, your value directions can change. For example, today most colleges are familiar with students who have returned to formal education after several years of absence. Many of these people failed to value education in their youth but grew to value it more and more.

Intensity We hold values with varying degrees of intensity. Most people in a given culture or subculture hold similar values. They don't all hold the same values with the same degree of intensity, however. For example, most of us value good health. But some of us value it intensely enough to work for it, and others do not. Value intensity often changes with circumstances. We usually value good health more intensely when we are ill or threatened with illness than when we are well.

Conflict Values do not exist in isolation. They exist in combinations. Each person's collection of values is called a *value system* or *value hierarchy*. Sometimes values within a person's value system are in conflict. You may, for example, value respect for and obedience to your parents while at the same time valuing your own independence and freedom of choice. Sometimes values do not conflict until circumstances focus upon them. To illustrate: a man may value patriotism and duty to country while at the same time valuing human life. These values do not conflict until, because of a national emergency, he is inducted into a branch of the armed forces with full knowledge that he may be called upon to kill.

Another interesting conflict lies in the discrepancy between our professed values and our behaviors. Some people, for example, profess to value certain religious precepts but remember to value them only on Sunday mornings. Some people say that they value freedom of speech but deny this freedom to those who do not agree with them. Some people say that they value enlightenment but stubbornly resist examining new ideas and concepts.

We should emphasize here that it is difficult to tell what people are valuing by merely observing their behavior. A single value can be served by an almost infinite number of behaviors. To illustrate: let's use the value of respect. Most people value being respected. In our culture there are a number of ways to gain respect. People gain respect by accumulating wealth, by becoming skilled, by being heavyweight champion of the world, by having the best car on the block, and so forth. In some gangs young people even gain respect by committing acts of violence and brutality.

Power is another value that many people share. They can achieve it in many ways. People secure power by being elected to office, by becoming supervisors, by having a large family and "running a tight ship," and by many other means.

The point is that sometimes conflicts occur between what individuals profess to value and their behavior. These discrepancies are not easy to discern, however, because so many different behaviors can serve the same values.

Permanence Are personal values lasting? The answer is yes and no. Values tend to be relatively permanent, but they do change. Sometimes the change is dramatic, but usually it is gradual. Some of our values may last a lifetime, while others undergo considerable change. Values grow out of experience; as we have new experiences, our values may change. In way of comparison, however, values do not change as readily as opinions. For example, Harriet values good health. She has had that value for some time, and it is likely to endure indefinitely. Last summer it was her opinion that her health would be served by periods of fasting. After a few experiences and a little reading on the subject, however, she

changed her opinion about fasting. After listening to some friends, she took up yoga as a health measure. Her opinion about fasting changed; the parent health value remained.

Values are relatively persistent because we tend to protect them. Our value systems are part of our self-concepts. As we learned in an earlier chapter, people are strongly motivated to preserve their concepts of self. We attempt to preserve our values by avoiding exposures and interactions that would threaten them and by seeking out situations that would reinforce them. We will talk more about value change later in the chapter when we consider how values are acquired.

Thus far we have noted that values are the attitudes we have toward the worth, importance, and desirability of various phenomena. Values may be held consciously or unconsciously. We can value both positively and negatively with varying degrees of intensity. Values are relatively enduring, but they do change.

Some Value Classifications

Another way to become aware of various kinds of values is to consider some of the ways in which they have been classified.

Operative, Conceived, Objective Charles Morris suggests three value classifications. These are operative values, conceived values, and objective values.[2]

People reflect *operative values* behaviorally when they select one phenomenon and reject another. There needn't be any cognitive or conceptual thinking involved in this choice. In other words, people reveal operative values when they demonstrate preference for one thing or another. When an infant pushes away a cold bottle and accepts a warm bottle, she or he is indicating an operative value for warm milk as opposed to cold milk. When you consistently order chocolate ice cream simply because it tastes the best, you are demonstrating an operative value.

Conceived values involve conceptual beliefs. The following statements reveal conceived preferences or values: Democracy is better than communism; people should be kind to animals; it is better to fight than to run; cooperation is good; it is better to drink Coca-Cola than water; it is better to read than to watch television; it is desirable to have a new car each year; we should love our neighbors.

Many of our conceived values are learned from sources outside of ourselves. Sometimes our ultimate best interests are served by our conceived values, and sometimes they are not.

An *objective value* expresses beliefs without any personal preference or involvement. For example, if you personally don't care one way or the other about space exploration but objectively decide it is for the best, you are expressing an objective preference or value. These categories of course overlap. An objective value for you could be a conceived value for me and vice versa.

Terminal, Instrumental   Milton Rokeach[3] has written a great deal about values. He categorizes them as *terminal values* and *instrumental values*. Terminal values are con-

cerned with what we hold to be ideal states to strive for during our lifetime: a world of peace, inner harmony, a comfortable life.

Instrumental values are concerned with desirable ways of behaving: being ambitious, being cheerful, being forgiving, being polite.

Primary, Secondary   Another way to approach values is to ask whether they are primary or secondary. From time to time, people have attempted to articulate the basic values. Harold Lasswell suggests the following eight.[4]

1. Respect (esteem, honor, recognition)
2. Rectitude (a sense of doing what is morally and ethically sound)
3. Affection (love, friendship, concern)
4. Skill (motor skills, intellectual skills, social skills, artistic skills)
5. Enlightenment (knowledge, understanding, wisdom)
6. Power (making choices, implementing decisions)
7. Wealth (accumulating goods and services)
8. Well-being (happiness, physical and mental health)

How would you rate these values? Can you think of any values that you hold that can't be related to these basic eight?

Whether Lasswell or anyone else has successfully articulated universally basic values is still up for debate. The point here is that some values are more basic than others. For example, some people value money not for its own sake but because it brings them respect. In this case, respect is the primary value and money is secondary. Other people value money because it brings them affection or power. In these cases affection and/or power are the primary values. Some people value athletic skills because they get satisfaction from doing something well. Skill would be the primary value here. Others value athletic skill because it contributes to health or brings respect, or wealth, or affection—or perhaps "all of the above." Sometimes a secondary value is rooted in a combination of primary values. Tracing secondary values back to primary values is like peeling the skins from an onion. Can you trace the things you value to one or more of Lasswell's basic eight?

There are, of course, additional ways to classify values. Perhaps we have made the point that there are many different kinds of values.

Thus far we have considered the nature of values. We have noted some of the ways in which values are classified and some general value characteristics.

Values Are Acquired

We are not born with values; we acquire them after we arrive. They are learned. Our values develop from a complex interaction between human needs, experience, the intervention of people and institutions, and—if we are fortunate—our own value analysis.

The process works like this: We have certain basic needs. Among these, for example, are survival needs. One survival need grows out of hunger. Through experience we learn that certain substances satisfy this need and that others do not. Also through experience we learn that, when we utilize certain food substances, we gain approval and affection from our parents and others. In this way, we learn to value substances that satisfy our hunger and that receive approval from others. In different words, we learn to value actions that are positively reinforced because they meet needs and/or because they win approval and respect from others. We learn to value negatively phenomena that bring negative reinforcement in the form of pain, punishment, and need deprivation. To further illustrate: Among our basic needs are psychological needs. Some of our psychological needs are related to self-esteem. Cecily learned as a youngster that she could gratify certain esteem needs by playing the piano. When she played the piano well she received approval and respect from her parents and others. In this way, she learned to value musical skill. As Cecily grows older, perhaps she will decide to satisfy these needs by other means. Perhaps her value for music will change. Perhaps, however, it will not. Let's consider some of the elements in this process separately.

Direct Experience

When by direct experience you learn that it feels better to be warm than to be cold, you learn to value warmth. When you learn that it feels good to look at sunsets, you learn to value sunsets. No one has to tell you to value warmth or sunsets; your own organism tells you. According to Carl Rogers, this direct kind of valuing process lies largely in the domain of the infant.[5] We soon learn to modify this process to accommodate the values of others. For example, were you to learn to value breaking your mother's china because it feels good, your mother would soon teach you to modify that value because it conflicts with her values and the values of others. Accommodations of this kind are necessary because people live in groups.

Unfortunately, from time to time some people internalize the values of others to such an extent that they deny the evidence of their own experience almost entirely. This ordinarily is not the case, however. Most of us hold to values interjected from the culture, but we continuously modify them in the light of our continuing experience. Louis Raths, Merrill Harmin, and Sidney Simon state, ''We therefore see values as consistently being related to the experiences that shape them and test them. They are not, for any one person, so much hard and fast verities as they are the results of hammering out the style of life in a certain set of surroundings. After a sufficient amount of hammering, certain patterns of evaluating and behaving tend to develop. Certain things are treated as right, or desirable, or worthy. These tend to become our values.''[6]

External Factors

As we have just noted, our direct experiences are modified by the influence of parents, peer groups, and the general community.

Parents and Other Significant Adults Parents and other significant adults influence our values in two basic ways. These are by direct intervention and by modeling. Parents reward values they approve of and punish or fail to reward others. Parents also serve as models that children consciously or unconsciously emulate. Even though most children rebel from time to time against parental values, studies show that many people retain parental values in such basic areas as politics and religion.[7]

Peer Groups Peer groups influence our values in much the same way that our parents do. They reward and punish by accepting and rejecting. To illustrate: many teenagers consider it a cardinal sin to be different. Walk into any junior high school class in the nation and odds are that 90 percent of the shoe styles as well as the hair styles will be similar. Do we adopt the values of our groups or are we attracted to groups that value the same things we do? It works both ways. We tend to internalize group values

We adopt group values and are attracted to groups that hold values similar to our own.

and at the same time we are attracted to people who hold values similar to ours.

The Community All cultures and subcultures develop their own value systems. Communities within a single state often demonstrate different values. For example, some communities consistently pass bond issues in support of education. Other communities consistently vote against such issues but support such things as parks and stadiums. A community's values are often articulated by its schools and churches and media outlets. These institutions, in turn, influence the values of the community. We learn values from the community in the same way we learn them from our family and friends. The community rewards and punishes by acceptance or rejection. Sometimes the punishment is subtle. For example, a person who fails to respect community values in regard to dress or moral conduct may have difficulty finding employment. Through its court systems, the community sometimes punishes more directly.

Self-Examination

Mature valuing is marked by conscious and deliberate value analysis. The word *mature* here is not meant to refer to any age level. Some people begin to examine their values at an early age. Others never question their own values. The point is we don't need to be helplessly married to values imposed upon us by others. We can examine and modify those values. We can settle on the values that work best for us within the con-

fines of our social and physical environments. Values arrived at in this way are usually the most satisfactory. As H. B. Gelatt, Barbara Varenhorst, and Richard Carey state, "Values are learned. Those learned through exploration and free choice may be more constant and consciously available for use in decision making than those learned through indoctrination."[8] Many of the exercises at the close of this chapter are designed to help you think about your own values.

In review, we have observed that values are learned. We acquire them by self-analysis and from parents, peer groups, the general culture, and direct experience.

Values Affect Communication

Our values have a profound effect on our communication. We avoid communication that threatens our values and we welcome communication that reinforces them. We are consequently attracted to and often seek out people who hold values similar to ours. We frequently react defensively when our values are threatened. Because our value system is an integral part of our self-concept, we are strongly motivated to protect our values. We commonly utilize several strategies for this purpose.

Exposure

Research indicates that we tend to avoid exposure to people and communication situations that would threaten our values.

We tend to seek friends and situations that would reinforce our values.[9] This process is known as *selective exposure*. Think about your own circle of close friends. Chances are your close friends and the organizations you have elected to belong to express values similar to your own.

Perception

In a previous chapter we observed that perception is selective. Studies show that we tend to perceive in any situation that which enhances and supports our own beliefs and values.[10] In message situations we have a tendency to attend to the portions of the message that would reinforce our own values.

Expression

Another way we support our values is by expressing them. Values are a central part of the personality. When we express our values, we are reinforcing and defining ourselves. We are consequently motivated to express our values. This is yet another way that values influence communication. The urge to express values seems to go beyond ego reinforcement. People enjoy expressing values in the same way that they enjoy expressing talents or special skills. As Daniel Katz observes, "The gratification obtained from value expression may go beyond the confirmation of self-identity. Just as we find satisfaction in the exercise of talent and abilities, we find rewards in the expression of any attributes associated with our egos."[11]

Consistency

We can also see the influence of values in a group of theories called *consistency theories* (balance theory, tension-reduction theory, congruity theory, dissonance theory). These theories state: (a) people need consistency in their beliefs, attitudes, and values; (b) tension results when people become aware of inconsistencies; (c) people usually do something to reduce these tensions.

For example, let's assume that you value self-discipline and the repression of feelings. You are proud that you are the "strong, silent type." One day your psychology teacher, whom you respect very much, states that people are foolish to repress feelings, that they would be better off to express feelings. The conflict between this new knowledge and your value produces tension. You will reduce this tension either by modifying your value or by discounting the new knowledge. You could, for example, change your opinion of the psychology teacher. You could decide that he doesn't know what he is talking about or simply that he has made a mistake in this instance. Perhaps you could find additional material to counteract his opinion. On the other hand, you could change your value. Which course of action you take depends on the intensity of the value and the intensity of your belief in the new knowledge. Incidentally, the process we have just described is one of the reasons that real education is often frustrating and upsetting.

In short, values affect communication because we enjoy expressing values and because we are protective of our values. We seek out people, groups, and situations that support our values. We avoid people, groups, and situations that threaten them. We tend to discredit messages that conflict with them.

In Section A we have considered the nature of values, how values are acquired, and how values influence communication.

Key Ideas in Review

- Values are conceptions we have concerning worth, desirability, and importance.
- Values are relatively persistent, but they do change.
- Values are acquired.
- Values grow from a complex interchange among human needs, experience, the intervention of people and institutions, and subjective value analysis.
- People sometimes hold conflicting values.
- Values acquired by exploration and free choice may be more consciously available for decision-making than values acquired through indoctrination.
- We enjoy expressing our values.
- We seek out people, groups, and situations that reinforce our values.
- We avoid people, groups, and situations that threaten our values.
- We tend to discredit messages that threaten our values.

Section B

Person-to-Group
Focus

A thousand heads, a thousand tastes.

Horace

In Section A we discussed personal values and some ways in which they are related to interpersonal communication. In this section we will consider some of the ways in which personal values can affect person-to-group communication. Specifically, we will talk about ways in which speakers can adapt to their listeners' values in order to encourage belief, and we will consider methods of audience analysis.

Adapting to Audience Values

Facts are of paramount importance. Unfortunately, in order to encourage belief, speakers often must do more than present facts. They must arrange and interpret them so that they have meaning and are acceptable to listeners. Facts alone sometimes have little meaning for listeners. Several studies show that mere information learned and retained has little relation to how people feel and act. What seems to matter is how listeners *feel* about information—how they interpret it and what they associate it with. Often, then, speakers must help listeners appreciate and interpret the information they present. One way to do this is to present material in accordance with the value beliefs of listeners. Before discussing specific techniques for accomplishing this, let's briefly review the relation between values and behavior that we discussed in Section A.

We recall that people are protective of their values. They seek out people and situations that support their values, and they avoid people and situations that threaten them. We also recall that people enjoy expressing their values by acting consistently with them. People tend to discredit and reject messages they feel are in conflict with their values and beliefs. The process by which people protect their values is explained in part by the various consistency theories.

Since the 1940s a group of theories have been developed and variously labeled *balance theory, congruency theory, dissonance theory, tension-reduction theory,* and *homeostatic theory*. These theories are predicated on the idea that people need consistency and balance in their ideas, beliefs, information, attitudes, and values. When something upsets the balance between certain of these factors, tension occurs. People usually act to reduce this tension by doing something to restore balance.

For example, when a respected speaker presents information, an idea or a theory that is in conflict with a listener's value, a state of tension or cognitive dissonance is induced in the listener. To reduce this tension and restore consistency the listener has many alternatives. One choice is to decide that she or he was wrong to respect the speaker. A change in attitude toward the speaker results. Another choice is to distort the speaker's message so that the apparent conflict is reduced. For example, the lis-

tener may decide that he or she has misunderstood the speaker's message, or that the speaker has somehow misspoken. In short, the listener says, "Here is what the speaker really meant to say —— —— ——.'' A third choice is sometimes called "leaving the field." With this alternative the listener withdraws from the situation either physically or psychologically. Usually it is the latter. A fourth choice, less likely, is for the listener to modify the value or belief or attitude that is in conflict with the speaker's message. A fifth choice, rarely chosen, is for the listener to recognize the conflict and to live with it.

In short, people are protective of their values. When the speaker's message conflicts with the listener's values, the message is apt to be ignored, distorted, or discredited. Speakers, then, will be wise to prepare and present their messages in ways that reduce the possibility of direct conflict with listener values. In the next few pages we will discuss three ways of avoiding such conflict while at the same time using listener values to encourage belief and support.

Show That Your Message Is Consistent with the Values of a Respected Person or Group

As we observed in Section A, we often adopt behaviors, beliefs, and values from persons and groups we admire. This process is sometimes called *identification*. Speakers can take advantage of identification by demonstrating that their propositions are consistent with the values of a person or group the listeners admire. For example, if your listeners are mostly dedicated union members, you can gain some acceptance for your product or policy or idea by showing that your proposition is consistent with the traditional values and aims of unionism.

Television advertisers use this method frequently. A famous athlete is shown shaving with a particular shaving cream on the theory that his admirers will buy the shaving cream he uses because they want to be like him. We are asked to join the "Pepsi generation" because theoretically most of us admire that generation (beautiful, handsome, healthy young adults) and want to be like them. One joins the Pepsi generation, of course, by drinking Pepsi-Cola. In presidential nomination conventions candidates are often associated with revered political leaders of the past. Knowledgable college professors and students might scoff at the idea of buying shaving cream on the endorsement of a baseball player, but they often accept arguments associated with prominent consumer, environmental, or political advocates.

A kind of reverse identification is also possible. We resist measures we feel conflict with the values of people and groups we admire. For example, Harold Kelley and Edmund Volkart found that Boy Scouts who most valued membership in the Scouts were the most resistant to messages attacking traditional scouting values and activities.[12]

Show That Your Message Is Consistent with the Value Beliefs of Listeners

It is helpful to demonstrate that your proposals are consistent with the values held directly by your listeners as well as by persons or groups they admire. If your listeners value health, show them how your message can lead to improved health; if they value wealth, show them how your message can result in more money; if they value the environment, show them how your message is related to environmental protection; if they value independence, show them how your message can help them gain independence.

Again advertisers provide numerous examples. Most of us admire sexual attractiveness. Think of the many messages you encounter each week suggesting that you will become more sexually attractive if you buy certain products. Americans seem to value youth. We are constantly told that washing with this soap or shining with this wax or dressing with these shoes will make us more youthful. Because most of us value security, insurance policies and investment programs frequently stress security.

Experienced speakers usually try to decide what audience values their message is related to and then try to adapt their message to those values. For example, many political analysts believe that President Carter won the 1976 presidential election because at that particular time a large number of Americans valued change in government. President Carter and his supporters skillfully utilized his being a Washington outsider representing change.

In short, listener values often affect how the speaker's message is received. Speakers then can ill afford to ignore audience values. As Charles Mudd and Malcolm Sillars point out, "Some audiences see greater value in religious ideas than others. Some audiences will give higher values to athletics, agriculture, politics or books than others do. A skillful speaker understands the system of values which is operative in an audience and adapts his speaking to it."[13]

Show How Listener Values Are Threatened

Sometimes it is useful to show how the values held by listeners are threatened. When the speaker is opposing an idea or a policy or a product, she or he can show how that proposal represents a threat to audience values. On the other hand, when the speaker is for an idea or policy or product, she or he can show that failure to adopt the proposal can represent a threat to listener values.

For example, proponents of unlimited nuclear energy often suggest that restrictions on it could result in energy shortages, economic failure, and overdependence on foreign powers. They are saying in effect: "If you value your economic well-being and the continued independence of this country, you will vote against measures to restrict nuclear energy." Opponents of nuclear energy often claim that it is unsafe and that nuclear wastes represent a health hazard for generations to come. They are saying in effect: "If you value your life and health and the life and health of your children and their children, you will vote for restrictions on nuclear energy."

Utilizing values in this way frequently arouses fear in listeners. If you don't buy this product, your friends will talk about you because your toilet bowl will be dirty. If you don't buy traveler's checks, your vacation will be ruined. If you don't brush with fluoride, your teeth will fall out; if you don't use this mouthwash, you won't have any sex life. If you vote for the Democratic candidate, the country will go further into debt; if you vote for the Republican candidate, social programs will suffer. If you vote for this candidate, she will ruin the environment; if you vote for this candidate, she will repress economic growth.

Does fear arousal work? Yes, sometimes. Considerable research has shown that fear arousal is often very effective. The question now is how much fear is most effective. A 1953 study by Irving Janis and Seymour Feshbach[14] suggests that moderate fear appeal is more effective than high fear appeal. Since that early study an avalanche of related studies has occurred. Many recent studies indicate that, when properly handled, high fear appeals are quite effective. After summarizing considerable research, Bert Bradley states, "On the basis of the most recent evidence, therefore, it appears that a persuasive speaker need have no concern about the amount of fear he arouses in his listeners, provided he offers a means for removing the cause of the fear."[15] Needless to say, appeals to fear must be believed in order to be effective. They therefore must be reasonable and well documented. As Bradley indicates, for them to be most effective, speakers must present fear appeals in connection with clear and obtainable alternatives. Speakers must supply listeners with a safe escape, a way out. For example, If you don't take care of your teeth, you will develop painful and expensive cavities (fear appeal). However, if you will brush with Brand X, your teeth will be fine (the safe escape).

In summary, the values listeners hold

affect how the speaker's message is received. Speakers can adapt to audience values by showing that their messages are
consistent with values held by the listeners
and/or with values held by persons or
groups esteemed by the listeners. Sometimes speakers can adapt to audience values
by showing that those values will be
threatened if listeners accept or fail to accept certain propositions. In brief, speakers
cannot afford to ignore the values listeners
hold. But how can speakers become aware
of audience values?

Audience analysis involves making inferences.

Methods of Audience Analysis

Although it is important, audience analysis
is not an exact procedure. Most of us hold
values both consciously and unconsciously;
that is, we are aware of some of our values
and unaware of others. We also frequently
hold conflicting values. Furthermore, some
of our values influence us on certain occasions and some on other occasions. Also,
audiences are made up of individuals. It is
unlikely that any two individuals in an audience will have exactly the same value
hierarchy. For these and many other
reasons, a completely accurate and reliable
prediction about listeners is probably impossible. We can, however, make some
surprisingly good guesses or inferences
about what our listeners think, feel, and
value. Fortunately we don't need to know
all about our listeners' values. We need only
to emphasize those that are relevant or salient to our message or purpose. For example, some people value their religious beliefs a great deal. If you were speaking

about abortion, capital punishment, or
prayer in school, the religious values of
your listeners would be relevant to your
topic. But if you were trying to sell a new
food processor, the religious values of
your listener probably would not be salient.
You would be more interested in how your
listeners valued nutrition, economy, or free
time. Relevant information of this kind is
not impossible to gather. In the next few
paragraphs we will consider the kind of information about audiences that speakers
usually seek and some ways of collecting it.

Types of Information

There are two general approaches to gathering information for audience analysis: the
standard questionnaire approach and the
specific purpose approach. Both of these
approaches require that the analyzer do a
great deal of inferring. In each approach,
the speaker gathers information and then
makes inferences from it concerning what

listeners think, feel, or value. For example, if you were to learn that the average age of your listeners was over forty, that most of them were registered Republicans, and that their average income was over $40,000 annually, you might infer that they shared those values commonly associated with "conservative Americans." Although this conclusion sounds logical, with so little information to act from, it could be a dangerous inference. It would be wise to gather more information before reaching such conclusions about the internal states of your listeners. Remember, although inferences sometimes are the best we have, they are frequently risky. It is best to base them on as much pertinent information as possible.

The Standard Questionnaire Approach With the standard questionnaire approach, speakers seek to learn about listeners by applying a standard set of questions regardless of the audience, the occasion, or the subject. Proponents of this system argue that speakers cannot know what questions will be important until the questions have been answered. Consequently, they say the same questions should be asked in every case. For example, a person preparing to speak on food budgets would normally not consider questions about the religious values of listeners to be relevant. Exceptions, however, do occur. Some religious groups have strict dietary laws. A knowledge of listener commitment to such laws could conceivably be helpful for such a speaker.

Questionnaires for audience analysis usually contain questions similar to the following:

1. Why will the audience be assembled?
2. What will be the size of the audience?
3. What will be the predominant sex of the audience?
4. What will be the predominant age level of the audience?
5. What are the religious commitments of the listeners?
6. What races will be represented?
7. What occupations will be represented?
8. What will be the educational level of the listeners?
9. What will be the socioeconomic level of the audience?
10. To what organizations do audience members belong?
11. What do audience members know about the subject?
12. What will be the attitude of the listeners toward my subject and purpose?
13. What will be the attitude of the listeners toward me?

Depending on the circumstances, the speaker can answer some of the preceding questions by collecting objective data and others by making inferences. With reasonably sound answers, we are better able to adapt our messages to the values, interests, and abilities of our listeners.

The Specific Purpose Approach Proponents of the specific purpose approach argue that, although it would be nice to answer a lengthy and standard list of questions for every audience, most speakers don't have the time or the means. Consequently, they say that speakers should concentrate on questions they assume will be most relevant to their speech purpose. With the standard questionnaire approach, speakers answer a number of questions and then take from those answers information they feel will be useful. With the specific purpose approach, speakers decide in advance what information they want and then they go after it with selected questions.

As an example of the specific purpose approach, let's assume that you have been invited to return to your high school to give a 40-minute speech to the drama club on applying stage makeup. You could decide that what you need to know about your listeners is: what the predominant sex of the club is, what club members already know about stage makeup, and what kind of makeup club members want to learn to apply. With answers to these questions, you probably could do a good job of preparing with your listeners in mind.

On the other hand, if you were preparing to convince a citizens' group to vote yes on a school bond issue, you would need considerably more information. Among other things, you would want to know what value premise to appeal to. Should you appeal to community pride? Should you assume that your listeners already value improved education? Should you stress the economic advantages of passing the bond issue at this time? Or should you talk about the relation between education and a strong democracy? To answer these questions you would need to know how your listeners felt about education and taxes, and whether they had children or grandchildren in

school. You would also need to know about their occupations, their economic position, their education, their political affiliation, their religious affiliation, and probably many other things.

In review, with the standard questionnaire approach to audience analysis, speakers ask standard questions regardless of the audience or the speech purpose. With the specific purpose approach, speakers ask only those questions they feel in advance are relevant to what they want to know. With each approach speakers are called upon to make inferences. Whether you decide to use the standard questionnaire method, the specific purpose method, or some combination of the two, you will eventually be faced with the task of obtaining the desired information. Let's turn our attention now to techniques for learning about audiences.

Ways of Collecting Information

Over the years many techniques have been developed for securing information about listeners. Some of these have been rather exotic. We will try to confine ourselves to methods that are practical for most speakers.

Information Pretests One way to find out what your listeners know about a subject is to give an information pretest. For example, teachers sometimes give diagnostic tests at the beginning of a course so that they can address subsequent instruction to what students need to know. Most speakers are not in a position to test every member of the audience. Representative testing, however, is sometimes possible. Often persons representative of potential audience members are willing to submit to a brief written or oral pretest. If this method is used, you should take care to see that persons taking the test are truly representative. Such tests can be administered by the speaker, by a representative of the speaker, or by mail.

Attitude Scales Attitude scales are similar to information tests except that they are geared to attitudes rather than to information. Questions on these scales usually attempt to locate the respondent's attitude at a point on a continuum. For example, How do you feel about the proposed law that would require all dogs in our city to be on a leash when not on or in their owner's property?

Strongly approve—Approve—Undecided— Disapprove—Strongly disapprove

To reduce the possibility of a momentary whimsical response, attitude scales usually consist of several questions of this kind arranged around a specific topic. Attitudes are then inferred from the average response.

Like information tests, attitude scales can be administered representatively. The speaker can give them to people who are committed to being audience members or to members of the larger group or community from which the audience will come. Once again, the important thing is to be sure that those questioned represent the potential audience in ways that are important to the speech subject For example, Mr. Jeffries, who dislikes football, may represent his community on many matters, but he

"Yes. No. Sometimes. No. No. Yes. Don't know. Sometimes. Yes. Yes. No."

does not represent it in a way that is relevant to the speech on defensive football that you plan to give to the Boosters Club this Thursday evening.

Public Opinion Polls Advertisers, television networks, politicians, corporations, and governments frequently commission professional public opinion polls. Most of us can't afford to have a professional poll conducted. We can afford, however, to utilize professional polls that others have commissioned. Newspapers and magazines frequently publish the results of such polls. Frequently, these polls categorize the respondents according to race, economic level, sex, occupation, education, geographical region, and other pertinent factors. For the price of a newspaper or a magazine, then, speakers can often learn a great deal concerning prospective audiences.

Interviews   Interviewing is well within the reach of most speakers. They can conduct interviews by phone or in person, either formally or informally. The interviewer can ask a few questions of several people or several questions of a few people. He or she can seek specific information or ask open-ended questions. Once again, questions can be addressed to committed audience members or to representatives from the larger group or community from which the audience will come. Through interviews, speakers can usually learn something about how audience members feel as well as what they know concerning the subject.

Local Newspapers, Magazines, Radio, and Television   Sometimes, when scheduled to speak in an unfamiliar community, speakers find it worthwhile to study local media outlets. For example, by reading local newspapers and listening to local news broadcasts, you learn of current issues and items of local interest. These are often valuable clues to audience values.

Statistical Sources   Almost every library contains statistical handbooks such as *The World Almanac* or the *Statistical Abstract*. Chambers of commerce, school districts, tourist bureaus, and other agencies often make available statistical brochures. From sources of this kind speakers can learn about such things as the number of schools in an area, religious affiliations, political affiliations, average incomes, and the percentages of workers in certain occupations.

In this way the speaker can often build a useful profile of the audience.

Show of Hands   One of the oldest methods of finding out about listeners is to ask for a show of hands. In some circumstances, this works very well. For example, let's assume you are speaking about gardening to a group you haven't had time to analyze. You might begin by asking: How many of you are familiar with gardening in this area? How many of you have had a garden in other areas? How many of you have a garden now? How many of you are interested in starting a garden? The answer to such questions could apprise you of what to emphasize and how much detail to present. This technique has the added advantage of involving listeners at the beginning.

We have been discussing ways of collecting information about audiences. We have considered information pretests, attitude scales, public opinion polls, interviews, local news media, statistical sources, and a show of hands.

In this section of the chapter we considered methods by which speakers can adapt to the values of listeners in order to secure belief, and we also considered some methods of audience analysis.

Key Ideas in Review

☐ The values held by listeners affect how the speaker's message is received.

☐ Speakers can adapt to audience values by showing that their proposals are consistent with values held by a person or group esteemed by the listeners.

☐ Speakers can adapt to audience values by showing that their proposals are consistent with values held directly by the listeners.

☐ Speakers can adapt to listeners' values by showing that those values will be threatened if listeners accept or reject certain propositions.

☐ Audience analysis involves making inferences.

☐ With the standard questionnaire approach to audience analysis, speakers seek answers to a number of standard questions and then select from those answers information that seems relevant.

☐ With the specific purpose approach to audience analysis, speakers decide in advance what information they want and they then go after it by asking selected questions.

☐ Devices for collecting information about listeners include information pretests, attitude scales, public opinion polls, interviews, local newspapers and radio and television stations, statistical sources, and a show of hands.

Suggested Assignments

Integrated Assignments

The integrated assignments in this section are designed to help you better understand the ideas presented in Section A while utilizing the ideas presented in Section B. Prepare and deliver a well-organized speech. Use supporting materials throughout. Before preparing and delivering the speech, analyze your class as an audience. Do your best to adapt your speech to the values of your audience. Select or adapt your topic from the following list.

Speech Topics

1. Describe a value you hold. Tell how it developed and how it has changed. Discuss whether or not you would like to maintain this value in the future. Describe how the value affects your behavior and what you do to achieve the value.

2. Discuss two or three people who have been instrumental in the development of your own value system. Be specific. Describe these persons and how they influenced you. Use examples and other supporting materials.

3. In Section A we learned that Milton Rokeach classifies values as terminal or instrumental. Discuss three of your own terminal values and three of your instrumental values. How did they develop? What do you do to achieve them? How do they affect your communication?

4. Sometimes within our personal values system we hold conflicting values. Describe a value conflict you have experienced. How

did you resolve the conflict? Would you handle it the same way again?

5. Each culture and subculture develops its own value system. Describe a culture or subculture that you have belonged to. What seemed to be its primary values? Which of these did you accept and which did you reject? Which of these do you maintain today?

6. Value projection occurs when we attempt to induce others to adopt our values. Discuss value projection. To what extent is it justified? Are parents, schools, and governments obliged to project values? If so, under what circumstances? Please give specific examples.

7. Select an item from your wallet, from your bedroom, and from your wardrobe. Discuss what these items might imply about your values.

8. Keep a diary of your daily activities for a few days. Speak about what your activities tell about your values. What are you valuing by doing the things that you do? Do you sometimes do things that are in conflict with what you value? Why? What could you do to better align your activities with your values?

9. In a speech answer one of the following questions and then show how your answer is related to your values.
   a. If someone were to give you a million tax-free dollars, what would you do with them?
   b. If the tooth fairy were to grant you one of the following, what would you accept and why?
      1) Unlimited wealth
      2) Great talent in one of the fine arts
      3) Great beauty
      4) Robust health for 100 years
      5) Exceptionally high intelligence
   c. List the three most important occupa-

tions and tell why they are the most important.

10. Discuss some values you hold as the result of deliberate value analysis. Contrast these with the values you have adopted from others without much thought.

Auxiliary Assignments

Interpersonal Focus

1. Each class member completes the following statements in writing. Next the class is divided into groups and group members discuss their completed statements. Focus on what the added material reveals about values.
   a. If I had three wishes I would _____.
   b. I feel most comfortable when _____.
   c. My greatest regret is _____.
   d. My advice to high school freshmen would be _____.
   e. If next weekend were a three-day weekend, I would _____.
   f. I can hardly wait to _____.

2. The class is divided into groups. Each group will develop a list of five basic values that elementary schools should seek to inculcate in their students. After 30 minutes the lists are read and discussed by the entire class.

3. This is an exercise you can do privately. No one will ever see your paper. In the lefthand margin of a sheet of notebook paper list 20 things you like to do. After you have completed the list, code it in the following way. Place a dollar sign by everything that costs more than five dollars every time you do it. Place the letter A by everything you do alone and the letter P by things you do with people. Next put down the approximate date you last did each thing. Put down the number of times

you have done each thing in the last two years. Next, check the items you would have included on your list five years ago. Put an *F* by each item your father would include on his list and an *M* by each item your mother would include on her list. Finally, rank the top five items in your order of preference. Study the completed sheet. Does it tell you anything about your values?

4. This exercise is accomplished in two stages. First, each class member lists the items he or she would take were a sudden departure from home necessary. Each class member can take only one suitcase full of items. After the lists are completed, the class is divided into groups and group members discuss their lists and what the lists reveal about values.

5. Each class member comes to class with an item or a representation of an item that he or she values. In a general class discussion, members explain the valued item.

Person-to-Group Focus

1. In a general discussion, the class develops an original standard questionnaire for audience analysis. Discussion should center on the importance of each question in the list.

2. Select a subject for your next classroom speech. Using either the standard questionnaire approach or the specific purpose approach, analyze your speech class as an audience for your next speech. Use at least three of the techniques for gathering information that we discussed in the chapter. In a general discussion share your analysis with the class. Amend the analysis as the need becomes evident.

3. Give the speech for which you analyzed the class in exercise 2. Try to utilize all the skills of person-to-group speaking you have learned thus far.

4. Give a speech demonstrating how a speaker could represent the same point of view to several different audiences holding different values. Demonstrate how the speaker could adapt to each audience.

5. Give a speech to the class on a controversial issue. Without compromising your own position, do your best to adapt to the values of the class as you perceive them.

Suggested Readings

Interpersonal Focus

McCroskey, James C. et al. *An Introduction to Interpersonal Communication.* Englewood Cliffs, N. J.: Prentice-Hall, 1971, pp. 54–76. An easy-to-read, straightforward chapter on the influence of attitudes, beliefs, and values.

Simon, Sidney B. et al. *Values Clarification: A Handbook of Practical Strategies for Teachers and Students.* New York: Hart Publishing Co., 1972. An easy-to-read book designed to help the reader think about values. Lots of examples and exercises.

Triandis, Harry C. *Attitude and Attitude Change.* New York: John Wiley & Sons, 1971. A fairly easy-to-read treatment of the major consistency theories and other attitude theories.

Person-to-Group Focus

Clevenger, Theodore. *Audience Analysis.* New York: Bobbs-Merrill, 1966. This short paperback is devoted entirely to learning about audiences and how that learning can be utilized in communication.

Hance, Kenneth G. et al. *Principles of Speaking.* 3d ed. Belmont, Calif.: Wadsworth Publishing Co., 1975, pp. 46–72. A clear and useful chapter on analyzing and adapting to the listener.

Miller, Gerald R. "Studies on the Use of Fear Appeals: A Summary and Analysis." *Central States Speech Journal* 14 (May 1963): 117–24. A very good summary of early research on the use of fear appeals.

Note Directory

1. Alvin Toffler, in *Values and The Future: The Impact of Technological Change On American Values,* ed. Kurt Baier and Nicholas Reacher (New York: The Free Press, 1969), p. 5.

2. Charles W. Morris, *Varieties of Human Value* (Chicago: University of Chicago Press, 1956), pp. 9–12.

3. Milton Rokeach, *The Nature of Human Values* (New York: The Free Press, 1973), p. 28.

4. Harold D. Lasswell and Abraham Kaplan, *Power and Society: A Framework for Political Inquiry* (New Haven: Yale University Press, 1950), p. 87.

5. Carl R. Rogers, "Toward a Modern Approach to Values: The Valuing Process in the Mature Person," *Journal of Abnormal and Social Psychology* 68, no. 2 (February 1964):160–67.

6. Louis E. Raths et al., *Values and Teaching: Working with Values in the Classroom* (Columbus, Ohio: Charles E. Merrill Publishing Co., 1966), p. 28.

7. Herbert Hyman, "The Value System of Different Classes: A Social Psychological Contribution to the Analysis of Stratification," in *Class, Status and Power: A Reader in Social Stratification,* ed. Reinhard Bendix and Seymour Lipset (New York: The Free Press, 1953), pp. 426–42.

8. H. B. Gelatt et al., *Deciding: A Leader's Guide* (New York: College Entrance Examination Board, 1972), p. 5.

9. Judson Mills, Elliot Aronson, and Hal Robinson, "Selectivity in Exposure to Information," *Journal of Abnormal and Social Psychology* 59, no. 2 (September 1959): 250–53.

10. James C. McCroskey et al., *An Introduction to Interpersonal Communication* (Englewood Cliffs, N. J.: Prentice-Hall, 1971), pp. 65–66.

11. Daniel Katz, "The Functional Approach to the Study of Attitudes," in *Foundations of Communication Theory,* ed. Kenneth K. Sereno and C. David Mortensen (New York: Harper & Row Publishers, 1970), p. 244.

12. Harold H. Kelley and Edmund H. Volkart, "The Resistance to Change of Group-Anchored Attitude,"

American Sociological Review 17, no. 4 (August 1952): 453–65.

13. Charles S. Mudd and Malcolm O. Sillars, *Speech: Content and Communication* (San Francisco: Chandler Publishing Co., 1962), pp. 158–59.

14. Irving L. Janis and Seymour Feshbach, "Effects of Fear-Arousing Communications," *Journal of Abnormal and Social Psychology* 48, no. 1 (January 1953): 78–92.

15. Bert Bradley, *Fundamentals of Speech Communication: The Credibility of Ideas* (Dubuque, Iowa: William C. Brown Co., 1974), p. 60.

Chapter Nine

**Nonverbal
Communication**

Much of our communication is nonverbal. In this chapter we will consider some nonverbal variables that affect communication. In Section A we will consider some elements of nonverbal communication that are especially relevant to most interpersonal situations. In Section B we will discuss elements that are especially important in person-to-group settings.

Section A: Interpersonal Focus

We send messages without words: a discussion of nonverbal cues in interpersonal communication.

■ The importance of nonverbal cues ■ difficulties with interpretation ■ types of nonverbal indicators ■ classifying nonverbal messages

Section B: Person-to-Group Focus

The speechmaker utilizes nonverbal language: a discussion of nonverbal cues in person-to-group communication.

■ Verbal and nonverbal cues interrelate ■ specific aspects of the visual picture ■ the audience sends the speaker nonverbal messages

Suggested Assignments

Section A

Interpersonal Focus

In every object there is inexhaustible meaning.

Thomas Carlyle

Any discussion of human communication would be incomplete without a consideration of what has come to be known as nonverbal communication. The study of communication is after all the study of messages and how they are sent and received. Words are only one message medium. In many circumstances other message mediums are as important as, or in some cases more important than, words. To illustrate: try to recall recent conversations you have had. Chances are you extracted meaning not only from the words the others spoke but from the way they spoke them and from their general appearance as well. Postures, gestures, facial expressions, and dress may have stimulated meaning. If the communication was intimate, touch, smell, and even taste may have conveyed messages. And you may have abstracted meaning consciously or unconsciously from the use of space or time or from furniture, lighting, or color. For example, Albert Mehrabian estimates that when it comes to communicating feelings, nonverbal components may carry as much as 90 percent of the meaning.[1] Other scholars have made similar estimates. It is probably unrealistic, then, to consider communication without consider-

ing its nonverbal elements as well as its verbal elements.

Conversely, it is probably as unrealistic to consider nonverbal factors without considering verbal factors. In his excellent book on nonverbal communication, Mark Knapp credits Birdwhistell with the remark "Studying nonverbal communication is like studying noncardiac physiology."[2] Knapp goes on to observe that "verbal and nonverbal communication should be treated as a total and inseparable unit."[3] In other words, although we can make a distinction between verbal and nonverbal components on paper or when we talk about them, in practice they usually appear together and combine in various ways to produce messages. In instances when nonverbal components appear in isolation, the observer usually interprets them in terms of verbal symbols. In speech courses and books of this kind, we often treat nonverbal communication separately for ease and clarity of study. Care must be taken, however, to remember that in the final analysis verbal and nonverbal elements are parts of the total communication process.

The study of nonverbal communication is at once old and yet new. Since the misty beginnings of civilization, dancers, dramatists, and other storytellers have studied and understood the importance of nonverbal communication. The very word *drama* is a Greek word meaning an action. In the nineteenth century, speech students and teachers were actively interested in nonverbal communication. Practitioners of the so-called elocution school of public address actually memorized postures, gestures, and facial expressions for com-

"I think he's attempting some form of nonverbal communication."

factors as movement, gestures, and facial expressions. In this section of the chapter, we will confine ourselves to those elements of nonverbal communication that are most relevant to most interpersonal situations. In Section B we will be concerned with elements especially relevant to person-to-group communication. Specifically, in Section A we will note some obstacles to interpretation, some nonverbal indicators, and one way of classifying nonverbal messages.

Obstacles to Interpretation

We begin with a note of caution. Recently, several popular books on nonverbal communication have been published. To the extent that these books suggest that nonverbal language can be interpreted uniformly, automatically, and consistently they have been premature and even misleading. Some of these books imply that every movement, gesture, and facial expression has a specific meaning and that all we need to do in order to read a person is to memorize the specific meanings for specific nonverbal cues. This idea is less than realistic. It is just not true that nonverbal cues always mean the same thing. For example, you may assume a certain posture in order subtly to shut someone out of the conversation. On the other hand, you may assume that posture because your back hurts, or because your clothes are tight fitting, or because the chair is uncomfortable, or because you have a hearing loss in one ear, or because you have a cold and you don't want to breathe on

municating shades of meaning to listeners. This practice led to such artificiality that it fell into disrepute. In other ways, the study of nonverbal communication is an infant. Only recently have the tools of modern scientific investigation been applied to the study of nonverbal communication. In the past two decades anthropologists, psychologists, sociologists, and communicologists, have been studying nonverbal communication with increasing scientific objectivity and skill. Their work is already beginning to bear fruit.

Modern students of nonverbal communication are interested in a wide range of topics. They consider such things as architecture, weather, lighting conditions, odors, colors, and shapes as well as such people, or because your muscles are tired and need a change, or because your father used to sit that way. The possibilities are endless.

Modern researchers have concentrated on identifying nonverbal elements that communicate something. Although attempts have been made, no one has progressed very far in codifying or standardizing meanings for various nonverbal cues. The obstacles are staggering. To use body movements, for example, Mario Pei estimates that people can produce some 700,000 distinct and elementary physical signs.[4] Furthermore, nonverbal behavior appears to be partly instinctive, partly taught, and partly imitated. Some evidence suggests that certain nonverbal behaviors are universal. Others are definitely cultural. Meanings, then, can vary from culture to culture, subculture to subculture, and in some cases from family to family. Additionally, context seems to be more important in nonverbal communication than in verbal communication. These factors and many others make the task of standardizing meaning almost overwhelming.

This is not to say that we should ignore nonverbal signals. This is simply to say that this wordless language is not as yet subject to exact and universally agreed-upon interpretations. There are exceptions, of course. In every culture certain signals have fairly specific and agreed-upon meanings. The sign language of the deaf is an excellent example. Furthermore, most of us can with reasonable accuracy apply general meanings to many nonverbal signals. However, when we act upon our interpretations with rote certainty, we are behaving unrealistically. To emphasize this point, let's look at

some of the obstacles to precise interpretation of nonverbal cues.

Causation

People usually wear certain clothes, sit in certain ways, present certain facial expressions, and gesture in certain ways for reasons. The difficulty in interpretation arises because the observers usually can't be certain about what reason is influential at any one time. In another example we observed that the posture a person assumes may be influenced by his or her feeling toward others in a group. A particular posture may also be caused by an injury, poor-fitting clothes, or fatigue. Often people sit the way they do because they have learned to sit that way by imitating others. For the observer to be aware of the causation at any one time is difficult and frequently impossible. When people get up in the morning, they often put on clothes that express the way they are feeling. On other occasions, they put on certain clothes because their other garments are at the cleaners or in the dirty clothes hamper. In short, nonverbal displays are usually stimulated by something. The difficulty is knowing what that stimulus is.

Perception

Another obstacle to consistent and uniform interpretation of nonverbal stimuli lies in the nature of human perception. As we observed in chapter 5, each of us perceives the world somewhat differently because of our unique perceptual filters. We noted that some of the factors in perception are the senses, past experiences, expectations, selectivity, and language. These factors also make us perceive nonverbal cues in a personal way. The smile and pat on the arm, which to you may be a sexual invitation, to the other person may simply mean "This is a fine day and thank you very much for returning my pen." Children from some subcultures in our country perceive eye contact with the teacher as a sign of respect. Children from other subcultures perceive eye contact with adults as a sign of disrespect.

Verbal Equivalence

Sometimes we have difficulty understanding phenomena because we lack the words with which to make distinctions and to assign meanings. Sometimes we are forced to use the same word or words to refer to separate phenomena. We tend to think about these phenomena, therefore, as if they were all the same. In referring to this tendency, general semanticists talk about the *elementalistic nature of language.* For example, to most Americans, ice is simply ice. By contrast, Irving Lee tells us that the Lapps have names for and consequently make distinctions between 20 kinds of ice.[5]

Lester Kirkendall, a noted scholar and lecturer in human sexual behavior, believes that one of the reasons Americans have difficulty understanding sexual behavior is that they have so few words to describe a great variety of different behaviors.

> The word "intercourse" is used to describe all heterosexual congress, and sometimes homosexual association as well. A sexual contact with a prostitute is intercourse; so is a sexual relationship between a loving husband and wife. A sexual association entered in a spirit of bravado or hostility is equated, so far as terminology is concerned, with one entered with an attitude of affectionate sharing, or in an earnest desire to procreate. Yet, qualitatively speaking, these are very different experiences.[6]

The elementalistic nature of language constitutes yet another obstacle to the interpretation of nonverbal cues. Some scholars believe that theoretically much of what we refer to as nonverbal communication is literally verbal communication. Frank Dance,[7] for example, takes the position that all symbols are verbal. While admitting that people engage in nonverbal behavior, he suggests that, when those behaviors are interpreted by observers as words, they become verbal phenomena. The point is that, to convey precise meaning, nonverbal cues must readily translate into language. Test this idea for yourself. Birdwhistell claims to have isolated at least 23 distinct eyebrow positions that have separate meanings. How many words do you have for eyebrow positions? How many different meanings can you assign to eyebrow positions?

We have been considering some obstacles to the interpretation of nonverbal cues. We have noted that it is often difficult to be aware of the stimulation that causes certain nonverbal behavior. We also noted that we each perceive nonverbal cues in a personal way because of the personal nature of perception. And finally, we observed that the elementalistic nature of language sometimes makes it difficult to give meaning to nonverbal stimuli. This does not mean that we can afford to ignore the nonverbal components of any communication situation. On the contrary, in many situations they carry a high percentage of the meaning. In every culture certain nonverbal phenomena have precise and agreed-upon meanings; since childhood most of us have been learning to give fairly reliable general meanings to many nonverbal cues. However, the study of nonverbal communication does not as yet make mind reading realistically possible. To date, we have not been able to codify nonverbal language to the extent of assigning specific and standardized meanings to most nonverbal cues. With this reservation in mind, let's turn next to some interesting nonverbal indicators.

Nonverbal Indicators

One of the difficulties in talking about nonverbal communication is the lack of a standardized vocabulary. In this chapter we are using *nonverbal indicators* to mean the nonverbal phenomena from which observers extract meaning. For example, facial expressions and gestures are nonverbal indicators—they provide observers with messages. Obviously a list of nonverbal indicators could be almost endless. We are going to confine ourselves to some elements that are relevant in *most* interpersonal situations.

Body Movement

The study of body movement is referred to as *kinesics*. The body is wonderfully expressive. For this reason, researchers have paid

it more attention than any other single nonverbal indicator. To date, the research is tentative and in some areas conflicting. Consider the following, then, to be a progress report on general tendencies. Body movements can be divided into three broad categories: gestures and body orientation, facial expressions, and eye behavior.

Gestures and Body Orientation   Gesture refers to movements of the head, torso, arms, hands, legs, and feet. In this context, the term also refers to general body orientation or posture. Researchers have been interested in gestures and body orientation as they relate to such things as courtship, attitude, mood, and status.

Albert Scheflen[8] made numerous sound films of business meetings, conferences, and therapeutic sessions. He then analyzed the films for courtship behaviors. He found that courtship readiness was characterized by high muscle tone, reduced jowl sag, reduced eye bagginess, and reduced abdominal sag. It was also characterized by reduced shoulder hunching and slouching. He found that preening behavior included such things as touching the hair, redoing makeup, and adjusting clothes. Invitational behavior included protruding the breasts, crossing the legs, rolling the pelvis, and exhibiting wrists and palms.

Mehrabian[9] studied body orientation as it relates to the attitudes people have toward one another. He found that seated males tend to assume a less direct body orientation when talking to someone they like very much. Seated females, on the other hand, assume very indirect body orientation with people they strongly dislike and very direct orientation with people about whom they feel neutral. Women assume relatively direct posture with those they like very much. Mehrabian also found that the arms akimbo position was most often assumed when people were talking with people they disliked. Michael Argyle[10] found that when people are cooperating they tend to sit side by side, and when they are competing they tend to sit face to face.

Paul Ekman[11] concludes that the head and face reveal information about the kind of mood one is experiencing while the rest of the body is more apt to indicate the intensity of that mood. A high degree of excitement is usually accompanied by considerable body movement.

People with high status in specific situations tend to slouch and assume relaxed positions, while lower status people sit more formally. The former use the arms akimbo position more often when they are relating to those they consider to have lower status. People in high-status roles keep their heads raised. People tend to lower their heads when talking to those they perceive to have higher status.

Facial Expressions The face is an extremely important nonverbal indicator. Some evidence indicates that some facial expressions are universally recognizable. For example, photos of faces were shown to people in several different countries, some of which were isolated and primitive. Subjects had no difficulty identifying expressions of happiness, fear, surprise, sadness, anger, disgust, and interest.[12] Many people feel that the face is the most accurate indicator of emotion. When making interpersonal judgments about others we frequently refer to the face. Thomas Stritch and Paul Secord

In some situations a high percent of the meaning is carried by nonverbal components.

found that slight changes in facial details can make significant differences in judgments of personality.[13]

Research into the meaning of facial expressions is very difficult. The face is exceedingly complex. Contradictory expressions can appear on the face simultaneously and some expressions appear only momentarily. Using slow motion film, researchers found that "micromomentary" facial expressions often change so rapidly that they are not detected in normal conversations.

While running films at slow motion, Ernest Haggard and Kenneth Isaacs noticed that facial expressions often changed completely within a few frames. These changes were not noticed when the film was run at normal speeds.[14] Another difficulty in researching facial expressions is that most of us learn to control our facial expressions at an early age. It has been said that the body doesn't lie. As far as the face is concerned, research doesn't support that statement. From the time we are infants we receive almost constant feedback concerning our facial expressions. After a while certain expressions become almost automatic.

Eye Behavior The eyes are perhaps the most expressive part of the body. Christopher Brannigan and David Humphries[15] use the word *flash* to describe the sudden raising and lowering of the eyebrows. They contend that we use this action to emphasize and to indicate interest. Several investigators have been interested in eye contact. Eye contact is used to indicate whether the channels of communication are open or closed. When we wish to start a conversation with someone, we often indicate it by establishing eye contact. When we wish to avoid conversation, we avoid eye contact. For example, when two people approach each other on the sidewalk, they normally look at each other from a distance. However, as they get closer, they avoid eye contact if they do not wish to speak. If eye contact is maintained in these circumstances, people normally feel obliged to exchange greetings. Usually when people wish to disassociate themselves socially from others, they avoid eye contact. Perhaps you have noted that, when strangers assemble in a crowded elevator, they avoid each other by looking straight ahead.

When two people are talking, the speaker usually maintains less eye contact with the listener than the listener does with the speaker. However, when the speaker has finished stating an important point, he or she usually seeks feedback by contacting the eyes of the listener. Eye contact increases as distance between communicators increases. It decreases when people become physically close to each other. Women seem to maintain more eye contact than men do. When we are talking with someone we consider to have high status, we tend to maintain more eye contact than when we are talking to someone we consider to have low status.

H. T. Moore and A. R. Gilliland[16] relate eye contact to aggressiveness. They report that an unaggressive person is three times more likely to feel uncomfortable when stared at than an aggressive person. On the other hand, lingering eye contact, particularly when accompanied by a smile, often signals the need for affection and inclusion.

Some researchers have been interested in pupil dilation. Pupil dilation seems to indicate the amount of interest the observer has for the observed. For example, Eckhard Hess and James Polt[17] found that male subjects experienced more pupil dilation when looking at pictures of female nudes than female subjects did. Females experienced more pupil dilation when looking at pictures of partially clothed muscular men. Other experiments demonstrated that the pupils of political conservatives dilated when looking at pictures of conservative politicians and constricted when looking at pictures of well-known political liberals.

Liberal subjects had the opposite reaction.

As dancers and actors have known for centuries, the body is extremely expressive.

Space

The way we use personal space is another subject of considerable research. The study of personal space is called *proxemics*. In a now famous study involving white middle-class Americans residing in northeastern America, Edward Hall[18] found that his subjects adhered to rather rigid conventions concerning personal space. They maintained consistently varying degrees of space or distance between themselves and others depending upon the activities and people involved. It is as though each of us were surrounded by invisible zones or bubbles of space of varying diameters. Certain relationships and activities seem to be appropriate to certain zones. We are uncomfortable when people violate our sense of distance or space.

While observing white middle-class Americans, Hall identified four major distances. He says that *intimate distance* is between 0 inches and 18 inches. At this distance personal contact is easy. Lovemaking and comforting occur here but very little vocalizing. Usually only intimate acquaintances are welcomed in this zone. Hall's second space is 18 inches to 4 feet. He calls this *personal distance*. This is the distance in which acquaintances talk about personal topics. Nonpersonal business is conducted between 4 feet and 12 feet. Hall calls this *social distance*. Touch is not usually possible here; impersonal or business topics appear appropriate at this distance. Contact can easily be discontinued at this distance. Hall's last category is *public distance*, 14 feet or further. At this distance topics are usually impersonal and often formal. Communicators have very little personal involvement. Public figures such as ministers, judges, and public officials often maintain this distance from their respective audiences.

We must remember that Hall's study involved white middle-class Americans. Other studies indicate that people in different cultures tend to maintain different distances. People in many Mediterranean countries, for example, consistently maintain closer distances than do most North Americans. This preference in personal distance is one of the many reasons why people from different cultures sometimes have difficulty relating to one another. The important thing to remember is that we all have a sense of distance and become uncomfortable when it is violated. Some people even become violent. One study noted that nonviolent prisoners in a federal penitentiary remained comfortable when others were as close as 18 inches. For violent men the comfortable distance was 34 inches in front and 42 inches in the rear.

Several studies have examined the relation between distances and the character of personal relationships. Kenneth Little[19] found that friends interact more closely than acquaintances and that acquaintances interact more closely than nonacquaintances. We seem to give more space to people we perceive as having high status than we do to people we perceive as having low status. Furthermore, according to Mehrabian,[20] high-status people or supervisors seem to have more freedom to move close to subordinates than subordinates have to move close to supervisors. Space or distance, then, often provides a clue as to the relationship of people in a given situation.

This has been a sampling of some of the research that has been done in the area of proxemics. Other studies have been and are being conducted into the relation of space to sex, age, race, physical appearance, and physical setting.

Paralanguage

The study of paralanguage focuses on the effects of the voice apart from the words it transmits. The word *paralanguage,* then, refers to characteristics of vocalization; it does not refer to words themselves. You might have difficulty thinking of vocal characteristics as nonverbal indicators. How words are said, however, often transmits more meaning than the words themselves. To illustrate: read the following sentence three times. Each time emphasize the underlined word.

George hurried to her.
George hurried to her.
George hurried to her.

Significant vocal characteristics include such things as pitch (height or depth of tones on a musical scale), force (loudness of tones), duration (length of time tones are held or continued), rate (rapidity with which sounds are uttered), and quality (overall sound and timbre, the individuality of voice). These and other vocal characteristics combine to produce meaning

above and beyond the words that are involved. It has been said, for example, that Sarah Bernhardt, could recite nonsense syllables or the letters of the alphabet so as to move her listeners to a variety of emotions. Researchers have been interested in how vocal cues affect perception of personal characteristics, judgments of emotion, and judgments of personality.

Perception of Personal Characteristics We often base inferences about the personal characteristics of others partly on vocal cues. Surprisingly, researchers have found that we can often make fairly accurate inferences from vocal cues alone. For example, one researcher found that from vocal cues listeners could distinguish among people with less than a high school education, a high school education, and a college education. The same study found that listeners could distinguish among people from the eastern, southern, and general American dialect regions. It also revealed that listeners could differentiate between male and female, Black and Caucasian, large and small speakers, and speakers twenty years old and thirty years old, forty and fifty years old, and sixty and seventy years old.[21]

Leroy Harms[22] reports that listeners are amazingly accurate in perceiving social class or status from brief recorded vocal samples. Incidentally, in most studies of this kind, either speakers voice nonsense symbols or various devices are used to block out distinguishable words so that judgments are made on vocal characteristics alone. Several studies have focused on whether listeners can discern body types from vocal cues. The results of these studies are inconclusive, but they seem to indicate that extreme body types can be perceived from vocal cues.

Judgments of Emotion   A number of studies have been directed toward the communication of emotion through vocal cues. As you might expect, the literature generally indicates that vocal expression often communicates emotional meanings accurately. Certain vocal stereotypes seem to be associated with various emotions. For example, a fast rate and frequent pauses indicate anger. High pitch and a fast rate suggest fear. Long pauses and a slow rate suggest grief.

This is not to imply that judgments of emotion based on vocal characteristics are invariably accurate. Accuracy seems to depend on the sender, the receiver, and the emotion involved. Apparently, some emotions are easier to identify than others. Anger, hate, and joy, for example, seem to be fairly easy to recognize; pride, shame, and love, more difficult. The accuracy with which people send and receive emotional meaning via vocal cues depends upon their intelligence, general sensitivity, and experience with the expression of emotions.

Judgments of Personality   We seem to associate certain vocal characteristics with certain personality characteristics. Perhaps we learn these stereotypes from folk literature, movies, television, and similar sources. Studies indicate that (1) people do hold these stereotypes (judges have agreed considerably concerning personality characteristics and vocal cues) and (2) auditors make more accurate judgments about some personality characteristics than about others.

In one study speakers read uniform manuscripts to 600 people. Listeners could not see nor did they know the speakers. Audience members were asked to match personality data and photographs of people with the voices. Audience members tended to respond uniformly. They were most accurate in choosing age and general personality sketches. They were least accurate in matching individual personality traits and photographs with voices.[23]

David Addington[24] had somewhat similar results. He found that judges were most successful in rating the following characteristics: masculine–feminine, young–old, enthusiastic–apathetic, energetic–lazy, good-looking–ugly. They were least reliable in such matters as extraverted–introverted, honest–dishonest, law-abiding–criminal, and healthy–sickly.

Physical Appearance

The adage you can't tell a book by its cover may be true, but in this culture physical appearance appears to be a factor in communication. For example, Donn Byrne, Oliver London, and Keith Reeves report that physical attractiveness is an element in interpersonal attraction.[25] Children who are perceived to be attractive are punished less than children who are perceived to be unattractive. College students who are perceived to be attractive receive higher grades than do students who are perceived to be unattractive. Attractive adults receive better jobs and more promotions than unattractive adults do. Whereas favoring attractive people may seem to be grossly unfair, this tendency does seem to be the fact.

Fortunately, there are also mitigating

factors. Our perceptions about another person's attractiveness are influenced by our feelings toward that person. Standards of beauty change from time to time and from culture to culture. Additionally, attractiveness can be learned to a certain extent. People can learn how to walk, dress, and pose themselves attractively. They can also learn to adopt attractive facial expressions. Finally, it should be emphasized that physical attractiveness is only one of the many elements that contribute to one's desirability. Others are intelligence, disposition, talent, interests, and character traits.

One reason that physical appearance is an important nonverbal indicator is that people often react to stereotypes associated with particular attributes of physical appearance. For example, we judge people to be more intelligent when they wear spectacles. We perceive women with heavy lip makeup to be more sexually accessible than women with light lip makeup. Daniel Freedman tentatively suggests that a beard might make a man appear more masculine to a woman.[26]

Several studies have associated certain stereotypes with certain body types. For example, William Wells and Bertram Siegel[27] showed drawings of three basic body types to a group of adults. The subjects perceived endomorph types (fat, round) as older, lazier, more talkative, more sympathetic, and more dependent upon others. Mesomorph types (athletic, muscular, bony) were seen as more self-reliant, stronger, more adventuresome, and more mature. The ectomorph type (thin, frail) was rated as ambitious, tense, nervous, suspicious of others, more stubborn, and

more quiet. Although these stereotypes may be inaccurate, they frequently influence how we react to others and how they react to us.

Dress constitutes another element of physical appearance. The way we dress, probably because of stereotypes, seems to communicate something to others about the kind of people we are. This is especially true when we meet others for the first time. The work of Thomas Hoult[28] in this area would indicate that, once we get to know people, we are less likely to be influenced by their dress. Leonard Bickman[29] conducted another interesting experiment in the same area. As subjects he used 206 people using phone booths. Aiding in his study were both male and female confidants. Some of these aides were dressed in high-status fashion and some were dressed in low-status fashion. For example, high-status men wore suits and ties, and low-status men wore work clothes. High-status women wore fashionable dresses, and low-status women wore shabby skirts and blouses. In every case, a dime was left in a phone booth. Shortly after a subject had entered the booth, one of the aides would approach and state that she or he had left a dime in the booth. Seventy-five percent of the subjects who were approached by a confederate dressed in a high-status manner returned the dime. Thirty-eight percent of the subjects approached by a confederate dressed in a low-status manner returned the dime. Monroe Lefkowitz, Robert Blake, and Jane Mouton[30] conducted a similar experiment in which they found that people dressed in high-status clothes were more influential in getting others to jaywalk than people dressed in low-status clothes were. Clothes and general personal appearance, then, do seem to make a difference.

We have been considering some important nonverbal indicators. We have noted some research concerning posture and gesture, facial expressions, eye behavior, space, paralanguage, and physical appearance. Other nonverbal indicators include lighting, color, architecture, odor, and touch. Let's turn our attention next to a way of classifying nonverbal cues.

Classifying Nonverbal Cues

When you were in elementary school or junior high, you studied the parts of speech. As you learned to make distinctions between nouns, verbs, and adjectives, you were learning a classification system—a system for classifying elements of our verbal language. No such thorough system for classifying nonverbal elements has yet been developed. Some beginnings have been made, however. We will consider a system developed by Ekman and Friesen.[31] An understanding of this system will help you appreciate the several ways that nonverbal acts contribute to the total communication process. This system is composed of five categories: emblems, illustrators, affect displays, regulators, and adaptors.

Emblems

Emblems are nonverbal acts that have a rather specific and generally understood meaning within a culture or subculture. They can be directly translated into words. They are usually consciously displayed. The fingers spread in a V for peace or for victory, depending on your generation, is an example. The sign language of the deaf and the signals used by officials during football games are other examples. People frequently employ emblems when verbal communication is impossible or impractical.

Illustrators

Illustrators are nonverbal acts used in conjunction with verbal speech in much the way that printed illustrations are used with written communication. They can repeat, substitute for, contradict, or augment spoken communication. They directly relate to and illustrate that which is being said verbally. When you spread your hands to show how long the fish was that got away or when you use your body to illustrate a dance step, you are using an illustrator. We are usually somewhat conscious of using illustrators when we use them but not to the extent that we are conscious of using emblems. Sometimes, in the excitement of conversation, we use illustrators without thinking about them.

Affect Displays

As used in this context, affect means emotion. Affect displays are usually facial expressions that display emotional states. Other parts of the body, however, are sometimes involved. Sometimes we are aware of these displays and sometimes we are not. Affect displays can be connected to the verbal message or they can be un-related to it. They can reinforce the verbal message or they can contradict it. When your face and body register fear, anger, joy, or disappointment, you are display-ing affect. Sometimes we are aware of affect displays and sometimes we are not.

Regulators

Regulators are like traffic signals; they help direct the flow of conversation. They say such things as: *please speak louder, explain that please, hurry up, would you repeat that, I want to talk now.* Regulators consist of eye movements, facial expressions, head nods, hand and arm gestures, posture shifts. We frequently use regulators without being aware of them.

Adaptors

Adaptors are less clearly defined than the other categories we have been discussing. They are fragmented, incomplete holdovers from movements learned in childhood. It is speculated that in childhood we learn cer-tain movements in order to adapt to prevail-ing conditions. These become habitual and emerge in adulthood as partial, incomplete, almost meaningless movements. Some rest-less movements of the feet and hands may fall into this category. These are uncon-scious movements, and usually neither the observer nor the observed understands them. They seem to have no significant communication function.

In review, most nonverbal behavior falls into one of the following categories: emblems, illustrators, affect displays, regu-lators, or adaptors.

In this section of the chapter we have considered the importance of nonverbal communication, some difficulties with in-terpretation, some nonverbal indicators, and a system for classifying nonverbal acts.

Key Ideas in Review

☐ In many communication situations the non-verbal components carry a high percentage of the meaning.

☐ Although we sometimes consider verbal and nonverbal communication separately for convenience of study, in the final analysis they should be treated as inseparable parts of the total communication process.

☐ We should exercise caution when interpreting the nonverbal aspects of a message because as yet we are unable to assign specific and standard meanings to most of them. (In the next chapter we will learn that the same caution is advised for verbal message components.)

☐ There is a great variety of nonverbal phenomena.

☐ Some nonverbal indicators that influence many everyday situations are body orientation and gesture, facial expression, eye behavior, the use of personal space, paralanguage, physical appearance, and dress.

☐ Most nonverbal acts can be placed in one of the following categories: emblems, illustrators, affect displays, regulators, adaptors.

Section B

Person-to-Group Focus

Thy actions to thy words accord.

John Milton

Nonverbal cues are as important in the person-to-group situation as in any other situation. Frequently speakers and listeners are not well known to one another in such situations, and usually opportunities for verbal interchange, questions, and clarification are limited. Consequently, nonverbal elements often take on added importance. In this section of the chapter we will discuss some aspects of nonverbal communication that are usually relevant in person-to-group settings. Specifically, we will consider some ways that the verbal and the nonverbal aspects of the speaker's message combine to create a total impression, we will consider some audible elements, we will discuss the picture that the speaker presents, and finally we will note the importance of the nonverbal messages that audiences send to speakers.

Verbal and Nonverbal Components Work Together

As we noted in Section A, verbal and nonverbal cues usually intermix to produce the total message effect. Nowhere is this seen more clearly than in person-to-group speaking. Ekman suggests several different rela-

tionships that can exist between the speaker's verbal and nonverbal behaviors.[32]

Repeating

Sometimes with nonverbal behavior the speaker simply repeats what has been said verbally. For example, let's say you tell your listeners that the best way to grip a tennis racket is to pretend to shake hands with it. Then you pick up a tennis racket and demonstrate. Your nonverbal behavior is repeating your verbal behavior. This kind of repetition is often extremely helpful to listeners.

Substituting

Sometimes nonverbal behavior substitutes for verbal behavior. When a speaker raises both hands for quiet, this nonverbal act may be substituting for a verbal request. When a teacher smiles and nods to a student who has just answered a question, the gesture may be a substitute for the words "Thank you, that was a very good answer." Often speakers refrain from saying, "Hey! I feel great about this idea," but their facial expressions and general body movement substitute for those words.

Contradicting

Unfortunately, sometimes the speaker's verbal and nonverbal behaviors are contradictory. For example, when a speaker verbally says, "This is a matter of grave importance, we should all be vitally interested

Listeners as well as speakers send nonverbal messages.

in it," but with posture, facial expressions, and other nonverbal means says, "Ho-hum, I can't get very excited about this," listeners are presented with conflicting messages. A further example is provided by the speaker whose words say, "I am delighted with the chance to talk to you today," but whose body language says, "I would rather be almost any place but here." Some research indicates that when listeners are confronted with conflicting messages of this kind, they tend to believe the nonverbal messages.[33] Regardless of how listeners resolve conflicts between verbal and nonverbal cues, their perception of those conflicts creates considerable confusion and doubt concerning the speaker's total message.

Complementing

Sometimes nonverbal behavior complements or amplifies the speaker's verbal message. In many respects, complementing is the opposite of contradicting. For exam-

ple, the speaker says, "I feel a deep loss at his passing" and the speaker's body registers this feeling of personal loss. Or another speaker says, "I am really happy to be able to show you this product" and the speaker's body reflects this great pride in the product. Then the verbal and nonverbal elements are complementary.

Accenting

Sometimes nonverbal acts serve as exclamation points—they accent parts of the speaker's verbal message. Often when a speaker makes a fist, snaps fingers together, pounds the rostrum, or stamps a foot, it is to accent a point.

Regulating

In interpersonal situations, nonverbal acts frequently regulate the back and forth flow of the conversation. A nod of the head, a shift in posture, a quizzical look, a change in eye contact are often signals. They show that it is someone else's turn to speak, that the speaker has not been understood, or that the listeners are not interested. In person-to-group settings, nonverbal acts often serve a similar function. For example, a speaker frequently signals readiness to begin a speech with a gesture or a nod or an appropriate facial expression. Speakers often signify the end of the speech by similar means. During question and answer periods speakers often recognize audience members by pointing or smiling and nodding. Furthermore, nonverbal acts often serve a kind of regulating function during the speech itself. Speakers frequently use some movement or gesture to indicate that they are going from one part of the speech to another. In other words, transitions can be indicated physically as well as verbally. Experienced speakers usually reinforce verbal transitions with some kind of movement.

Audience members, of course, also use nonverbal acts to indicate agreement or disagreement, understanding or lack of understanding, interest or lack of interest. We are going to talk more extensively about how audiences communicate nonverbally with speakers later in this chapter.

Thus far we have noticed that nonverbal statements work with verbal statements to produce the total message effect. Sometimes nonverbal elements repeat, substitute for, contradict, complement, accent, and regulate verbal elements. Now that we have noticed some of the ways in which nonverbal messages intermix with verbal messages, let's turn our attention to some nonverbal indicators that influence this process.

Audible Elements

As we noted in Section A, the audible aspects of speech, minus words, are considered to be nonverbal elements. Sometimes how we say words is more important than the words themselves. In person-to-group settings these audible, nonverbal aspects have been studied primarily in connection with comprehension, retention, and persuasion.

Considerable research data indicates that vocal variety is significant in increasing audience comprehension and retention.[34] Other data implies that relatively poor vocal quality and even "nonfluencies" have little effect on comprehension. These characteristics, however, may affect listener perception of speaker personality. Apparently, listeners are quite adaptable in respect to comprehension. Studies in rate indicate that listeners can comprehend a wide range of speech rates. The average speaker speaks at an average rate of between 120 and 140 words a minute. Comprehension does not seem to fall until the rate approaches 225 words a minute.

Research into the relationship between vocal cues and persuasion suggests that vocal characteristics are important to persuasion. Mehrabian and Williams[35] found that increased intonation, increased volume, increased rate, and less halting speech enhanced persuasiveness. Some studies indicate that so-called good vocal delivery encourages positive judgments concerning speakers' credibility. Barnett Pearce and Forrest Conklin,[36] for example, were able to relate vocal cues to judgments about trustworthiness and likeableness but not competence. The conversational style of delivery receives higher ratings on such things as honesty and trustworthiness than the more oratorical styles of delivery do.

Important elements of the auditory code include force, pitch, rate, and quality. Let's discuss each of these briefly.

Force

Force or volume is determined by the energy of the sound waves. It is important that speakers adjust volume to the circumstances. Obviously, if the speaker doesn't use enough volume, listeners won't be able to hear the message. On the other hand, too much volume is distracting and it may cause listeners to withdraw psychologically if not physically. Volume should not be forced. People don't like to be shouted at. For many people excessive volume has unpleasant associations, such as anger and loss of control. Incidentally, there are some indications that lowering the volume is more effective for emphasis than is raising the volume. As we noted earlier, variety in delivery increases comprehension and retention. This observation applies to volume as well as to the other elements of the vocal code.

Pitch

Pitch involves the placement of the voice on a musical scale. Every voice has a normal pitch level. It is determined by the length and thickness of the vocal folds. Optimum pitch varies greatly from person to person. To find your own optimum, strike notes on a piano until you locate a note that corresponds with the normal pitch level of your voice. Now, still matching your voice with notes from the piano, work up the scale until you reach the highest pitch you can achieve without straining. Next, work down the scale in the same manner until you reach the lowest pitch you can achieve without straining. The highest and lowest levels outline your pitch range. Your optimum pitch should be three or four notes above your lowest pitch. If your habitual pitch level is significantly different from

your optimum, you should make a conscious effort to adjust your pitch so that it more closely coincides with the optimum pitch. If you strain to reach an unnatural pitch, you can injure the vocal folds. Vocal nodes sometimes develop when people consistently use an unnatural pitch. Nevertheless, most of us possess a greater pitch range than we utilize. Sometimes speakers fall into a pitch rut. Appropriate variations in pitch help listeners comprehend and retain material. Variations in pitch also stimulate attention.

Rate

Rate is the speed at which sounds are uttered. Modern studies indicate that people can comprehend speech at a greater range of rates than was first believed. Studies indicate that, within a range of 100 to 225 words per minute, there is no significant difference in comprehension or retention. Speakers are advised to achieve variety with rate as well as with the other aspects of the audible code.

Quality

Quality refers to the overall sound and timbre of the voice. It is the distinctive and individual property that enables us to distinguish between voices. A voice with good quality is pleasant, rich, and resonant. Several common defects in quality occur. The nasal voice results from too much resonance in the nasal cavities. Conversely, the denasal voice results from too little nasal resonance. The muffled voice comes from too much resonance in the throat cavity. The hoarse or husky voice usually results from an overly tense vocal mechanism. A breathy voice carries the sound of breath in addition to the vocal tones. Specific defects such as these should be treated by a speech therapist. According to Kenneth Andersen, a pleasant voice doesn't affect comprehension when the material is simple; however, "When material is difficult to comprehend, those people who are judged more effective in the use of voice gain an advantage in comprehension."[37]

We have considered some audible nonverbal elements that are relevant in person-to-group settings. Let's turn our attention next to some important visual elements.

Important Aspects of the Picture

In a sense, speakers are like television sets—they present both sound and picture. In most person-to-group situations, listeners see as well as hear the speaker.

That we communicate something with the pictures we present is almost inescapable. Any time someone is watching us we are saying something with our bodies whether we want to or not. As William Brooks states, "All observed behavior has message value. Behavior has no opposite. There is no such thing as nonbehavior. Hence it follows that one cannot avoid communicating. One can avoid communicating verbally, but nonverbal communication cannot be avoided."[38] Before we discuss specific aspects of the picture that the speaker presents, let's consider

some general suggestions for improving that picture.

General Suggestions

Using the body effectively in communication is not difficult because it is perfectly natural. Most people use the body effectively in informal communication every day. But this tendency is sometimes inhibited in more formal person-to-group situations. Usually, however, people become somewhat accustomed to speaking before an audience. When they do and their desire to communicate is great enough, effective nonverbal communication occurs spontaneously. It grows from the situation and the desire to communicate. The first and most important suggestion, then, for improving the picture is *to concentrate on communicating your message to your listeners.* When you do, effective bodily action or nonverbal behavior usually takes care of itself. Problems, however, sometimes develop. It is appropriate, therefore, to consider these suggestions:

Physical Behavior Should Be Appropriate First of all physical behavior should be appropriate to the message. As we noted earlier, contradictory verbal and nonverbal cues make listeners confused and doubtful. When your words are "I have always been interested in this subject," but your body says that you are not interested, your listeners don't know what to believe. However, they are most apt to believe your body.

Physical behavior should also be appropriate to the speaker. Bodily action that is natural for someone else may not be appropriate for you. Try to refrain from imitating the movements of other speakers. Do what is appropriate for you.

Finally, physical behavior should be appropriate to the audience and the setting. Expansive movements and gestures that would be appropriate before a large audience in a large auditorium might seem exaggerated in more intimate circumstances.

Physical Behavior Should Be Natural   To be effective physical activity should be natural. It should grow spontaneously out of the speaker's desire to communicate. Gestures and movements that seem forced are artificial and distracting. For this reason, you probably should not rehearse specific gestures and movements in connection with a particular speech. It is desirable to use bodily activity while rehearsing, but it is usually advisable to refrain from planning and memorizing specific gestures, expressions, and movements for specific places in the speech. Memorized gestures and movements seldom seem natural.

Physical Behavior Should Be Varied   If physical behavior is not varied, it becomes repetitious and distracting. It is appropriate to move about in front of the audience, but to move back and forth continuously is distracting. It is appropriate to move your hands when you speak, but to move them continuously in the same fashion is distracting. No one will notice if you scratch your head once or twice during the speech, but to scratch continuously would be dis-

tracting. Bodily activity, then, should be varied if it is to be effective.

We have noted that it is natural to use the body in communication. When speakers are concentrating on communicating their messages, effective bodily action often occurs spontaneously. Bodily action should be appropriate, natural, and varied. Let's look now at some specific aspects of the picture that the speaker presents.

Posture

Posture is an important part of the picture. It often is perceived to indicate the speaker's attitude toward the audience and the subject. Your posture, then, should indicate that you are comfortable, alert, confident, and interested. To accomplish this, try to avoid extremes. Don't stand or sit at rigid attention, and don't slouch excessively. Posture should not call attention to itself; it should be unforced and natural. Posture that is natural for someone else may not be appropriate for you.

Posture must also be appropriate to the message and the occasion. More formal settings call for more sedate and formal posture. Less formal settings allow posture to be more relaxed and informal. Posture should not contradict the message. If you are trying to impress your listeners with the seriousness of a matter, your posture should reflect that attitude. If your message is lighter and chatty, your posture can be more informal. Remember also that posture should be varied. It should change as the mood and the message changes. Don't be afraid to shift position from time to time.

Avoid appearing to be rooted in one position during the entire speech.

Gestures

Gestures are usually considered to be movements of the head, shoulder, torso, arms, and hands. These movements often prove to be valuable visual aids. Gestures can be used to amplify, emphasize, clarify, repeat, and in some cases substitute for the verbal message. Most people use gestures extensively every day. To be effective, gestures too must be natural, appropriate, and varied. For example, large and expansive gestures appropriate for a large audience in a large auditorium would be inappropriate for a smaller audience in a smaller setting, gestures appropriate for a pep talk would be inappropriate for a memorial service, and gestures appropriate for some people might not be appropriate for others.

Gestures should never call attention to themselves. The speaker should consider them not as separate phenomena but as an integral part of the message. The most effective gestures grow naturally out of the speaker's impulse to communicate. A gesture made for its own sake usually calls attention to itself and is distracting. For this reason, you should not memorize specific gestures for insertion at specific points in the speech. In the classroom or in private it is often desirable to practice exercises and movements in order to reduce physical inhibitions and to cultivate the use of gestures. In actual speaking situations, however, memorized gestures usually seem artificial.

Gestures should also convey meaning—they should not be aimless. Sometimes speakers "saw the air" with random and repetitious gestures. Such motions usually result from tension and they are distracting. Gestures, then, should emerge naturally from your desire to communicate, but you should discipline them to the point that they have meaning. With effective gestures speakers clarify, amplify, and explain.

Movement

Speakers should try to avoid extremes in movement. The speaker who stands rooted in one spot throughout the speech appears

". . . third word . . . two syllables . . . table . . . sounds like table . . . stable . . . ."

almost as unnatural and is almost as distracting as the speaker who paces back and forth. Generally, it is desirable for speakers to vary their positions on the platform from time to time. Movement, like gestures, should never be forced. It should grow naturally from the speaker's desire to communicate. Also like gestures, movement should be meaningful. It should never be aimless or repetitive. Natural, controlled movement not only promotes interest through visual variety, but it helps to communicate meaning as well.

Speakers frequently use movement to indicate a shift in mood or content. For example, it can amplify and emphasize verbal transitions. At points of transition speakers often pause and move to another part of the platform before beginning the next point. Some speakers simply move to one side of the speaker's stand, others move several feet, and some shift their positions only slightly. You must do what is natural for you. Generally, movement should be relaxed, comfortable, and confident.

Facial Expressions

A smile and a pleasant expression of goodwill and interest will usually put listeners at ease and establish rapport. As we observed in Section A, some authorities believe that the face is especially expressive of mood and feelings. We also observed that some evidence indicates that some facial expressions have cross-cultural or universal meaning. It is probably natural, then, that listeners frequently look to the speaker's face for evidence of attitude or feeling. When the speaker's face contradicts the verbal message, listeners are more apt to believe the face than the words. You should have no difficulty with appropriate facial expressions as long as your speech reflects your real attitudes and beliefs. If you try to mislead your audience, your face may betray you.

Eye Contact

As we noted in Section A, eye contact is important for indicating that channels of communication are open. When we establish eye contact with someone, we signal a desire to relate, to be involved, to communicate. By avoiding eye contact, we indicate a desire to disassociate ourselves from others. Is it any wonder, then, that eye contact is one of the most important links between the speaker and the audience?

Eye contact holds attention, and it facilitates the feeling of personal involvement between the speaker and the listeners. Obviously, most of the time you won't be able to maintain eye contact with everyone in the audience. You should, however, distribute your eye contact throughout the audience. When you spend most of your time talking to one section of the group, people in other sections may feel excluded. Eye contact should be maintained throughout the speech. Because speakers are preoccupied with notes or visual aids or the microphone, they sometimes neglect eye contact at the start of the speech. This is particularly unfortunate. Try to establish eye contact before you begin talking. Before your listeners "tune you out," tell them with your eyes that you want to become involved and want to talk to them personally and directly.

Personal Appearance

As we indicated earlier, although it may seem unfair, dress and general appearance do influence how others respond to us. For example, employment counselors report that one of the most frequent reasons for failure in job interviews is that people fail to dress and groom themselves appropriately. As you will recall, experimentation indicates that dress and physical appearance are more influential before people become acquainted than afterward.

In person-to-group communication situations, where speakers and listeners are often not well known to one another, personal appearance is particularly important. Whether you like it or not, your appearance will say something to listeners above and beyond what you say with words. This is because people have stereotypes concerning certain attributes of personal appearance. Try, then, to avoid extremes in makeup, fashion, or jewelry. Try to dress appropriately for yourself, the audience, and the occasion—avoid dressing up or dressing down. Any aspect of your clothing or makeup or hairdo that calls attention to itself can distract from and compete with your message. Remember, how listeners judge you as a person will determine to a degree how they receive your ideas. Furthermore, their opinion of you will depend partly on the impression they receive from your personal appearance. Personal ap-

pearance, then, is an important part of the picture you present to listeners.

Mannerisms

Unfortunately, annoying mannerisms can sometimes enter the picture that speakers present. Any physical activity that clashes with the speaker's message or is repeated until it distracts can be classified as an annoying mannerism. Following are some typical mannerisms:

> pacing back and forth
>
> rubbing hands together
>
> scratching the nose or head
>
> jingling keys
>
> staring vacantly at the floor or out a window
>
> rocking back and forth
>
> tugging at an item of clothing

Usually speakers who are guilty of such mannerisms are not aware of their action. Your speech class offers an ideal place for you to learn about mannerisms of your own that might be annoying. Once you are aware of such mannerisms, you can discard them with conscious effort.

In review, we have observed that, when speakers are concentrating on communicating an important message, physical activity usually occurs spontaneously. Bodily activity should be appropriate, natural, and varied. We discussed posture, gestures, movement, facial expression, eye contact, personal appearance, and mannerisms as parts of the picture that speakers present to listeners. In the final paragraphs of this chapter, let's consider the importance of the nonverbal messages that audiences send to speakers.

Audiences Communicate Nonverbally with Speakers

Real communication is a dynamic, two-way transaction. Listeners as well as speakers simultaneously send and receive messages. For the most part, in person-to-group situations audience members send messages to the speaker with nonverbal cues. These cues do or should have a vital effect on the speaker's message.

Earlier we noted that nonverbal acts often serve as regulators. They sometimes regulate the pace and direction of communication. For example, in interpersonal settings a shift in posture, a puzzled expression, or a nod of the head can indicate that the listener is restless, or does not understand, or is in agreement or disagreement with the speaker. In person-to-group situations the bodily actions of audience members serve much the same purpose. Sensitive speakers search for and respond to this important feedback. As Theodore Clevenger states, "Much of the presumed audience control of skillful public speakers resides not so much in their ability to manipulate audiences as in their adroitness at fitting speeches to ongoing behavioral patterns and tendencies in the audience."[39]

It is not difficult to respond to audience feedback. When listeners indicate by cupping their hands to their ears that they can't hear, you can ask them to move closer, or you can speak more loudly, or you can turn up the public address system. When puzzled facial expressions indicate that you have failed to make yourself clear, you can back up and explain the matter differently. When toward the end of your speech you note that your listeners are becoming restless, you can work toward a swift and graceful conclusion. In reacting to audience feedback, you must be careful not to overreact. Nor should you generalize about the entire audience from the actions of two or three listeners. However, to ignore audience feedback is to ignore the personal interaction that makes face-to-face communication exciting.

In this section of the chapter, we considered ways in which verbal and nonverbal cues work together, we noted some aspects of the audible code, we talked about the picture that speakers present to listeners, and we discussed the nonverbal messages that audiences send to speakers.

Key Ideas in Review

☐ In person-to-group communication settings, verbal and nonverbal cues interact to produce the overall message.

☐ Sometimes nonverbal elements repeat, substitute for, contradict, complement, accent, and regulate the verbal elements.

☐ Sometimes how we say words is as important as the words themselves.

☐ It is natural to use the body when communicating.

☐ When people are concentrating on communicating messages, effective bodily action often occurs spontaneously.

☐ Physical activity should be appropriate, natural, and varied.

☐ Important parts of the picture that speakers present to listeners are posture, gesture, movement, facial expressions, eye contact, personal appearance, and mannerisms.

☐ Audience members often send important nonverbal messages to speakers.

Suggested Assignments

Integrated Assignments

The assignments presented in this section are designed to help you further explore the subject matter presented in Section A, while you are utilizing the ideas presented in Section B. In a well-organized, well-supported speech, utilize all the suggestions for improved communication that your class has considered thus far. Try your best to reflect what you have learned about nonverbal communication as it applies to person-to-group speech. Select or adapt your topic from one of the following:

Speech Topics

1. Section A presented a limited sampling of research that has been done in some areas of nonverbal communication. Go beyond the chapter. Select and research a nonverbal component such as architecture, color, furniture arrangement, or territoriality. In a well-organized speech present your findings to the class.

2. Describe a well-developed system of nonverbal communication such as the sign language used by the deaf, the signals used by football officials, the signs used in baseball, or the signals used by television and radio directors.

3. Pick another culture and talk about how its people use nonverbal symbols. Talk about such things as color, ornaments, personal space, gestures, and facial expressions.

4. Observe a number of interpersonal transactions. Analyze them for the influence of non-

verbal factors. Report your observations to the class.

5. On your campus or in some other public place, spend a few hours watching people. From your observations learn what you can about the relationship of nonverbal elements to courtship, status, self-esteem, mood, occupation, the attitudes of people toward one another, and so forth. Organize your observations and tell the class about them. Use specific examples. If you are a camera buff, photographs would be helpful.

6. Conduct an experiment with some aspect of nonverbal communication. For example, experiment by manipulating the personal space of others, or by wearing unusual clothes in different situations. Explain your experiment and interpret the results for the class.

7. In a park or some other public place, observe three or four people separately. Take notes and, on the basis of nonverbal cues only, write a one-paragraph biography of each person. From her or his posture, clothing, physical appearance, facial expressions, gestures, and other nonverbal cues, speculate about the person's occupation, mood, interests, marital status, age, place of birth, and so forth. If possible, after quickly writing each biography introduce yourself to the subject and check on its accuracy. Report about these experiments to the class.

8. Select one or more common emotions such as anger, boredom, fear, or happiness. Explain and demonstrate several of the ways in which the emotion or emotions can be displayed nonverbally. Consider such things as color, lighting, and furniture arrangement as well as gestures, postures, and facial expressions.

9. Explain what several different environments communicate to you nonverbally. For exam-

ple, talk about the effects of various classrooms, retail outlets, homes, and offices.

10. Through actual experience discover the limits of your personal space or distance bubbles. How much space do you need to keep between yourself and others in various circumstances? Explain and illustrate for the class.

Auxiliary Assignments

Interpersonal Focus

1. The class is divided into five groups. Each group selects as the setting for a role-playing scene one of the following: a park bench, the college library, the college cafeteria, the office of the president, a busy streetcorner, a neighborhood bar, a fashionable restaurant, a busy department store. Without using words each group will present a role-playing scene illustrating nonverbal communication appropriate to the selected setting. A wide variety of nonverbal cues should be illustrated.

2. The class is divided into groups of four or five. Group members exchange the impressions they had of one another when the course began. Comments should be confined to impressions derived from nonverbal cues.

3. A chair is placed in front of the class. Each class member in turn goes to the chair and sits in it for a few moments. No two class members can sit in exactly the same way, and consequently each class member should communicate something different to the class by the way he or she uses the chair.

4. Each class member tells a short story to the class twice. The story can be a joke, a proverb, a parable, or something similarly short. The first time through the storyteller will use pantomime only. The second time the storyteller will use both words and action.

5. This exercise is accomplished in three stages. First, class members list on a piece of paper five or six nonverbal behaviors they feel are typical of themselves. Secondly, the class divides into groups of four or five and group members list nonverbal behaviors they feel are characteristic of other members of the group. Finally, the lists are compared and discussed.

Person-to-Group Focus

1. Give an action speech in which you demonstrate how to do something. Pick a topic that will require lots of bodily activity. Sample topics are: how to swing a tennis racket, how to square dance, how to shoot baskets with a basketball.

2. To reduce physical inhibitions and to become accustomed to moving about on the speaker's platform, give a short pantomimic scene to the class. The scene should be filled with physical activity. Each scene should be complete; that is, it should have a beginning, a middle, and an end.

3. Give a speech about how public speakers utilize bodily activity. Demonstrate different kinds of annoying mannerisms, different styles of gesture and movement, and so forth.

4. In a class discussion, with the help of your classmates and teacher, list the annoying physical mannerisms of which you are guilty. In future speeches do your best to eliminate those physical distractions.

5. Give a speech on any suitable topic. Try to reflect everything you have learned thus far about communication. Use nonverbal cues to support your verbal behavior. Be sure your bodily action is appropriate, natural, and varied.

Suggested Readings

Interpersonal Focus

Hall, Edward T. *The Hidden Dimension*. Garden City, N.Y.: Doubleday, 1969. Hall has been a pioneer in the study of proxemics, and this easy-to-read book provides a good survey of the field. It includes chapters on how different cultures handle space.

Knapp, Mark L. *Nonverbal Communication in Human Interaction*. New York: Holt, Rinehart & Winston, 1972. A very readable, comprehensive treatment of nonverbal communication. A fine summary of research in most areas of nonverbal study. Highly recommended for both the beginning and advanced student.

Montagu, Ashley. *Touching: The Human Significance of the Skin*. New York: Columbia University Press, 1971. A fascinating book about the importance of touch, especially in childhood. A must for parents of small children.

Person-to-Group Focus

Bormann, Ernest G., and Bormann, Nancy C. *Speech Communication: An Interpersonal Approach*. New York: Harper & Row Publishers, 1972, pp. 62–98. How to improve nonverbal communication in person-to-group situations through vocal emphasis and body language is the subject of these two chapters. Easy reading level, appropriate for the beginning student.

Ross, Raymond S. *Speech Communication: Fundamentals and Practice*. 4th ed. Englewood Cliffs, N.J.: Prentice-Hall, 1977, pp. 128–

39. An easy-to-read chapter on body language as it applies to person-to-group communication.

Note Directory

1. Albert Mehrabian, *Silent Messages* (Belmont, Calif.: Wadsworth Publishing Co., 1971), p. 44.

2. Mark L. Knapp, *Nonverbal Communication in Human Interaction* (New York: Holt, Rinehart & Winston, 1972), p. 3.

3. Ibid., pp. 8–9.

4. Mario Andrew Pei, *The Story of Language* (Philadelphia: J. B. Lippincott Co., 1949), p. 13.

5. Irving J. Lee, *Language Habits in Human Affairs: An Introduction to General Semantics* (New York: Harper & Row Publishers, 1941), pp. 91–92.

6. Lester Kirkendall, "Semantics and Sexual Communication," in *Communication Vibrations,* ed. Larry L. Barker (Englewood Cliffs, N.J.: Prentice-Hall, 1974), p. 45.

7. Frank E. X. Dance, "Toward a Theory of Human Communication," in *Human Communication Theory: Original Essays,* ed. Frank E. X. Dance (New York: Holt, Rinehart & Winston, 1967), p. 290.

8. Albert E. Scheflen, "Quasi-Courtship Behavior in Psychotherapy," *Psychiatry* 28, no. 3 (August 1965): 245–57.

9. Albert Mehrabian, "Significance of Posture and Position in the Communication of Attitude and Status Relationships," *Psychological Bulletin* 71, no. 5 (May 1969):359–72.

10. Michael Argyle, "Non-Verbal Communication in Human Social Interaction," in *Non-Verbal Communication,* ed. Robert A. Hinde (Cambridge: Cambridge University Press, 1972), p. 247.

11. Paul Ekman, "Differential Communication of Affect by Head and Body Cues," *Journal of Personality and Social Psychology* (1965):726–35.

12. Paul Ekman and Wallace V. Friesen, "Constants across Cultures in the Face and Emotion," *Journal of Personality and Social Psychology* 17, no. 2 (February 1971): 124–29.

13. Thomas M. Stritch and Paul F. Secord, "Interaction Effects in the Perception of Faces," *Journal of Personality* 24, no. 3 (March 1956):272–84.

14. Ernest A. Haggard and Kenneth Isaacs, "Micromomentary Facial Expressions as Indicators of Ego Mechanisms in Psychotherapy," in *Methods of Research in Psychotherapy,* ed. Louis A. Gottschalk and Arthur H. Auerbach (New York: Appleton-Century-Crofts, 1966), pp. 154–65.

15. Christopher Brannigan and David Humphries, "I See What You Mean—," *New Scientist* 42, no. 650 (22 May 1969):406–08.

16. H. T. Moore and A. R. Gilliland, "The Measure of Aggressiveness," *Journal of Applied Psychology* 5, no. 2 (June 1921):101–02.

17. Eckhard H. Hess and James M. Polt, "Pupil Size as Related to Interest Value of Visual Stimuli," *Science* 132, no. 3423 (5 August 1960):349–50.

18. Edward T. Hall, *The Hidden Dimension* (Garden City, N. Y.: Doubleday, 1966), pp. 116–25.

19. Kenneth B. Little, "Cultural Variations in Social Schemata," *Journal of Personality and Social Psychology* 10, no. 1 (September, 1968):5.

20. Mehrabian, "Significance of Posture and Position," pp. 359–72.

21. G. P. Nerbonne, "The Identification of Speaker Characteristics on the Basis of Aural Cues," Knapp, *Nonverbal Communication,* p. 155.

22. Leroy S. Harms, "Listener Judgements of Status Cues in Speech," *Quarterly Journal of Speech* 47, no. 2 (April 1961):164–68.

23. Gordon W. Allport and H. Cantril, "Judging Personality From Voice," *Journal of Social Psychology* 5, no. 1 (February 1934):37–55.

24. David W. Addington, "The Relationship of Selected Vocal Characteristics to Personality Perception," *Speech Monographs* 35, no. 4 (November 1968): 492–503.

25. Donn Byrne, Oliver London, and Keith Reeves, "The Effects of Physical Attractiveness, Sex and Attitude Similarity on Interpersonal Attraction," *Journal of Personality* 36, no. 2 (June 1968):259–71.

26. Daniel G. Freedman, "The Survival Value of a Beard," *Psychology Today* 3, no. 5 (October 1969): 36–39.

27. William D. Wells and Bertram Siegel, "Stereotyped Sematotypes," *Psychological Reports* 8, no. 1 (February 1961):77–78.

28. Thomas F. Hoult, "Experimental Measurement of Clothing as a Factor in Some Social Ratings of Selected American Men," *American Sociological Review* 19, no. 3 (June 1954):324–28.

29. Leonard Bickman, "Social Roles and Uniforms: Clothes Make the Person," *Psychology Today* 7, no. 11 (April 1974):49–51

30. Monroe Lefkowitz et al., "Status Factors in Pedestrian Violation of Traffic Signals," *Journal of Abnormal and Social Psychology* 51, no. 3 (November 1955): 704–06.

31. Paul Ekman and Wallace V. Friesen, "The Repertoire of Nonverbal Behavior: Categories, Origins, Usage, and Coding," *Semiotica* 1 (1969):49–98.

32. Paul Ekman, "Communication through Nonverbal Behavior: A Source of Information about an Interpersonal Relationship," in *Affect, Cognition and Personality,* ed. Silvan S. Tomkins and Carroll E. Izard (New York: Springer Publishing Co., 1965), pp. 440–41.

33. Mehrabian, *Silent Messages,* pp. 40–56.

34. Knapp, *Nonverbal Communication,* pp. 165–66.

35. Albert Mehrabian and Martin Williams, "Nonverbal Concomitants of Perceived and Intended Persuasiveness," *Journal of Personality and Social Psychology* 13, no. 1 (September 1969): 37–58.

36. W. Barnett Pearce and Forrest Conklin, "Nonverbal Vocalic Communication and Perceptions of a Speaker," *Speech Monographs* 38, no. 3 (August 1971): 235–41.

37. Kenneth E. Andersen, *Introduction to Communication Theory and Practice* (Menlo Park, Calif.: Cummings Publishing Co., 1972), p. 153.

38. William D. Brooks, *Speech Communication* (Dubuque, Iowa: William C. Brown Co., 1971), p. 176.

39. Theodore Clevenger, *Audience Analysis* (New York: Bobbs-Merrill, 1966), p. 7.

Chapter Ten

Verbal Communication

In this chapter we will be concerned with some verbal language variables and how they affect communication. In Section A we will note some characteristics of verbal language and language usage that often contributes to communication confusion. In Section B we will concentrate on some positive language practices and how they apply in person-to-group situations.

Section A: Interpersonal Focus

Our words are important: a discussion of some semantic concepts.

■ Word magic ■ meanings are in people ■ bypassing ■ observations and inferences

Section B: Person-to-Group Focus

The speechmaker uses words: a discussion of language usage in speechmaking.

■ Clarity ■ vividness ■ correctness ■ appropriateness

Suggested Assignments

Section A

Interpersonal Focus

Be not the slave of words.

Thomas Carlyle

Language is a magnificent and powerful gift. It shapes our perception of the world and of ourselves. It enables us to know others and to be known by them. We use it for work and for play, for inspiration and for insight. Language can move us to violence or to compassion, to laughter or to tears. Sometimes language also misleads and befuddles. In this section of the chapter we will consider some characteristics of language and language usage that often contribute to communication confusion. An understanding of these elements can promote reliable and satisfying communication. Specifically, we will discuss word magic, meanings and words, and observations and inferences. In the last chapter we sometimes used the word language for both verbal and nonverbal elements. In this chapter the term will refer to verbal elements exclusively.

Word Magic

The most fundamental of language lessons can be stated quite simply: a word is not the thing that it represents. Words, written or spoken, are symbols. A symbol is some-

thing that represents something else. The word *chair*, for example, represents the object chair. The two are not the same, however. You can't sit on the word *chair*. The word *apple* represents a fruit that is edible, but you can't eat the word. Similarly, the map is not the territory that it represents. To hold a map of the city of Chicago in your hands is not to hold the city of Chicago in your hands.

Surprisingly, from time to time some of us neglect the distinction between words and things. We treat symbols as if they were what they represented. We assign the properties of whatever it is a word is representing to the word itself. This kind of behavior is called word magic. It is unrealistic. For example, some people avoid using words that represent dread diseases. They treat the words as if they were the diseases. Public health officials tell us this tendency has been a real obstacle in the fight against venereal disease. Because people have avoided the words, it has been difficult to communicate information concerning the diseases. During the Second World War, several Japanese citizens were decorated for rescuing pictures of the emperor from bombed and burning buildings. In these cases, the emperor's picture was treated as if it were the emperor.

Most of us don't have to look very far to find examples of word magic. Perhaps you have known students who are interested in receiving high grades but are not interested in learning. This is a kind of word magic. Grades are symbols. They are symbols for a degree of achievement and learning. To rejoice in the symbol without having received what the symbol represents is to practice

"Getting an 'A' or a star is all right, but I'd like some sort of profit-sharing plan around here."

word magic. Small children are usually more realistic in this regard than are some college students. When children ask for candy, they usually aren't satisfied with symbols; they want the real thing. Tragically, sometimes people spend much of a lifetime striving for the symbols of happiness before learning that the symbol is not the thing that the symbol represents.

Often when we deal with problems symbolically, we assume that we have dealt with them in other ways as well. This is another manifestation of word magic. For example, in so-called primitive cultures before going into battle warriors would often draw images of the enemy in the dirt and then disfigure them with spears and stones. The reasoning seemed to be that the enemy would somehow be weakened if the image or symbol was weakened. We frequently

engage in similar reasoning today. That is, we sometimes assume that when a problem has been treated symbolically, it somehow has been solved in reality. Public officials wave their wands and give speeches, pass laws, and appoint commissions, and the rest of us breathe a sigh of relief and assume that problems have been solved. Often speeches, laws, commissions, and similar devices are mere symbols that are used to create for a gullible public the illusion of action. As Amitai Etzioni states, "Modern shamans dazzle us with a variety of magic. Speech making, the modern equivalent of the witch doctor's mumbo-jumbo, seeks to create around words the illusion of deeds."[1] Promises given in speeches are sometimes not followed up with actions. Commission reports are often not read or utilized. Laws are frequently not funded or enforced. A law that is not enforced is simply a piece of paper. Of course, giving speeches, appointing commissions, and passing laws are often important first steps. The error lies in assuming that, because these steps have been taken, the problem has been solved.

A few years ago in a small university town, a citizens' group brought pressure to bear on university officials to establish a strong affirmative action program. University administrators adopted an elaborate and impressive affirmative action statement. They had it distributed as a colorful brochure. The citizens' group appeared satisfied. The statement was so impressive that government officials praised the university for its affirmative action policy. Two years later members of the original citizens' committee were surprised to learn that in spite of the impressive affirmative action statement university hiring and promotion practices had changed very little. In way of further illustration, a high school principal once fell into the habit of evaluating teachers solely on the basis of the lesson plans they handed in each week. He did not visit classes. He assumed that the lesson plans accurately represented class activity. Actually in many cases there was little correlation between the lesson plans and what happened in the classroom. Teachers who learned to write the best lesson plan received the highest evaluations.

Word magic is sometimes used to transform the old into the new. Sir James Frazer[2] reports that in some ancient cultures people often assumed the names of the young, the strong, or the swift in the belief that the names themselves could transform the persons named. On occasion, we utilize the same kind of reasoning today. Old products that are no longer selling well are simply given new names and new packaging, and buyers respond as if the products themselves were new. College courses that are no longer attracting students are often given new titles and new catalog descriptions. Sometimes even though these changes are not accompanied by significant changes in content, the courses enjoy renewed popularity.

In summary, a symbol is something that represents something else. The symbol is not the thing that it represents. Sometimes, however, people react to symbols as though they were the things they were representing. We call this word magic. Word magic assumes many forms, but always at its heart is this confusion between symbols and what symbols represent.

Meanings and Words

What is a word? A word is a symbol—something that stands for something else. It usually takes the form of a mark on paper or a sound in the air. What is meaning? Meaning is the relationship we create between words and the phenomena that we have words represent. Meaning is arbitrary. We can have words represent anything we want them to represent. Words have communication value only to the extent that people agree upon what they represent. Words, then, in and of themselves do not have meaning; people supply the meaning. Words do not contain meaning, people contain meaning. The frequent question "What does that word mean?" is actually a poor question. A better question is "What does that person mean with that word?"

Because words do not contain inherent meaning, language does not transform meaning directly. The process of translation is always involved. When you transmit words to others, you are not directly transmitting your meanings with those words. Others receive your words and put their own meanings on them. If the meaning they give to your words is the same as the meaning you gave to your words, communication has been successful. The process can be diagrammed as follows: (a) Beth has some thoughts she wants to express to John. (b) She thinks of some words to express her thoughts. (c) She transmits the words to John. (d) John receives the words and puts his own meaning on them. If John's meanings for Beth's words are the same as Beth's meanings, communication has worked. We all know, however, that frequently Beth and John have different meanings for the same words. This is to say that people frequently interpret words differently. In the next few paragraphs let's consider some of the reasons that people often assign different meanings to the same words.

Factors That Affect Meanings

People give different meanings to the same words for a number of reasons. The primary reason is that no two people have identical past experiences. Other reasons are that meanings change, that there are regional differences in meanings, and that most words have many referents. Context and connotation and denotation also affect meaning.

Past Experiences We assign meanings to words as a result of our experiences with words and with the phenomena that words represent in the culture or subculture in which we live. Frequently people assign different meanings to words because they have had different past experiences. I was reminded of this fact early in my marriage. My wife was born and raised in the small island of Kauai in the Hawaiian chain. We were living in California after our marriage and my wife suggested that we return to Hawaii for her sister's wedding. We agreed to stay for a few days after the wedding for a brief vacation in Hawaii. Having read travel posters about Hawaii since I was a small boy in the Midwest, I pictured a vaca-

tion in Hawaii as lying on the beach and playing in the surf. To my wife it meant quite another thing. The small community in which she was raised was very close-knit. A vacation in Hawaii to her meant visiting friends and relatives. Needless to say, we experienced some conflict about this matter. Who was right? The point is that nobody was right or wrong. We gave different meanings to the term *Hawaiian vacation* because we had different backgrounds and past experiences.

A father and son provide another example. The son, who is in his mid-twenties, has shown no great interest in holding a steady job or beginning a career. His father can't understand this attitude, and they have difficulty communicating about the matter. They give different meanings to terms such as *success, job, security,* and *money*. Their meanings are different because their past experiences are different. The father grew up during the depression when jobs and money were very scarce. The son grew up during more affluent times. If the generations have difficulty communicating, surely one of the reasons is their different past experiences.

Meanings Change An additional reason for misunderstandings concerning word meanings is that sometimes people change the meanings they have for words rather rapidly. Can you remember when grass was something you mowed, when hippie was to be large in the hips, when neat was orderly, and when bad was something undesirable? When meanings are shifted rapidly, confusion sometimes results. A year or so ago a young man introduced himself to a girl's parents and said, "I think your daughter is bitchen." He meant the remark as a compliment; the parents were incensed.

A father was once shocked to hear his preteen daughter report that she and her friend had enjoyed the matinee at a local movie theater because they "sat behind a high school couple who were making out." The father was relieved to learn that the term *making out* had a much less specific meaning for his daughter's generation than it had for his own.

Regional Differences   Sometimes words mean different things in different regions of the country. "Let's stop for a soda" means let's stop for a soft drink in some regions of the country. In other regions soda used in this context refers to an ice cream concoction similar to a malted milk. In some parts of the country when you order a "danish" with your morning coffee, you are specifying a particular type of breakfast pastry. In other regions the same term is used for any kind of breakfast pastry.

Most Words Have Many Referents   Compared to the almost infinite number of phenomena in our world that we would like to name, we have a limited number of words with which to do the naming. This is true in spite of the fact that we are constantly developing new words. This means, of course, that most words must represent more than one phenomenon. To put it simply, for most of us most words have more than one meaning. Take the word *strike* for example. A strike in bowling is different from a strike in baseball. We strike a match, we hope for a strike while fishing, we strike

up a conversation, and employees sometimes strike against employers. That most words have more than one commonly accepted meaning is sometimes the cause of communication confusion.

Context   Because words are frequently given more than one meaning, we are forced to rely heavily on context to determine intended meaning in a particular situation. The words "I struck out" suggest something entirely different in a baseball context from the same words in a bowling context. Part of a line about Shakespeare attributed to Ben Jonson reads: "Thou hadst small Latin and less Greek." Unfortunately, this is the part that is usually quoted. Taken out of context, these words give the impression that Jonson was depreciating Shakespeare. However, the entire line—"And though thou hadst small Latin and less Greek"—and the lines that follow indicate that Jonson was paying Shakespeare a compliment. He was suggesting that the masters of Latin and Greek could very well come to Shakespeare for lessons in playwriting. Context is so important in determining meaning that it is foolhardy to speculate on meaning without knowledge of context. As S. I. Hayakawa states, "It is clear then that the ignoring of context in any act of interpretation is at best a stupid practice. At its worst, it can be a vicious practice. A common example is the sensational newspaper story in which a few words by a public personage are torn out of their context and made the basis of a completely misleading story."[3] Ignoring context, then, is yet another reason for occasional communication mixups.

Connotation and Denotation   Another reason that the speaker and the listener may put different meanings on the same words is that words have both connotative and denotative meanings. Denotative meanings are the objective, publicly agreed-upon, "dictionary" meanings that we give to words. Connotative meanings are the more personal, subjective, emotional meanings that we have for words. Sometimes when people are successful in supplying the same denotative meaning to words, their connotative meanings fail to match up. For example, you and your classmates will probably give similar denotative meanings to the word *father* in the following sentence. "My father was a carpenter." Your connotative meanings may vary widely, however, depending upon the personal feelings of class members concerning their own father or fathers they have known. That we respond to words both connotatively and denotatively is another complicating factor in their interpretation.

In short, words do not contain meaning—people supply the meaning. Because people do not have identical past experiences, because usage sometimes changes rapidly, because regional differences in usage exist, because most words come to have many meanings, because people sometimes ignore context, and because we react to words both connotatively and denotatively, different people sometimes assign different meanings to the same words. Let's turn our attention now to what happens when people are unaware that they are assigning different meanings to the same words.

Bypassing

When people are aware that their meanings differ, they can make adjustments and avoid misunderstandings. The most serious difficulties arise when people are unaware that their meanings differ. When people assume they are understanding one another but in fact are missing one another with their meaning, the occurrence is called bypassing. It is called bypassing because people are passing by one another with their meanings.

There are two types of bypassing. One type occurs when people use different words for the same thing and are unaware that they are referring to the same thing. To illustrate: two college faculty members once argued for over a half hour in the mistaken belief that they were in disagreement. One was saying that the general education requirements at their college needed to be changed radically. The other wanted to retain the status quo while making some adjustments. Eventually they realized that what one person meant by radical changes

Meanings are in people.

was the same as what the other meant by adjustments. Frequently people argue unnecessarily because they are unaware that they are using different words for the same things.

A more common type of bypassing happens when people are unaware that they have different meanings for the same words. For example, your roommate says, "I am having a friend over and I am late. Will you pick up the apartment while I take a shower?" You say, "Sure." However, "picking up" the apartment to you means stacking the dishes in the sink and straightening the magazines and newspapers. To your roommate it means doing the dishes and running the vacuum cleaner. Hard feelings could result because you and your roommate gave different meanings to the same words. This kind of bypassing sometimes occurs in the classroom. The professor says, "Hand in a short paper on Friday." Short to you means one and a half pages; short to your professor means eight pages—result: trouble. An office executive once asked a new secretary to "burn" a newly typed report. "Burn" in the jargon of that office meant "make a Xerox copy." The secretary, thinking she had understood her supervisor, threw the report in the trash for burning.

Sometimes the results of bypassing are humorous, but on other occasions they are tragic. Late in the Second World War a young, inexperienced replacement was ordered to escort two prisoners down the road and "take care of them." The officer who gave the order meant for the replacement to take the prisoners to a compound where prisoners were being held and to turn them over to whomever was in charge. The young soldier, thinking he was following orders, took the prisoners down the road and shot them. David Frost asked former President Nixon why the Watergate tapes hadn't been destroyed. The former President replied that he had ordered some of the tapes destroyed. He further stated that his order may have been misunderstood. This particular bit of bypassing may have changed the course of American history.

Preventing Bypassing

The first step in preventing bypassing is simply to develop an awareness that it can occur. Experience shows that the best communicators are often those who realize that communication frequently breaks down. When one realizes that communication frequently fails, one is more apt to take measures to avoid breakdowns. Conversely, poor communicators are sometimes those who presume communication to be infallible. Sometimes people are poor communicators because they assume, "If it's been said, it's been understood." Good communicators, then, often expect to be misunderstood and expect to misunderstand.

When we are aware that bypassing is not only possible but often probable, we are more likely to utilize a second prevention, feedback. As we discovered in the chapter on listening, feedback occurs when people take the time to check on whether their meanings are coinciding. Feedback consists of querying and paraphrasing. When using feedback people say in effect, "I think this is important, here is what I think you meant—am I right?" Or they say, "Hey, this is important to me. Did I make myself clear? What did you understand me to say?" Both speakers and listeners should feel responsible for initiating and supplying feedback. (For further suggestions concerning the use of feedback, see chapter 6). Feedback goes a long way toward preventing bypassing. It is useful on the job, at school, at home, and in social situations.

In summary, meanings are not contained in words, they are contained in people. Meaning is arbitrary; words can mean anything we want them to mean. Words have communication value only to the extent that people agree on what words mean. For several reasons people often disagree concerning the meanings of words. Bypassing is a serious communication problem. It occurs when people are unaware that they are using either different words to refer to the same things or the same words to refer to different things. Bypassing can be prevented by developing an awareness of its possibility and by utilizing feedback.

Observations and Inferences

Consider the following two sentences: (1) Mary is running. (2) Mary is late for class. Structurally these are both declarative sentences. However, one statement is observational and the other is inferential. That is, one statement reports an observation and the other reports an inference. These two statements represent another characteristic of our language that is sometimes misleading. Our language doesn't help us much in distinguishing between observational and inferential statements. There is nothing in its structure or in spelling or in punctuation that distinguishes between them. Observational statements report what one has observed. Inferential statements go beyond that. They report what one concludes or guesses from what one has observed. In the preceding example the first sentence is an observational statement because the speaker actually observed Mary running. The second sentence is an inferential statement because it goes beyond what the speaker observed and reports what the speaker guessed from what she or he had observed. After all, Mary may have been running simply because she felt good, or because she was anxious to meet a friend, or because class had been dismissed and she wanted to get home early, or for many other reasons.

Distinguishing between Observations and Inferences

Both inferential and observational statements are important, necessary, and desirable. We use both kinds of statements daily. Both kinds are necessary and important in science, in art, in business, in politics, and in everyday affairs.

In actual practice, observations grow out of inferences and inferences grow out of observations. Trying to decide which comes first in any situation is a little like trying to decide about the chicken and the egg. For example, you *observe* that traffic on Fourth Street is heavy, and you *infer* because of the time of day that it would be lighter on Sixth Street. You decide to go home by way of Sixth Street. As you are driving down Sixth, you *observe* that a large number of people are waiting for Caesar's Restaurant to open. You *infer* from this that Caesar's is a good restaurant. You come back a few days later to try Caesar's. You *observe* that your soup and coffee are cold and that your steak is well done, in spite of your request that it be medium-rare. You *infer* from these *observations* that Caesar's is not a good restaurant after all. The chain of inference and observation, observation and inference goes on and on. We check on our inferences by making observations, and from our observations we develop inferences.

Since observational statements and inferential statements are both necessary, it is not the purpose here to discourage the use of either. Rather we want to emphasize the importance of recognizing the differences between the two types of statements. It serves our best interest to know when we are dealing with an observation and when we are dealing with an inference. Inferences, after all, are nothing more than guesses. When we are working with a guess, we should be aware of it. It is true that in some areas some people are expert inference makers (guessers). Physicians, for example, often arrive at diagnoses by means of inferences. These inferences are usually based on careful observation and years of training. Furthermore, it is also true that observations are often not foolproof. As we observed in chapter 5, human perception is fallible. Nevertheless—even though inferences are sometimes accurate and observations are sometimes faulty— it is unwise to act on most inferences with the same degree of certainty that we demonstrate when acting on observations. It

is advantageous to be aware of inferences, because then we can assess the probability appropriate to them.

When we are unaware of the differences between observations and inferences, we often act on inferences with unrealistic certainty. A student was walking toward class when in the distance she observed two of her classmates walking away from the classroom area. She inferred that the class had been dismissed, and, without taking the time to check on the accuracy of her inference, she turned around and returned to the library. The class had not been dismissed. By acting on her inference without checking on it, she missed an important surprise quiz. Because the road was lonely, a motorist inferred it would be safe to pass on a hill. He met another car head on, and all concerned were seriously injured. Hamlet accidentally and impulsively killed Polonius by acting on an inference without checking on it. The plot of Othello is built on Othello's inferring that Desdemona has been unfaithful to him. In his jealous mind, the inference becomes a fact and tragedy results. A more positive example is provided by a woman whose physician told her, on the basis of EKG readings, that she had developed a heart problem and would need to reduce her daily activities and take medication. Although she respected her physician, she realized his diagnosis was an inference, and she sought the opinion of two other doctors. They both pronounced her health perfect. Further inquiry revealed that the first doctor's tests had been distorted by a medication the woman had temporarily been taking for another illness. If she had not bothered to check on the original inference, she might have undergone needless inconvenience and expense. In short, it is wise to recognize the differences between observations and inferences, because it is unwise to treat them in exactly the same way.

Separating Observation and Inference

As we observed earlier, nothing in the nature of our language helps us distinguish between statements of observation and statements of inference. Grammatically and structurally they both look and sound the same. The way to distinguish between the two is to remember that an observational statement reports only what has actually been observed. It can be made only after the observation and only by the observer. It cannot go beyond what has been observed. An inferential statement, on the other hand, reports what the speaker infers from what has been observed. It can be made at any time, it goes beyond what has been observed, and it can be made by anyone. To understand these distinctions further, study the following examples. Decide which of the italicized statements are observational and which are inferential.

1. At 10:30 in the morning you notice that Mr. Gillespie's car is parked in front of his house. You remark, *"Gillespie stayed home again this morning."*

2. You are sitting in class and you notice that for the third day in a row Bill is wearing a blue shirt. You say to the girl next to you, *"Bill sure likes blue shirts."*

3. Same situation as above and you say, *"Bill wore a blue shirt to school again today."*

4. You read in this morning's paper that Professor Sanchez has been in an accident. When you get to class you see a notice on the board stating that Professor Sanchez will not meet with classes this week. You say to a friend, *"Sanchez was in an accident."*

5. Same situation as above and you say, *"I read in this morning's paper that Sanchez was in an accident."*

6. You are lying in a hospital bed and a nurse puts a thermometer in your mouth. After five minutes she removes the thermometer and notices that the mercury has registered 101. She remarks to herself, *"This person has an elevated temperature."*

7. Same situation as above. The nurse says to herself, *"This person has a temperature of 101."*

8. You notice dark clouds on the horizon and in the distance you see lightning. You say to a friend, *"It is going to rain."*

You are correct if you decided that only one of the statements is observational. Let's discuss them.

1. This statement is inferential. All you actually observed was Mr. Gillespie's car parked in front of his house. He might have accepted a ride from someone else; he might have gone out and come back; or maybe his wife took him to work so she could have the car.

2. This is a statement of inference.

Perhaps Bill wears the shirts because someone gave them to him or because they are required for a job he must go to after class. There are many possibilities.

3. Unless you actually saw Bill wearing the shirt on the way to school, this statement is also inferential. All you have actually observed is that Bill is wearing the shirt in class.

4. This statement is inferential. You observed an article in the paper and a notice on the board. You did not observe an accident involving Professor Sanchez.

5. Right—this statement is observational. It reports only what you observed—a statement in the paper. You are not claiming that the statement is correct.

6. This statement is inferential. Maybe your normal temperature is 101.

7. This is also a statement of inference. The nurse can't see your temperature; she can see only the thermometer. She makes an inference about your temperature from what she observes on the thermometer. There is a strong possibility that this is an accurate inference; however, it is still an inference. Professional nurses know this and they frequently use more than one thermometer. If they get a surprising reading on one, they check it with the other.

8. This statement is inferential. No matter how probable, any statement about the future is a statement of inference.

Once again, observational statements can be made only after the observation, they can be made only by the observer, and they cannot go beyond what has been observed. Inferential statements can be made at any time, they go beyond what has been observed, and they can be made by anyone. Perhaps the following story will help you remember these distinctions. It is often told about Calvin Coolidge. One day when Mr. Coolidge was riding in the country, his companion pointed to some cows and said, "Look at those beautiful spotted cows." Mr. Coolidge responded, "On this side." Old Cal was not willing to make an inference about the side of the cows that he could not see.

In summary, both observational and inferential statements are important. However, it is beneficial to recognize the differences between the two. Wisdom would suggest that both kinds of statements be treated with appropriate caution.

In this section of the chapter we discussed word magic, the relationship between words and meaning, and the distinction between statements of inference and statements of observation.

Key Ideas in Review

☐ A symbol is not the thing that it represents.

☐ Word magic occurs when people respond to symbols as though they were the things they were representing.

☐ Meaning is the relationship we establish between words and the phenomena we want words to represent.

☐ Meanings are contained in people, not in words.

☐ Words have communication value only to the extent that people agree upon what they represent.

☐ People do not have identical past experiences; word usage sometimes changes rapidly; regional differences in word usage exist; most words represent more than one thing; people sometimes ignore context; and people react to words both connotatively and denotatively—therefore, people often interpret words differently.

☐ Bypassing occurs when people are unaware that they are using different words to refer to the same things or using the same words to refer to different things.

☐ Bypassing can be reduced by developing an awareness of its possibility and by utilizing feedback.

☐ An observational statement reports on what has been observed.

☐ An inferential statement reports on what has been inferred from what has been observed.

☐ It is important to distinguish between observational statements and inferential statements because different degrees of probability are associated with each kind of statement.

☐ The nature of our language fails to distinguish between observational and inferential statements.

☐ Observational statements can be made only after the observation, only by the observer, and must not go beyond what has been observed.

☐ Inferential statements can be made by anyone at any time and they go beyond what has been observed.

Section B

Person-to-Group Focus

Eloquence is a painting of the thoughts.

Blaise Pascal

In Section A of this chapter we considered some language factors that sometimes contribute to communication confusion. In this section we will shift the emphasis slightly and discuss some positive language practices. Much of what we observed about language in Section A can be applied in both interpersonal and person-to-group settings. Much of what we will discuss in this section is relevant to both settings also. However, in person-to-group situations listeners usually don't have the opportunity to interrupt and ask for clarification. Furthermore, person-to-group situations ordinarily require relatively long periods of listening. When speaking in person-to-group situations, then, you must take particular care to hold attention and to be understood. The degree to which your listeners pay attention to you and understand you often depends on your use of language. In this section we will consider four aspects of good language usage: clarity, vividness, correctness, and appropriateness.

Clarity

One of the basic requirements for good language usage is clarity. Clarity involves using words that produce the same meanings in the minds of listeners that the speaker intended. Clarity is always important, but it is particularly important in person-to-group situations. As we have already noted, in these situations listeners normally don't have the opportunity to ask for clarification. When listeners have difficulty understanding, they often become discouraged and stop listening. Speakers, then, should strive for instantaneous understanding. As Bernard McCabe and Coleman Bender state, "The listener must immediately comprehend the meaning of the language used by the speaker. Since speech is invisible and momentary, there is no time for the listener to contemplate."[4] These are three suggestions for promoting clarity: practice simplicity, be specific, and be conscious of translation.

Practice Simplicity

Readers can usually select the most ideal circumstances for reading. When readers fail to understand a word or a phrase, they can stop, think, and seek help if necessary. In informal conversation and in most interpersonal communication situations, listeners enjoy some of these advantages. They can interrupt, question, and ask for clarification. In person-to-group situations, however, as we have already observed, listeners usually don't have the opportunity to question, to discuss, to ponder the meaning of words and phrases. To compensate for this factor, successful speakers learn to use simple, uncomplicated language. The meanings of short, simple words are more apt to be immediately apparent than are the meanings of longer, more complicated words. The meanings of short, simple sentences are more apt to be immediately clear than are the meanings of longer, more complicated sentences. This is probably why studies that have compared oral and written communication have found that oral style is marked by shorter average sentence lengths, shorter words, and less complex sentences than written style is.

Simplicity does not rule out eloquence. Indeed, the opposite is true. Truly eloquent speakers achieve eloquence by learning to put together short, simple words and sentences effectively. The moving phrases that have come ringing down to us over the years are amazingly simple. Consider the following:

"Give me liberty, or give me death."—Patrick Henry. Speech in the Virginia Convention, 1775.

"The only thing we have to fear is fear itself."—Franklin Delano Roosevelt. First inaugural address, 1933.

"I have nothing to offer but blood, toil, tears and sweat."—Winston Churchill. Speech, 1940.

"Ask not what your country can do for you: Ask what you can do for your country."—John Fitzgerald Kennedy. Inaugural address, 1961.

"I have a dream."—Martin Luther King, Jr. Speech at the Lincoln Memorial, Washington, D.C., 1963.

Be Specific

Another way we can promote clarity is by being specific. Remember that some words and terms are general and others are specific. A general term refers to a whole class or a group of objects. A specific term refers to one particular thing. The word *school* is general. It refers to all schools—private schools, public schools, preschools, elementary schools, junior high schools, high schools, two-year colleges, four-year colleges, universities. Sometimes general terms are valuable; they enable us to refer to many things with one word. For example, without the general word *school* we could not make this simple statement: "We have many schools in our area." The term *Notre Dame University* is relatively specific. It refers to a specific school—a particular university. Even though general words are sometimes useful, specific words ordinarily provide greater clarity. General words are sometimes too vague to promote instantaneous understanding—they represent so many things. For this reason experienced speakers usually strive for specificity. In chapter 7 we learned that degrees of specificity can be represented with an abstraction ladder. Study the following abbreviated abstraction ladder:

object
manufactured object
item of hardware
utensil
kitchen utensil
spoon
tablespoon

Please note that the terms toward the top of the ladder tend to be vague because they represent many things, whereas the terms toward the bottom of the ladder are more specific because they represent fewer things. Generally, you can improve the clarity of your communication by trading general terms, which mean many things, for specific terms, which mean fewer things. "Bring home some stuff for tonight" is not as clear as "Bring home a quart of whole milk, a head of iceberg lettuce, one bunch of carrots, and a pound of calf's liver."

Be Conscious of Translation

It will be easier for you to achieve clarity if you will remember that words do not transfer meaning directly from one mind to another. The process of translation is always involved. With an ink pad and a rubber stamp, you could, after properly inking the stamp, transmit an image directly to any receptive substance. You cannot, however, ink up a word and transfer an image directly from your mind to the minds of your listeners. You send words to your listeners and listeners endow them with their own meanings. Communication is successful to the degree that the listeners' meanings are the same as the meanings you intended. This is often not the case, however. As we noted in Section A, people translate words differently for many reasons: they do not have identical past experiences, usage changes rapidly, regional differences in usage exist, words come to have many meanings, people sometimes ignore context, and we react to words both connotatively and denotatively.

If you are to achieve clarity, you must be conscious of these factors. You must be aware that listeners are providing their own meanings for your words. You must select words to which your listeners can attach the intended meaning. Obviously, the closer together speakers and listeners are in background and previous experience, the better the chances for clarity are. Consequently, communication within subgroups is usually easier than communication between subgroups.

In this country most of us share a common language; however, most of us also utilize one or more sublanguages. Teenagers often have their own jargon. So do teachers, typesetters, plumbers, pharmacists, army officers, surfers, fishermen, and hunters. These special languages are made possible by the common experiences shared by members of the respective subgroups. Keep this in mind when speaking to people whose education, occupation, avocation, generation, and general background is different from yours.

You can be sensitive to listeners' providing their own meanings for your words by selecting words that fit the experiences and consequently the vocabularies, of your listeners. Avoid using technical jargon with listeners who do not have the experience to understand it. Avoid using faddish words that might be easily misunderstood. Avoid regional terms when your listeners are not from the appropriate region. Take the time to explain and define terms you feel your listeners might not understand. In short, help your listeners translate your words in an appropriate manner.

In review, an important aspect of good language usage is clarity. Speakers can promote clarity by practicing simplicity, by being specific, and by being conscious of translation.

Vividness

As speakers we want to be listened to as well as understood. Indeed, we will not be understood unless we are listened to. Clarity of language helps us make meanings clear; vivid language helps us hold the attention of our listeners. Vivid language is language that is exciting and interesting. In the next few paragraphs, we will consider some practical suggestions for developing vivid language.

Avoid Unnecessary Repetition

Sometimes language is boring because speakers repeat the same word or sound over and over. To illustrate: consider the speaker who punctuates every sentence with an "uh," or an "okay," or a "you know." Sometimes we become infatuated with certain words and phrases and use them to the point of boredom. Your language will be more interesting if you avoid these habits.

Avoid Clichés

When expressions are overused, they often lose their effectiveness. When an expression has been used so often that people are accustomed to hearing it, it no longer stimulates interest. Exhausted expressions of this kind are referred to as clichés. The following fall into this category: "We had a ball." "She is as pretty as a picture." "And in conclusion, ladies and gentlemen." "Last but not least." "The next speaker needs no introduction." "I am into ———." "Right on." "The wave of the future." These phrases were probably wonderfully expressive for the first person who used them. We have heard them so often, however, that now they evoke little more than boredom. Our language usually becomes more interesting when we eliminate trite expressions.

Be Specific

Besides contributing to clarity, specific words help make expression more interesting. Specific words and phrases focus attention on definite things; they help create sharp mental images. We are attracted to the tangible, to the definite, to the specific. We lose interest in the speaker who becomes overly vague, general, and abstract. The statement "We had a salad for lunch" is not as stimulating as "We had a very cold salad made from three kinds of fresh lettuce, bits of sweet onion, crisp bacon crumbles, pieces of blue cheese, and a fresh grind of coarse black pepper." Advertisers know the value of being specific. A newspaper ad might say, "A store full of bargains," but it also mentions specific items and prices. Most students know that the best sleeping pill yet discovered is the teacher who, without ever coming down to ground level, fills the hour with generalizations and high-level abstractions. If you will develop the habit of using specific words and terms, your language will be more interesting.

Use Figurative Language

The occasional use of a fresh figure of speech can add zest to language. The most commonly used figures of speech are the simile, the metaphor, and personification. A simile is an expressed comparison between two things of unlike nature. It is usually indicated by the conjunctions *like, as,* or *than.* In other words, we say something is like or as something else. "The guy playing opposite me was like a concrete garage with legs," or "Their halfback was as slippery as a bucket full of boiled okra." A metaphor is an implied comparison between two things of unlike nature. The words *as* or *like* are omitted. "To me he was Christmas, Easter, and the tooth fairy all rolled into one," or "When it comes to facts, she is flypaper." Personification occurs when we give inanimate objects or lower animals the characteristics of persons. "My textbooks sit in the room and mock me when I watch television," or "My car just looked at me and said, 'Hey, partner, it's time for a trip.'"

Figurative language is not only colorful, it also often promotes clarity by enabling us to compare new concepts with more familiar ones. Figures of speech should not be forced, nor should we use too many. When techniques of this kind call attention to themselves, they are distracting and they often diminish the speaker's credibility. Of course, we should also avoid overused figures of speech that have become clichés.

"It's good to be here, folks, and before I start I'd like to suggest you pick up a copy of the program, which will help to explain a lot of my obscure bits of metaphor and imagery, and my double entendres."

Fresh figures of speech judiciously used, however, can add excitement to language. Lamar Reinsch[5] conducted a study in which a speech was given with and without figurative devices. One version used four metaphors, another used four similes, and the third was without any figurative devices. The speech with metaphors caused significantly more attitude change than the literal speech did. The speech with similes caused less attitude change than the speech with metaphors did, but it caused more attitude change than the speech without figurative devices caused. In short, the speech without figurative devices caused less attitude change than the two forms with figurative language did. Carefully used, figurative devices then can be important language tools.

In review, the degree to which our listeners pay attention to us is often related to the language we use. Language becomes more vivid when we eliminate clichés and excessive repetition, when we use specific words and terms, and when we use fresh figures of speech.

Correctness

Unlike the speaker, the writer usually has time to evaluate and rewrite. Similarly, the reader has time to study and evaluate the writer's work. Such, however, is not the case with speaker and listener. For both the speaker and the listener, spoken language is of the moment. It is no wonder, then, that grammatical standards for spoken English are less rigid than they are for written English. Speakers are usually dismayed when presented with an exact transcript of their spoken remarks. The fact is that spoken language just can't be as consistently correct as written language. Nevertheless, speakers should strive to maintain grammatical correctness because most listeners will react unfavorably to a speaker whose use of language does not meet acceptable standards. Even listeners who themselves use faulty grammar often notice grammatical errors in others. Remember, correctness seldom calls attention to itself. Incorrect usage, however, tends to be conspicuous.

Appropriateness

The element of appropriateness overlaps the language factors we have discussed thus far. Correctness is often related to appropriateness. Clarity and interest also sometimes depend on appropriateness. Language should be appropriate to the speaker, the subject, the occasion, the listeners, and the medium used for transmission.

Speakers should use language that is appropriate to themselves. We should be comfortable with the language we use. Sometimes when we borrow language from others simply because it sounds good, our speech lacks sincerity. Language must also be suited to the subject, the listener, and the occasion. Jargon and technical terms that might be appropriate in some circumstances may not work in others. If you were explaining a medical breakthrough to a group of doctors, you could use technical language that would be inappropriate for a

Language must be appropriate to the listeners.

more general audience. Language suited to the courtroom might seem awkward in other settings. Slang words and phrases appropriate to informal discussions might seem out of place in more formal speaking situations.

Language that is appropriate for the printed page is often not suited to oral speech. When written material is translated directly to the speaker's platform, it often seems stilted and artificial. This is why it is not advisable for most people to write speeches word for word. Generally, oral usage when compared to written usage appears to have shorter words and sentences, fewer different words, more personal pronouns, more qualifying terms, and more slang words and phrases.

In short, language should be appropriate to the medium, the speaker, the subject, the occasion, and the listeners.

In this chapter we have noted that speakers should strive for clarity, vividness, correctness, and appropriateness in language usage.

Key Ideas in Review

□ The degree to which listeners understand and pay attention is often related to the speaker's use of language.

□ Clarity is promoted when speakers practice simplicity, use specific words and terms, and remain conscious of translation.

□ Language becomes more vivid when speakers eliminate clichés and excessive repetitions, use specific words and terms, and use fresh figures of speech.

□ Grammatical standards for spoken English are less rigid than they are for written English. Even so, speakers should strive to maintain grammatical correctness. Most listeners react unfavorably to speakers who do not meet acceptable standards.

□ To be effective, language usage must be appropriate to the speaker, the subject, the listeners, the occasion, and the medium of expression.

Suggested Assignments

Integrated Assignments

The assignments presented in this section are designed to help you understand and put into practice what you have learned about language in this chapter. Give a speech to the class. Try to utilize everything you have learned about communication thus far. Pay particular attention to the language you use. Strive for clarity, vividness, correctness, and appropriateness. Select or adapt your topic from one of the following.

Speech Topics

1. Describe modern word magic. Illustrate your speech with specific examples that you have experienced or observed.

2. Do a little research about ancient word magic and then give a speech of contrast. Compare ancient word magic with modern practices.

3. Illustrate how past experiences influence the meanings we bring to words and events.

4. The meanings we give to words change over the years. Relate the history of certain words. Show how meanings have changed.

5. Illustrate regional differences in word usage.

6. Talk about bypassing. Give examples of bypassing you have experienced or observed.

7. Feedback can be utilized to reduce bypassing. Select a specific situation at home, at school, or at work and show how the people involved could encourage feedback and reduce bypassing.

8. Describe what happens when people neglect the distinction between observations and inferences. Give many specific examples.

Auxiliary Assignments

Interpersonal Focus

1. One student is designated as the leader. The leader is given a sheet of paper upon which four or five geometric figures have been drawn. Class members will try to reproduce those figures by following oral directions given by the leader. No questions or feedback are allowed. The leader should have her or his back turned to the class while giving the directions. The process is repeated with a different set of geometric figures. The second time, the leader faces the class and feedback and questions are allowed. Results of the two efforts are compared and discussed. What do the results suggest about bypassing and feedback?

2. The class is divided into small groups and each group will develop an observation-inference quiz similar to the one presented in Section A of this chapter. Quizzes will be administered to the class and discussed.

3. Analyze a short newspaper or magazine article for inferential and observational statements. Are inferences clearly labeled as inferences, or are they presented as observations? What is the percentage of inferential statements to observation statements? In a general discussion share your findings with the rest of the class.

4. The class is divided into six small groups. Two of the groups will develop examples of word magic, two groups will develop examples of bypassing, and the remaining two groups will develop examples of inference-observation confusion. All examples will be presented to the class.

5. The class is divided into six groups. Two of the groups will develop and present role-playing scenes illustrating word magic, two groups will develop and present role-playing

scenes illustrating bypassing, and two groups will develop and present role-playing scenes illustrating inference-observation confusion.

Person-to-Group Focus

1. Prepare and deliver a three-minute speech. During the speech whenever your classmates do not understand you, they will raise their hands. When this happens, rephrase your ideas and try to make yourself clear.

2. This assignment is an exercise in clarity. Give a speech on a very abstract topic, such as justice, love, or honor, or give a speech on a technical subject, such as the operation of a jet engine or the process of making and playing back stereophonic recordings. Do your best to use language that your listeners will understand.

3. This assignment will give you experience in using vivid descriptive language. Prepare and deliver to the class a short descriptive speech. Try your best to use colorful, exciting language. After you have finished your speech, invite the class to suggest ways by which you could have improved your language usage. Suitable topics for this assignment: (a) a parade, (b) a locker room after an important game, (c) a Christmas dinner, (d) a snowstorm, (e) a formal dance, (f) a garden, and (g) a crowded intersection.

4. Prepare and deliver a speech on any appropriate subject. Utilize everything you have learned about communication thus far. Take particular care to see that your language is clear, vivid, correct, and appropriate.

5. With the help of your teacher and classmates, compile a list of grammatical errors that you frequently commit. Consciously strive to eliminate these errors.

Suggested Readings

Interpersonal Focus

Johnson, Wendell. *People in Quandaries: The Semantics of Personal Adjustment*. New York: Harper & Row Publishers, 1946. This book has become a standard. It is a must for students who want to understand the practical value of general semantics in dealing with the problems of daily living. It is extremely readable.

Lee, Irving J. *Language Habits in Human Affairs: An Introduction to General Semantics*. New York: Harper & Row Publishers, 1941. Although some of the examples are dated, this highly readable book remains one of the best introductory texts in the area of general semantics. The author focuses on how language affects human behavior in everyday situations.

Sapir, Edward. *Language: An Introduction to the Study of Speech*. New York: Harcourt Brace Jovanovich, 1921. Don't let the date discourage you. This is another must for serious students of language and meaning. It is a classic work in its field.

Person-to-Group Focus

Aly, Bower, and Aly, Lucile F. *A Rhetoric of Public Speaking*. New York: McGraw-Hill Book Co., 1973, pp. 204–51. An authoritative chapter on the uses of language in person-to-group communication.

Oliver, Robert T. *Making Your Meaning Effective*. Boston: Holbrook Press, 1971, pp. 114–32. A very useful chapter on style. It focuses on making style reflect the speaker. Written for the beginning student.

Note Directory

1. Amitai Etzioni, "The Grand Shaman," *Psychology Today* (November 1972): 89–92, 141–43.

2. Sir James George Frazer, *The Golden Bough: A Study in Magic and Religion* (New York: Macmillan Publishing Co., 1958). Every chapter of this fascinating well-documented book provides examples of ancient symbolism.

3. Samuel I. Hayakawa, *Language in Thought and Action,* 2d ed. (New York: Harcourt Brace Jovanovich, 1964), p. 62.

4. Bernard P. McCabe and Coleman C. Bender, *Speaking Is a Practical Matter,* 2d ed. (Boston: Holbrook Press, 1973), p. 48.

5. N. Lamar Reinsch, "An Investigation of the Effects of the Metaphor and Simile in Persuasive Discourse," *Speech Monographs* 38, no. 2 (June 1971): 142–45.

Index

To the owner of this book:

I hope you enjoyed reading *People to People* as much as I enjoyed preparing it. I would like to learn as much as possible about your experiences with the book. Through your comments and the comments of others, I can learn how to make *People to People* a better book for future readers.

School _____ Title of Course _____

1. What did you like most about *People to People?* _____

_____

2. What did you like least about *People to People?* _____

_____

3. Were all of the chapters assigned for you to read?   Yes   No   (If not, which ones were not?)

_____

4. What chapter sections were usually assigned?

    A Sections   B Sections   Both Sections

5. What kind of assignments were usually assigned?

    Integrated   Interpersonal   Person-to-group   Other

6. What kinds of assignments did you gain the most from? Please explain. _____

_____

_____

7. How useful were the Key Ideas in Review? _____

8. How useful were the quotations, photographs, and cartoons in stimulating interest and helping

you to understand communication? _____

_____

_____

9. In the space below or in a separate letter please make any additional observations you think will be useful. I'll be delighted to hear from you. Thank you for your help.

Optional:

Your Name _____ Date _____

May Wadsworth quote you in future promotion of *People to People?*

Yes _____ No _____

Sincerely,

Jack McAuley

Jack McAuley

Fold Here

Cut Page Out

Fold Here

First Class
Permit No. 34
Belmont, CA

BUSINESS REPLY MAIL
No Postage Necessary if Mailed in United States

Mr. Jack G. McAuley

**Wadsworth Publishing Co., Inc.
10 Davis Drive
Belmont, CA 94002**